BLITZ
SCALING

BLITZ
SCALING

THE LIGHTNING-FAST PATH
TO BUILDING MASSIVELY
VALUABLE BUSINESSES

Reid Hoffman and Chris Yeh

CURRENCY
NEW YORK

Published in the United States by Currency, an imprint of the Crown Publishing
Group, a division of Penguin Random House LLC, New York.
currencybooks.com

CURRENCY and its colophon are trademarks of Penguin Random House LLC.

Currency books are available at special discounts for bulk purchases for sales
promotions or corporate use. Special editions, including personalized covers,
excerpts of existing books, or books with corporate logos, can be created in large
quantities for special needs. For more information, contact Premium Sales at
(212) 572-2232 or e-mail specialmarkets@penguinrandomhouse.com.

Library of Congress Cataloging-in-Publication Data
Names: Hoffman, Reid, author. | Yeh, Chris, author.
Title: Blitzscaling : the lightning-fast path to creating massively valuable
businesses / by Reid Hoffman and Chris Yeh.
Description: First edition. | New York : Currency, [2018] | Includes bibliographical
references and index.
Identifiers: LCCN 2017058413 | ISBN 9781524761417
Subjects: LCSH: New business enterprises. | Small business—Growth. |
Entrepreneurship.
Classification: LCC HD62.5.H624 2018 | DDC 658.4/063—dc23
LC record available at https://lccn.loc.gov/2017058413

ISBN 978-1-5247-6141-7
Ebook ISBN 978-1-5247-6142-4

Printed in the United States of America

Book design by Elina Nudelman
Jacket design by Josh Smith

10 9 8 7 6 5 4 3

First Edition

CONTENTS

Conclusion

I've known Reid Hoffman for years. Our friendship started on my visits to Silicon Valley to meet with Greylock Partners, the venture capital firm where Reid is a partner, so I could learn about the companies they were investing in. I was always impressed by his sharp mind and brilliant business sense. Reid is famous for hosting long dinners where the conversation runs late into the night, and we've spent many meals breaking down the technology industry, analyzing the promise of artificial intelligence, and more. When Microsoft CEO Satya Nadella started talking about acquiring LinkedIn, I knew it would be an amazing fit.

Of all the things I've discussed with Reid, the most thought-provoking might be blitzscaling. It is an idea that applies to many different industries, as he and Chris explain in the last section of this book. But prioritizing speed over efficiency—even in the face of uncertainty—is especially important when your business model depends on having lots of members and getting feedback from them. If you get in early and start getting that feedback and your competitors don't, then you're on the path to success. In any business where scale really matters, getting in early and doing it fast can make the difference.

This is especially true for two-sided business models, where you have two user groups that create positive network effects for each other. For example, LinkedIn wants to attract people who are looking for work as well as employers who want to hire them. Airbnb wants guests looking for a place to stay as well as hosts with space to rent. Uber wants to attract drivers as well as riders.

And a software company with an operating system to sell wants app developers as well as end users. Microsoft definitely went through a blitzscaling phase (although we didn't call it that at the time). We got on the learning curve early and were able to build a reputation as a serious company. We had an extreme culture of working hard and getting things done fast.

The ideas behind blitzscaling aren't just for startups and scale-ups. They're important for big, established companies too. The window for action can be tiny and it can close quickly. Even a few months of hesitation can mean the difference between leading and chasing.

Reid and Chris's ideas are more practical than ever, because it is now possible to get big fast in a way that simply wasn't feasible a few decades ago. There is a rich ecosystem of service providers and outsourcing companies to support rapid growth. Many companies have gone through their own big growth spurts, so there are lots of examples to learn from. User feedback comes in a constant stream of data. Product cycles have dropped from yearly to weekly or daily. And good reviews can spread in an instant online, so a strong product can quickly attract a big audience.

In other words, the case studies you're about to explore and the tools you're about to gain have never been more relevant. This is an ideal moment to be reading this book. I'm glad Reid and Chris are sharing their insights.

Introduction

"They're probably going to kill you."

The year was 2011, and in the offices of Airbnb, then a scrappy little forty-person start-up, its cofounder and CEO Brian Chesky had just received some very bad news.

Brian pondered the implications of the ominous prediction he'd just heard from Andrew Mason, the cofounder and CEO of Groupon. He didn't like it.

Brian and his cofounders, Joe Gebbia and Nathan Blecharcyzk, had already fought their way through plenty of obstacles to build Airbnb, a website that makes it easy for people to rent out their rooms or homes for the night. In the beginning, every investor the founders approached had turned them down or, worse, ignored them. The company was on the upswing now, but the painful early days were still fresh in their minds, and they weren't looking for another battle.

When the Airbnb founders first met, Paul Graham, the highly regarded founder of the start-up accelerator Y Combinator (YC), told them flat out that their idea was terrible. "People are actually doing this?!" he incredulously asked. When Brian told him yes, people were, in fact, renting out their living spaces for a night, Graham's response was "What's *wrong* with them?"

Still, Graham had accepted the Airbnb guys into the three-month-long YC program. Not because he was inspired by their Airbnb business, but because he was impressed by the hustle of the founders. He loved the (now famous) story about how Chesky and his cofounders managed to pay the bills while trying to get Airbnb off the ground. It was 2008, a US presidential election year, so they created and sold special-edition cereals called "Obama O's" and "Cap'n McCains"—a sugary parody of (or tribute to, depending on how you look at it) that year's candidates Barack Obama and John McCain. The creativity and persistence displayed by the Airbnb founders as "cereal entrepreneurs" got them in the door at YC; once in the program, they refined their business and were able to persuade two leading venture capital firms, Sequoia Capital and Greylock Partners (where I am a general partner), to invest.

Now, nearly four years later, it seemed like all the hard work was finally starting to pay off. Having celebrated its millionth booking, Airbnb had plenty of working capital, and it was clear that the concept was valuable.

But when you're successful, you attract competition. And sometimes that competition represents a deadly threat.

In Airbnb's case, that threat was three brothers from Cologne, Germany: Oliver, Marc, and Alexander Samwer. They had become billionaires by analyzing successful US companies, rapidly creating copycats in Europe, and, in many cases, selling those "cloned" companies to their original American inspirations. In other cases, the Samwers actually held on to and built out their clones; Zalando, the "Zappos of Europe," had over ten thousand employees and was worth more than $10 billion in 2017.

Their first success was Alando, an eBay knockoff that they were able to sell to eBay for $43 million, just one hundred days after launching it. The Samwer brothers then invested in the German versions of YouTube (MyVideo), Twitter (Frazr), and Facebook (StudiVZ) before founding their own start-up studio, Rocket Internet.

In early 2011, Brian and his team started noticing that Airbnb users were being spammed by a new company named Wimdu. Wimdu had apparently just received $90 million—the largest investment in a European start-up to date—from none other than Rocket Internet and Kinnevik, a major Swedish investment company that had partnered with the Samwer brothers.

The problem? Wimdu's business model and website looked like a knockoff of Airbnb's.

Wimdu was founded in March 2011, and, within weeks, the Berlin-based company had hired a staggering four hundred employees and opened twenty offices across Europe. Meanwhile, the original, but much smaller, Airbnb had raised only $7 million, had just forty employees, and operated out of a single office in San Francisco. As a first-time CEO, Brian wasn't even sure what was involved in opening a *second* office, let alone dozens more on another continent.

Brian also knew that if Wimdu was able to capture and dominate the European market, Airbnb might not survive. "If you're a travel site and you don't cover Europe, you're dead," he told us in 2015, when he visited the Technology-Enabled Blitzscaling class we taught at Stanford University.

The Samwer brothers had named their price: Airbnb could have Wimdu in exchange for a 25-percent stake in Airbnb. Now

Brian faced a difficult decision, with painful consequences regardless of what option he chose.

In response, Brian turned to one of his favorite decision-making techniques: reaching out to the world's leading experts. His first call was to the CEO of Groupon at the time, Andrew Mason. The leading daily deals company had had a similar experience the previous year: In December 2009, the Samwer brothers had launched CityDeal, their Groupon lookalike. Six months later, Groupon paid a nine-figure price, roughly 10 percent of its valuation at that point, to acquire this competitor.

Here was the question weighing heavily on Brian and his team: Should Airbnb follow Groupon's strategy and just buy the knockoff company? Brian's gut instinct was to say no. Integrating Wimdu's finance-centric and metric-driven team could harm Airbnb's design-driven culture. He was also reluctant to reward what he saw as a legal extortion racket rather than a sincere attempt to create value in the market.

Yet Brian felt he had an obligation to consider the offer. Mason had told him that despite the many problems the City-Deal acquisition had brought, it had also accelerated Groupon's progress into the European market, which ended up accounting for nearly 30 percent of its global sales. It could easily be argued that giving up 10 percent of Groupon for CityDeal was actually a good deal. But perhaps emboldened by their successful City-Deal gambit, the Samwers were asking for a far larger share of Airbnb—a full 25 percent.

On the other hand, Airbnb could reject the offer and instead take on the aggressive Samwer brothers in a head-to-head competition. But Wimdu had the home-turf advantage, not to mention ten times the number of employees and more than ten times the amount of invested capital. Competing against them would be one hell of an uphill battle.

Tired of the fund-raising grind, especially its emotional toll, Brian wondered whether he had it in him to take on this new and likely bruising fight. But he and his team had spent eighteen seemingly fruitless months working on Airbnb before entering Y Combinator, racking up tens of thousands of dollars in credit card debt. After all the blood, sweat, and tears, were they really willing to give up a quarter of their company?

Ultimately, Brian decided not to buy Wimdu, swayed in part by the arguments of his key advisers. Facebook founder Mark Zuckerberg counseled him to fight. "Don't buy them," he said. "The best product will win."

YC's Paul Graham gave similar feedback. "They're mercenaries. You're missionaries," he told Brian. "They're like people raising a baby they don't actually want."

When Brian reached out to me for my advice on the situation, I too advised him not to buy Wimdu. The key issue wasn't the price and dilution, but the way a merger could pose impediments to speed and success. "Buying [Wimdu] adds a substantial amount of integration risk, which tripped up Groupon after buying CityDeal," I told him. "Merging company cultures and company management could create potentially fatal risks, especially if it slows us down. With Airbnb, we have a business that is already benefiting from network effects. We can win." I stand by that advice today.

In the end, Airbnb's founders realized that they wanted to take on the Samwers—and they wanted to win. But how?

The key was an aggressive, all-out program of growth that we call *blitzscaling*. Blitzscaling drives "lightning" growth by prioritizing speed over efficiency, even in an environment of uncertainty. It's a set of specific strategies and tactics that allowed Airbnb to beat the Samwer brothers at their own game.

Just a few months later, determined to acquire the resources needed to outscale the Samwers, Brian raised $112 million in additional venture capital. Airbnb then embarked on an aggressive international expansion plan, including the acquisition of Accoleo, a smaller and more affordable German Airbnb clone, that allowed Airbnb to compete directly with Wimdu in its home market. By the spring of 2012, Airbnb had opened nine international offices, setting up shop in London, Hamburg, Berlin, Paris, Milan, Barcelona, Copenhagen, Moscow, and São Paulo. Bookings had grown ten times since that previous February, and in June 2012 Airbnb announced its ten millionth booking.

"The Samwers gave us a gift," Brian admitted many years later in our Blitzscaling class. "They forced us to scale faster than we ever would have." By choosing to grow at a breakneck pace, Airbnb had achieved a dominant position in its market. Despite the initial advantages that the Berlin-based Wimdu had in human resources, financial capital, and European market knowledge, the techniques that Brian and his cofounders implemented allowed Airbnb to meet and ultimately defeat its challenger.

2010: SHENZHEN, CHINA, TENCENT HEADQUARTERS

About a year before Airbnb embarked on its blitzscaling journey, in a different CEO's office on the other side of the world, the message that would change everything arrived in the middle of the night.

It was the fall of 2010, and Pony Ma (Chinese name: Ma Huateng) was trying to figure out what came next for Tencent, the company he had run since founding it in 1998 with four classmates from Shenzhen University. Thanks to its core product, the QQ instant messaging service, which had 650 million monthly active users, Tencent had become one of China's most valuable Internet companies with revenues of nearly $2 billion, a market capitalization of over $33 billion, and more than ten thousand employees. However, QQ was now a mature desktop product based on late-1990s technology, and its user base had stopped growing. Its American counterpart, AOL Instant Messenger, was already in a swift decline.

Ma was convinced that Tencent had to develop a new breakthrough product for the emerging smartphone platform—or else. "Internet companies that can react will survive," he said, "and those who can't will die."

The message Pony Ma read that night was from one of Tencent's employees, Allen Zhang (Chinese name: Zhang Xiaolong), a fellow entrepreneur whose company, Foxmail, Tencent had acquired five years earlier. Zhang now ran the company's Guangzhou R&D division, which was a two-hour drive from Tencent's Shenzhen headquarters. He had been monitoring the rapid growth of a new social messaging product called Kik, which was especially popular among young people. He decided that Tencent needed to create its own social messenger for smartphones—and quickly.

Zhang's proposal represented not only a huge opportunity but also a huge risk, with equally huge uncertainty about the outcome. While a new messenger service might appeal to young consumers, it was probably going to cannibalize QQ, which was, after all, Tencent's core business. Furthermore, Tencent had partnered with leading mobile carriers like China Mobile to receive 40 percent of the SMS charges that QQ users racked up when they sent messages to mobile phones. A new service could hurt Tencent's financial bottom line and at the same time risk its relationships with some of China's most powerful companies.

It was the sort of decision that publicly traded, ten-thousand-person companies typically refer to a committee for further study. But Ma wasn't a typical corporate executive. That very night, he gave Zhang the go-ahead to pursue the idea. Zhang put together a ten-person team, including seven engineers, to build and launch the new product.

In just two months, Zhang's small team had built a mobile-first social messaging network with a clean, minimalistic design that was the polar opposite of QQ. Ma named the service Weixin, which means "micromessage" in Mandarin. Outside of China, the service became known as WeChat.

What came next was staggering. Just sixteen months after Zhang's fateful late-night message to Ma, WeChat celebrated its one hundred millionth user. Six months after that, it had grown to two hundred million users. Four months after that, it had grown to three hundred million users.

Pony Ma's late-night bet paid off handsomely. Tencent reported 2016 revenues of $22 billion, up 48 percent from the previous year, and up nearly 700 percent since 2010, the year before WeChat's launch. By early 2018, Tencent reached a market capitalization of over $500 billion, making it one of the world's most valuable companies, and WeChat was one of the most widely and intensively used services in the world.

Fast Company called WeChat "China's app for everything," and the *Financial Times* reported that more than half of its users spend over ninety minutes a day using the app. To put WeChat in an American context, it's as if one single service combined the functions of Facebook, WhatsApp, Facebook Messenger, Venmo, Grubhub, Amazon, Uber, Apple Pay, Gmail, and even Slack into a single megaservice. You can use WeChat to do run-of-the-mill things like texting and calling people, participating in social media, and reading articles, but you can also book a taxi, buy movie tickets, make doctors' appointments, send money to friends, play games, pay your rent, order dinner for the night, plus so much more. All from a single app on your smartphone.

Ma himself recognized the importance of the decision he had made, saying in an interview, "Looking back, those two months were a matter of life and death."

These stories of extreme growth, whether in California or halfway around the world in China, are perfect examples of why it's valuable to study what blitzscaling is and how it works.

Throughout this book, we will be telling the stories of various blitzscalers. Appendix B: The Blitzscalers includes brief profiles of these companies that provide more context. For even more background, visit Blitzscaling.com.

BLITZSCALING: THE SECRET WEAPON FOR BUILDING SCALE-UPS

When a start-up matures to the point where it has a killer product, a clear and sizable market, and a robust distribution channel, it has the opportunity to become a "scale-up," which is a world-changing company that touches millions or even billions of lives. Often, the fastest and most direct path from start-up to scale-up is the hypergrowth produced by blitzscaling.

The enterprise software company Slack reached this critical stage once it was able to demonstrate the rapid and accelerating adoption of its team messaging apps by its initial market of software development teams. Nearly five years passed between the time when Slack was founded and the initial launch of its product. But once it launched, Slack users themselves drove user growth by adding many colleagues at a time, aided by a frictionless process that allowed new users to jump in with a simple

Web application or by downloading a mobile app from iTunes or Google Play. After the company reached this point, it began to scale rapidly, adding employees, capital, and customers at a blistering pace. Slack had raised $17 million during the first five years of its life; within eight months of launch, it had raised another $163 million and a total of $800 million by late 2017.

Any company, whether a global giant or a start-up in a cofounder's garage, would love to launch and grow killer businesses like Airbnb, WeChat, and Slack. Yet those who actually manage to do so, especially to the degree that Brian Chesky and Pony Ma did, are still exceedingly rare. Why is that? What sets these companies apart from the rest?

In this book, we will argue that the key to rapidly building massive businesses in today's environment is the aggressive growth strategy of blitzscaling: a set of techniques that allows both start-ups and established companies to build dominant, world-leading businesses in record time.

ENTERING THE BLITZSCALING ERA

Over the past two decades, the Internet has completely reshaped both our daily lives and the world of business. Netscape's blockbuster IPO on August 9, 1995, marked the beginning of both the dot-com boom and what I call the Networked Age. At the time, the rising stock prices of the dot-com boom attracted the most attention, but, in retrospect, the biggest change was that the Internet was beginning to connect all of us to people, information, resources, and other networks. There have been other revolutions in the past—steam, electricity, and radio spring to mind—but what makes the impact of the Internet so unique and so far-reaching is the fact it has made everything so much faster.

Today, every individual can connect to any other individual immediately; that increased velocity is what makes blitzscaling possible and so powerful.

The speed of the Internet has generated a number of second-order effects that have changed how businesses and organizations can grow. For example, the Internet has made it possible to access global markets and tap into massively scalable distribution channels in a way that wasn't feasible during earlier eras. But perhaps the most important impact for businesses has been the rising significance and prevalence of so-called network effects that occur when increased usage of a product or service boosts the value of that product or service for other users. For example, each additional Airbnb host makes the service a tiny bit more valuable for every other Airbnb guest and vice versa. Each additional WeChat user makes the service a tiny bit more valuable for every other WeChat user, and so on.

Network effects generate a positive feedback loop that can allow the first product or service that taps into those effects to build an unassailable competitive advantage. For example, eBay was founded in 1995, yet network effects keep it a dominant player in peer-to-peer commerce two decades later. Airbnb offers over three million listings in sixty-five thousand cities around the world; think of how difficult it would be for a new entrant to offer anywhere close to the same selection and value.

We're reminded of the famous scene from the movie *Glengarry Glen Ross,* in which Alec Baldwin's character, Blake, is speaking to a group of salesmen:

> As you all know, first prize is a Cadillac Eldorado. Anyone wanna see second prize? Second prize is a set of steak knives. Third prize is you're fired. Get the picture?

First prize in the first wave of consumer social networking went to Facebook; second prize to MySpace; third prize to Friendster. Remember Friendster? You need to win first prize in order to survive in the Internet era.

The level of competition can seem overwhelming at times, but the Networked Age also allows companies to reap incredible rewards much more rapidly than at any other point in history. We call the strategy and mindset they can use to get there "blitzscaling."

Blitzscaling is a strategy and set of techniques for driving and managing extremely rapid growth that prioritize speed over efficiency in an environment of uncertainty. Put another way, it's an accelerant that allows your company to grow at a furious pace that knocks the competition out of the water.

Blitzscaling requires hypergrowth but goes beyond the blunt strategy of "get big fast" because it involves purposefully and intentionally doing things that don't make sense according to traditional business thinking. In the Blitzscaling Era, you have to make a tough call:

- Take on the additional risk and discomfort of blitzscaling your company,

- Or accept what might be the even greater risk of *losing* if your competition blitzscales before you do.

Was Airbnb's decision to expand into European markets—a move that could have stretched the company so thin as to destroy its core business—either efficient or certain? Hardly. Airbnb could easily have failed, burning through all its capital while essentially ceding the European market to its copycat competitor Wimdu. Yet the risky decision proved the right one.

Blitzscaling disrupts entire industries, such as music, video games, and telephony, with both new technologies and new business models . . . and those are examples from just a single company. (You know, the one that produced the iPod, iTunes, the iPhone, and the iPad, to name just a few.) These waves of disruption affect every aspect of our daily lives, from the jobs we work, to the products we use, to the way we connect with one another.

Disruption on its own is neither good nor bad, but it always involves change. Replacing a $10 product with a $1 product of equal or better quality looks like a disaster to an incumbent player, but, for society as a whole, it means greater productivity. The buyer gets the desired product, and now also has $9 available to invest in other things. Netflix has been bad news for broadcast and cable networks, but it has been great news for fans and creators of movies and television. Yes, disruption produces losers as well as winners, but, as a whole, it is a vital source of growth and opportunity that you can't afford to ignore.

It's good to keep in mind that those who extoll the virtues of disruption tend to be—coincidentally enough—the ones in the winners' circle. But disruption that spreads its benefits and new opportunities broadly is better for society. Fortunately, most disruption falls into this category. In a 2004 working paper, "Schumpeterian Profits in the American Economy: Theory and Measurement," Yale economist William Nordhaus examined the US economy from 1948 to 2001. Based on the data he collected, he concluded that only 2.2 percent of "profits that arise when firms are able to appropriate the returns from innovative activity" went to the disrupters. "Most of the benefits of technological change are passed on to consumers rather than captured by producers," he concluded. Like it or not, change is inevitable—but it doesn't have to be wholly unexpected.

In their book *Future Shock,* the futurists Alvin and Heidi Toffler wrote that "change is the only constant," and "to survive, to avert what we have termed future shock, the individual must become infinitely more adaptable and capable than ever before." Those words were originally published in 1970. The pace of change has only accelerated since then.

Everyone should have the opportunity to learn how blitzscaling works, because it is already impacting their lives. And once they know how it works, they can use it to reshape the world. People should *be part of building the future* rather than feeling like the future is being forced upon them.

Blitzscaling is what separates the start-ups that get disrupted and disappear as the world changes from the ones that scale up to become market leaders and shape the future.

This book was born out of a class we taught at Stanford in which we dissected the process that went into growing the world's largest technology companies and then codified a series of tactics and choices that made it work. The result was a specific set of principles that describes how to grow multibillion-dollar companies in a handful of years.

While writing this book, we talked to hundreds of entrepreneurs and CEOs, including those of the world's most valuable companies, such as Facebook, Alphabet (Google), Netflix, Dropbox, Twitter, and Airbnb. (You can hear a number of these conversations on my podcast, *Masters of Scale.*) Even though the stories of their companies' rise were very different in many ways, the one thing they all had in common was an extreme, unwieldy, risky, inefficient, do-or-die approach to growth.

In this book, we draw lessons from these world-leading companies to explain the nuts and bolts of how to blitzscale, when to blitzscale, why to blitzscale, and the global impact of the companies that are blitzscaling all around you right this second.

This quest will take us all over the globe, but one place in particular stands out.

SILICON VALLEY: THE PERFECT PLACE TO DECODE BLITZSCALING

Although companies have successfully blitzscaled on every continent except for Antarctica, the most prominent and most concentrated set of examples comes from California's Silicon Valley. And while we can't simply copy and paste the techniques that work in Silicon Valley and expect them to work the same way in Shanghai, neither can we cut and paste from Shanghai to Stockholm, nor from Stockholm to São Paulo. Instead, we try to extract some universal lessons and then explore how they apply across the world.

As of this writing at the end of 2017, there are only fourteen publicly traded technology companies in the world that have a market capitalization of over $100 billion. Want to guess how many of those are in Silicon Valley? Seven—that's *half* of the world's most valuable tech companies.

Taken together, Silicon Valley's 150 most valuable publicly traded technology companies are worth $3.5 *trillion*. That number is so big it doesn't mean anything to most of us. So consider this: those 150 companies alone make up 50 percent of the value of the NASDAQ, and they account for over 5 percent of the entire world's market capitalization. That's a lot of value created by a region with an estimated 3.5 to 4 million residents, or roughly 0.05 percent of the world's population.

While we fully accept that this may change in the future, the historical and current success of Silicon Valley makes it the perfect place to examine this question: What is the most effective way to rapidly build massively valuable companies?

When outsiders look at Silicon Valley, they often think that the key to this question is innovative technology. But as you'll read, technological innovation alone doesn't make for a thriving company.

Silicon Valley insiders and well-read outsiders believe that the key is the combination of talent, capital, and entrepreneurial culture that makes it easy to start new companies. This too is wrong.

Sure, Silicon Valley is the leading hub for high-tech talent and venture capital, but it didn't start out that way. Sure, it is blessed with great universities, such as Stanford and Berkeley, but so are plenty of other regions. The answer can't be simply the combination of venture capital, research universities, and smart people. This combination of ingredients is *far* from unique. In fact, the same basic ingredients can easily be found in numerous start-up clusters in the United States and around the world: Austin, Boston, New York, Seattle, Shanghai, Bangalore, Istanbul, Stockholm, Tel Aviv, and Dubai.

To discover the secret to Silicon Valley's success, you need to look beyond the standard origin story. When people think of Silicon Valley, the first things that spring to mind—after the HBO television show, of course—are the names of famous start-ups and their equally glamorized founders: Apple, Google, Facebook; Jobs/Wozniak, Page/Brin, Zuckerberg.

The success narrative of these hallowed names has become so universally familiar that people from countries around the world can tell it just as well as Sand Hill Road venture capitalists. It goes something like this: A brilliant entrepreneur discovers an incredible opportunity. After dropping out of college, he or she gathers a small team who are happy to work for equity, sets up shop in a humble garage, plays foosball, raises money from sage venture capitalists, and proceeds to change the world—after which, of course, the founders and early employees live happily ever after, using the wealth they've amassed to fund both a new generation of entrepreneurs and a set of eponymous buildings for Stanford University's Computer Science Department.

It's an exciting and inspiring story. We get the appeal. There's only one problem. It's incomplete and deceptive in several important ways.

First, while "Silicon Valley" and "start-ups" are used almost synonymously these days, only a tiny fraction of the world's start-ups actually originate in Silicon Valley, and this fraction has been getting smaller as start-up knowledge spreads around the globe. Thanks to the Internet, entrepreneurs everywhere have access to the same information. Moreover, as other markets have matured, smart founders from around the globe are electing to build companies in start-up hubs in their home countries rather than immigrating to Silicon Valley.

Second, simply starting a company is obviously insufficient. The start-ups that achieve massive value are those that have found a way to grow into scale-ups at an exponentially faster pace than their competitors.

So what secret alchemy is at work in Silicon Valley to fuel such rapid-fire growth of so many of the world's most valuable tech companies? And if there *is* a secret, can it be identified, analyzed, understood, and, most important, applied elsewhere?

Blitzscaling is that secret. And the reason blitzscaling matters so much is that *nothing* about it is inherent to Silicon Valley.

There's a common misconception that Silicon Valley is the accelerator of the world. The real story is that the world keeps getting faster—Silicon Valley is just the first place to figure out how to keep pace. While Silicon Valley certainly has many key networks and resources that make it easier to apply the techniques we're going to lay out for you, blitzscaling is made up of basic principles that do not depend on geography. We're going to show you examples from overlooked parts of the United States, such as Detroit (Rocket Mortgage) and Connecticut (Priceline), as well as from international companies, such as WeChat and Spotify. In the process you'll see how the lessons of blitzscaling can be adapted to help build great companies in nearly any ecosystem, albeit with differing degrees of difficulty.

That's the mission of this book. We want to share the secret weapon that has allowed Silicon Valley to punch so much (more than a hundred times) above its population index so that those lessons can be applied far beyond the sixty-mile stretch between the Golden Gate Bridge and San Jose.

It is sorely needed.

Here's a startling fact: the global economy will need to create *six hundred million new jobs* by 2030 to meet the United Nations' sustainable development goals. That's less than fifteen years away. The world needs more than just new companies and new jobs; it's going to need entire new industries.

Those industries better generate scale-ups as well as start-ups. It seems to us that it will be a lot easier to add six hundred million new jobs worldwide by creating sixty thousand new ten-thousand-person companies rather than sixty million new ten-person companies.

The late, great Andy Grove, Intel's legendary CEO, understood and explained this when he wrote in a 2010 op-ed for Bloomberg:

> Start-ups are a wonderful thing, but they cannot by themselves increase tech employment. Equally important is what comes after that mythical moment of creation in the garage, as technology goes from prototype to mass production. This is the phase where companies scale up. They work out design details, figure out how to make things affordably, build

factories, and hire people by the thousands. Scaling is hard work but necessary to make innovation matter.

Recognizing what powers the rapid growth from start-up to scale-up, and understanding the principles behind how it works, will help entrepreneurs and companies apply these principles not just in small pockets of the United States and China but around the world.

WHO SHOULD READ THIS BOOK?

This book is for anyone who wants to understand the techniques that allow a business to grow from zero to a multibillion-dollar market leader in a handful of years.

These techniques should be of interest to entrepreneurs who want to build massive companies, venture capitalists who want to invest in them, employees who want to work for them, and governments and communities who wish to encourage the growth of these companies in their own regions. And even if you don't want to build, invest in, or work for any of these companies, you'll still need to navigate the world that they're building.

If you are a manager or a leader who is trying to rapidly scale a project or a business unit within a larger company, blitzscaling can help you too. And while we draw these lessons primarily from the world of high tech, many of the principles and frameworks the book lays out (especially regarding people management) are applicable to high-growth companies in most industries worldwide, from European fast-fashion retailers to Texan oil shale companies.

Even organizations outside the business world can use blitzscaling to their advantage. Upstart presidential campaigns and nonprofits serving the underprivileged have used the levers of blitzscaling to overturn conventional wisdom and achieve massive results. You'll read all these stories, and many more, in the pages of this book.

Whether you are a founder, a manager, a potential employee, or an investor, we believe that understanding blitzscaling will allow you to make better decisions in a world where speed is the critical competitive advantage.

With the power of blitzscaling, the adopted son of a Syrian immigrant (Steve Jobs), the adopted son of a Cuban immigrant (Jeff Bezos), and a former English teacher and volunteer tour guide (Jack Ma) were all able to build businesses that changed—and are still changing—the world.

The strategy and techniques we describe in this book are based on my experiences as a member of the founding team at PayPal; as the cofounder, CEO, and now executive chairman at LinkedIn; as a leading investor in Facebook and Airbnb; and as an investor at Greylock Partners, where I worked with many other billion-dollar companies, such as Workday, Pandora, Cloudera, and Pure Storage. My partners at Greylock and I have helped these companies go from garage to global dominance, and, in this book, we'll share with you what we believe are important frameworks for understanding and addressing the challenge of blitzscaling across the different elements of your organization.

Yet as many good business books disclaim, while this is a playbook and a strategy guide, it isn't a book of precise recipes. Regardless of how the popular press portrays things, each formula for building a great company is unique and depends on the market opportunity, the founders, and the network in which they operate. The truth is there is absolutely nothing guaranteed as a one-size-fits-all, must-follow *rule*book for everyone. However, there *are* patterns. So in addition to individual tips and tricks, this book offers a set of frameworks and strategies for leaders, entrepreneurs, and intrapreneurs to adapt to their own needs and circumstances.

A QUICK NOTE ON THE TERM "BLITZSCALING"

The term "blitzscaling" derives from the twentieth-century usage of "blitz" as a way of describing a sudden, all-out effort. The first usage of blitz in this way was to describe the "blitzkrieg" ("lightning war") strategy that General Heinz Guderian devised for the initial military campaigns of Nazi Germany during World War II. Ironically enough, Guderian was heavily influenced by British military thinkers like Basil Liddell Hart and J. F. C. Fuller, and the term "blitzkrieg" was actually popularized by the British press; the German military never formally adopted it.

The advancing armies in these campaigns abandoned the traditional approach of moving at the slow pace at which they could establish secure lines of supply and retreat. Instead they fully committed to an offensive strategy that accepted the possibility of running out of fuel, provisions, and ammunition, risking potentially disastrous defeat in order to maximize speed and surprise. The speed of these armies' advance shocked and overwhelmed their opponents, allowing the blitzkriegers to outmaneuver and outfight the defending forces.

The early success of the German army helped spread the lessons of blitzkrieg to all the forces in the war. For example, the American general George S. Patton later put these lessons to good use in leading the US Third Army's advance from the beaches of Normandy all the way to Berlin. Since then, the term "blitz" has been used to describe everything from an American football play to the way in which large corporations roll out new products. Like the all-out blitz defense in football—which involves the risky move of sending every available defender to pursue the quarterback—or the proverbial marketing blitz of television, print, and online advertising that accompanies the release of a new blockbuster movie, blitzscaling strives for a relentless and dizzying speed that overwhelms the market.

While we are wary of the negative connotations of "blitz," especially in those nations that felt the effects of blitzkrieg in World War II, we believe that the strength of the metaphor and the widespread and colloquial use of the term in nonmilitary contexts make it the best fit for the concepts discussed in this book.

PART I

What Is Blitzscaling?

Blitzscaling is what we call both the general framework and the specific techniques that allow companies to achieve massive scale at incredible speed. If you're growing at a rate that is so much faster than your competitors that it makes you feel uncomfortable, then hold on tight, you might be blitzscaling!

Amazon's incredible growth in the late 1990s (and up through today) is a prime example of blitzscaling. In 1996, a pre-IPO Amazon Books had 151 employees and generated revenues of $5.1 million. By 1999, the now-public Amazon.com had grown to 7,600 employees and generated revenues of $1.64 billion. That's a 50 times increase in staff and a 322 times increase in revenue in just three years. In 2017, Amazon had 541,900 employees and was forecast to generate revenues of $177 billion (up from $136 billion in 2016).

Dropbox founder Drew Houston described the feeling produced by this kind of growth when he told me, "It's like harpooning a whale. The good news is, you've harpooned a whale. And the bad news is, you've harpooned a whale!"

While blitzscaling may seem desirable, it is also fraught with challenges. Blitzscaling is just about as counterintuitive as it comes. The classic approach to business strategy involves gathering information and making decisions when you can be reasonably confident of the results. Take risks, conventional wisdom says, but take calculated ones that you can both measure and afford. Implicitly, this technique prioritizes correctness and efficiency over speed.

Unfortunately, this cautious and measured approach falls apart when new technologies enable a new market or scramble an existing one.

Chris earned his MBA from Harvard Business School in the late 1990s, during the dawn of the Networked Age. Back then, his MBA training focused on traditional techniques, such as using discounted cash flow analysis to make financial decisions with greater certainty. Chris also learned about traditional manufacturing techniques, such as how to maximize the throughput of an assembly line. These methods focused on achieving efficiency and certainty, and the same emphasis was reflected in the broader business world. The world's most valuable company during that time, General Electric, was beloved by Wall Street analysts for its ability to deliver consistent and predictable earnings growth. But efficiency and certainty, while innately appealing, and very important in the context of a stable, established market, offer little guidance to the disrupters, inventors, and innovators of the world.

When a market is up for grabs, the risk isn't inefficiency—the risk is playing it too safe. If you win, efficiency isn't that important; if you lose, efficiency is completely irrelevant. Over the years, many have criticized Amazon for its risky strategy of consuming capital without delivering consistent profits, but Amazon is probably glad that its "inefficiency" helped it win several key markets—online retail, ebooks, and cloud computing, to name just a few.

When you blitzscale, you deliberately make decisions and commit to them even though your confidence level is substantially lower than 100 percent. You accept the risk of making the wrong decision and willingly pay the cost of significant operating inefficiencies in exchange for the ability to move faster. These risks and costs are acceptable because the risk and cost of being too slow is even greater. But blitzscaling is more than just plunging ahead blindly in an effort to "get big fast" to win the market. To mitigate the downside of the risks you take, you should try to focus them—line them up with a small number of hypotheses about how your business will develop so that you can more easily understand and monitor what drives your success or failure. You also have to be prepared to execute with more than 100 percent effort to compensate for the bets that don't go your way.

For example, anyone who knows Jeff Bezos knows that he didn't simply mash his foot down on the gas pedal; Amazon has intentionally invested aggressively in the future, and, despite its accounting losses, generates a ton of cash. Amazon's operating cash flow was over $16 billion in 2016, but it spent $10 billion in investments and $4 billion paying down debt. Its seemingly meager profits are a feature of its aggressive strategy, not a bug.

Blitzscaling requires more than just courage and skill on the part of the entrepreneur. It also requires an environment that is willing to finance intelligent risks with both financial capital and human capital, which are the essential ingredients for blitzscaling. Think of them as fuel and oxygen; you need both to propel the rocket skyward. Meanwhile, the infrastructure of your organization is the actual structure of your rocket, which you're rebuilding on the fly as you rise. Your job as a leader and an entrepreneur is to make sure that you have sufficient fuel to propel your growth while making the necessary mechanical adjustments to the actual rocket ship to keep it from flying apart as it accelerates.

Fortunately, this is more possible today than it has ever been in the past.

SOFTWARE IS EATING (AND SAVING) THE WORLD

Historically, stories of breakneck growth involved either computer software, which offers nearly unlimited scalability in terms of distribution, or software-enabled hardware, such as the Fitbit fitness tracker or Tesla electric car, whose software component allows the company to innovate on software timescales (days or weeks) rather than hardware timescales (years). Moreover, the speed and flexibility of software development allow companies to iterate and recover from the inevitable missteps of haste.

What's especially exciting these days is that software and software-enabled companies are starting to dominate industries outside of traditional high tech. My friend Marc Andreessen has argued that "software is eating the world." What he means is that even industries that focus on physical products (atoms) are integrating with software (bits). Tesla makes cars (atoms), but a software update (bits) can upgrade the acceleration of those cars and add an autopilot overnight.

The spread of software and computing into every industry, along with the dense networks that connect us all, means that the lessons of blitzscaling are becoming more relevant and easier to implement, even in mature or low-tech industries. To use a computing metaphor, technology is accelerating the world's "clock speed" (the rate at which Central Processing Units [CPUs] operate), making change occur faster than previously thought possible. Not only is the world moving faster, but the speed at which major new technology platforms are being created is reducing the downtime between the arrivals of each wave of innovation. Before, individual waves would sweep through the economy one at a time—technologies like personal computers, disk drives, and CD-ROMs. Today, multiple major waves seem to be arriving simultaneously—technologies like the cloud, AI, AR/VR, not to mention more esoteric projects like supersonic planes and hyperloops. What's more, rather than being concentrated narrowly in a personal computer industry that was essentially a niche market, today's new technologies impact nearly every part of the economy, creating many new opportunities.

This trend holds tremendous promise. Precision medicine will use computing power to revolutionize health care. Smart grids use software to dramatically improve power efficiency and enable the spread of renewable energy sources like solar roofs. And computational biology might allow us to improve life itself. Blitzscaling can help these advances spread and magnify their sorely needed impact.

THE TYPES OF SCALING

Blitzscaling isn't simply a matter of rapid growth. *Every* company is obsessed with growth. In any industry, you live and die by the numbers—user acquisition, margins, growth rate, and so on. Yet growth alone is not blitzscaling. Rather, blitzscaling is *prioritizing speed over efficiency in the face of uncertainty.* We can better understand blitzscaling by comparing it to other forms of rapid growth.

	Efficiency	Speed
Uncertainty	Classic Start-up Growth	Blitzscaling
Certainty	Classic Scale-up Growth	Fastscaling

Classic start-up growth prioritizes efficiency in the face of uncertainty. Starting a company is like jumping off a cliff and assembling an airplane on the way down; being resource-efficient lets you "glide" to minimize the rate of descent, giving you the time to learn things about your market, technology, and team before you hit the ground. This kind of controlled, efficient growth reduces uncertainty and is a good strategy to follow while you're trying to establish certainty around what the authors Eric Ries and Steve Blank call product/market fit: your product satisfies a strong market demand for the solution to a specific problem or need.

Classic scale-up growth focuses on growing efficiently once the company has achieved certainty about the environment. This approach reflects classic corporate management techniques, such as applying "hurdle rates" so that the return on investment (ROI) of corporate projects consistently exceeds the cost of capital. This kind of optimization is a good strategy to follow when you're trying to maximize returns in an established, stable market.

Fastscaling means that you're willing to sacrifice efficiency for the sake of increasing your growth rate. However, because fastscaling takes place in an environment of certainty, the costs are well understood and predictable. Fastscaling is a good strategy for gaining market share or trying to achieve revenue milestones. Indeed, the financial services industry is often happy to finance fastscaling, whether by buying stocks and bonds or lending money. Analysts and bankers feel confident that they can create elaborate financial models that work out to the penny the likely ROI of a fastscaling investment.

Blitzscaling means that you're willing to sacrifice efficiency for speed, but without waiting to achieve certainty on whether the sacrifice will pay off. If classic start-up growth is about slowing your rate of descent as you try to assemble your plane, blitzscaling is about assembling that plane faster, then strapping on and igniting a set of jet engines (and possibly their afterburners) while you're still building the wings. It's "do or die," with either success or death occurring in a remarkably short time.

Given these definitions, you might wonder why anyone would ever pursue blitzscaling. After all, it combines the gut-wrenching uncertainty of start-up growth with the potential for a much bigger, more embarrassing, more consequential failure. Blitzscaling is also hard to implement. Unless you're like Microsoft or Google and can finance your growth from an exponentially growing revenue stream, you'll need to convince investors to give you money, and it's much harder to raise money from investors for a calculated gamble (blitzscaling) than for a sure thing (fastscaling). To make matters worse, you usually need *more* money to blitzscale than to fastscale, because you have to keep enough capital in reserve to recover from the many mistakes you're likely to make along the way.

Yet despite all of these potential pitfalls, blitzscaling remains a powerful tool for entrepreneurs and other business leaders. If you're willing to accept the risks of blitzscaling when others aren't, you'll be able to move faster than they will. If the prize to be won is big enough, and the competition to win it is intense enough, blitzscaling becomes a rational, even optimal strategy.

Once you convince the market for capital and the market for talent—which include clients and partners, as well as employees—to invest in your scale-up, you have the fuel required to start blitzscaling. At that point, your objective switches from going from zero to one to going from one to one billion in an incredibly compressed time frame.

A company might employ different types of scaling at different points in its life cycle. The canonical sequence that companies like Google and Facebook have gone through begins with classic start-up growth while establishing product/market fit, then shifts into blitzscaling to achieve critical mass and/or market dominance ahead of the competition, then relaxes down to fastscaling as the business matures, and finally downshifts to classic scale-up growth when the company is an established industry leader. Together, this sequence of scaling generates a classic "S-curve" of growth, with slower initial growth followed by rapid acceleration, eventually easing its way into a gentle plateau.

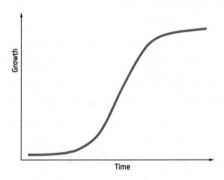

Of course, this canonical sequence is greatly simplified. The scaling cycle applies not just to whole companies but to individual products and business lines; the aggregate curves of these scaling cycles generate the overall scaling curve for the company.

For example, Facebook began as a classic blitzscaling story. The year-over-year revenue growth during its first few years of existence were 2,150 percent, 433 percent, and 219 percent, going from zero to $153 million in revenue in 2007. Then the company went through a key transition, and growth dropped into the double-digit range as Facebook struggled with both monetization and the shift from desktop to mobile. Fortunately, Facebook founder Mark Zuckerberg made two important moves: he personally led a shift from desktop-first to mobile-first, and he hired Sheryl Sandberg as the company's COO, who in turn built Facebook into an advertising sales juggernaut. Growth rose back into the triple-digit range, and, by 2010, these moves had pushed Facebook's revenues to over $2 billion. We'll examine both of these key moves in greater detail later in the book, with Facebook's shift to mobile featured in our analysis of Facebook's business model, and Facebook's hiring of Sheryl Sandberg in the section on the key transition from contributors to managers to executives.

Apple illustrates how this overlap looks over multiple decades. In its storied history, Apple went through complete scaling cycles for the Apple II, the Macintosh, the iMac, and the iPod (with the cycle for the iPhone still under way). It's worth noting that Apple failed to launch any blitzscalable products after the Apple II and the Mac until Steve Jobs returned and launched the iMac, iPod, and iPhone. It was part of Steve's rare genius that time and time again he was able to pick the right product for Apple to blitz-scale, even without slowing down for a period of classic start-up growth to gather feedback from the market.

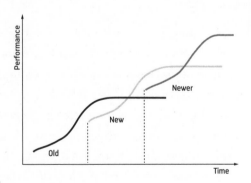

The scaling curve applies to every blitzscaler, regardless of industry or geography. The same multiple S-curve graph that describes Facebook or Apple also describes Tencent, which launched with QQ, then added a second curve for WeChat after QQ reached maturity in 2010. Just when you've finished blitzscaling one business line, you need to blitzscale the next to maintain your company's upward trajectory. And as blitzscaling continues to spread, established companies with mature business lines should consider turning to intrapreneurs to blitzscale new business units.

THE THREE BASICS OF BLITZSCALING

Blitzscaling requires you to move at a pace that is almost certainly uncomfortable for your team. You will definitely make many mistakes as you navigate an environment full of uncertainty; the art lies in developing the skill to learn quickly from those mistakes and return to a relentlessly rapid advance. But first, it's critical to understand three basics.

1. BLITZSCALING IS BOTH AN OFFENSIVE STRATEGY AND A DEFENSIVE STRATEGY.

On offense, blitzscaling allows you to do several things. First, you can take the market by surprise, bypassing heavily defended niches to exploit breakout opportunities. For example, Slack's rapid growth after its launch blindsided a host of entrenched competitors like Microsoft and Salesforce.com. Second, you can leverage your lead to build long-term competitive advantages before other players are able to respond. We'll explore this concept in greater detail later on. Third, blitzscaling opens up access to capital, because investors generally prefer to back market leaders. You can win this mantle if you blitzscale, and with it raise more money more easily and more quickly than your lagging competitors.

On defense, blitzscaling lets you set a pace that keeps your competitors gasping simply to keep up, affording them little time and space to counterattack. Because they're focused on responding to your moves, which can often take them by surprise and force them to play catch-up, they don't have as much time available to develop and execute differentiated strategies that might threaten your position. Blitzscaling helps you determine the playing field to your great advantage.

2. BLITZSCALING THRIVES ON POSITIVE FEEDBACK LOOPS, IN THAT THE COMPANY THAT GROWS TO SCALE FIRST REAPS SIGNIFICANT COMPETITIVE ADVANTAGES.

In April 2014, McKinsey & Company published a report entitled "Grow fast or die slow," which analyzed the life cycles of three thousand software and Internet companies, and found that positive feedback loops made rapid growth the key factor in financial success:

> First, growth yields greater returns. High-growth companies offer a return to shareholders five times greater than medium-growth companies. Second, growth predicts long-term success. "Supergrowers"—companies whose growth was greater than 60 percent when they reached $100 million in revenues—were eight times more likely to reach $1 billion in revenues than those growing less than 20 percent.

We believe that the mechanism behind the power of blitzscaling is "first-scaler advantage." Once a scale-up occupies the high ground in its ecosystem, the networks around it recognize its leadership, and both talent and capital flood in.

For one, top professionals understand that they can have a

greater impact working for the market leader. Meanwhile, joining a scale-up that is clearly a "rocket ship" offers many of the financial rewards of working for an early-stage start-up, with far more certainty and far less risk. Scale-up employees are paid market salaries, receive equity upside, and have a very good chance of becoming rich, if not filthy rich. By attracting the best people, scale-ups increase their ability to build and bring to market great products, which in turn increases their ability to rapidly scale.

A parallel calculus applies to investors. Venture capitalists (VCs) make investment decisions based on the confidence interval they have in their investment thesis. Achieving scale shrinks those intervals and makes it easier to decide to invest. And because the network that connects investors—especially within a tight-knit ecosystem like Silicon Valley—can disseminate this information quickly and broadly, a blitzscaling company can raise capital on a massive scale. This capital infusion can fuel explosive growth, which shrinks the confidence intervals even further.

Paradoxically, globalization has both leveled the playing field for entrepreneurs around the world *and* increased the value of being in a premier scaling hub like Silicon Valley or China. Because the rest of the world believes that these ecosystems have an advantage in scaling up start-ups, those start-ups and their investors attract capital (human and financial) from all over the world, further bolstering their ability to keep growing. This is a key reason why scale-ups like Uber and Pinterest have achieved a scale and valuation that dwarf those of most publicly traded companies. Due to my role at Greylock Partners, I can't comment on the valuations of Dropbox and Airbnb, but they occupy a similar place in the ecosystem.

Consider the case of two very similar companies, Twitter and Tumblr. Both had brilliant, product-oriented founders in Evan

"Ev" Williams and David Karp. Both were hot social media start-ups. Both grew at a remarkable rate after establishing product/market fit. Both had a major impact on popular culture. Yet Twitter went public and achieved a market capitalization that peaked at nearly $37 billion, while Tumblr was acquired by Yahoo!—another start-up that used blitzscaling to become a scale-up, only to decline and fade away—for "only" $1 billion.

Was this dumb luck on Twitter's side? Perhaps. Luck always plays a larger role than founders, investors, and the media would like to admit. But a major difference was that Twitter could draw on numerous networks for advice and help that Tumblr could not. For example, Twitter was able to bring in Dick Costolo, a savvy executive with prior scaling experience at Google. In contrast, even though Tumblr was arguably the most prominent start-up in its New York City ecosystem, it couldn't easily draw upon a pool of local talent who had experience dealing with rapid growth. According to Greylock's John Lilly, for every executive role that Tumblr needed to fill, there were less than a handful of candidates in all of New York City. This paucity of talent made hiring difficult; the company was reluctant to replace existing employees due to a lack of better alternatives. Without the ability to hire an executive team that could blitzscale, Tumblr decided to sell the company.

Of course, while geography can present challenges to blitzscaling, they become much more solvable if you're aware of them. For example, over the past decade, Priceline—the world's most successful online travel company—has been able to blitzscale from its headquarters in Connecticut. The CEO who led Priceline during its growth phase, Jeffery Boyd, saw advantages to this geographic isolation, noting that the company's location meant that it faced fewer bidding wars for the key software engineers and designers needed to support the rapid growth of the business.

It's extremely difficult for later entrants to compete directly with a blitzscaling company that has first-scaler advantage. Unless these players find a different game in which they can capture this advantage, they'll simply become irrelevant.

3. DESPITE ITS INCREDIBLE ADVANTAGES AND POTENTIAL PAYOFFS, BLITZSCALING ALSO COMES WITH MASSIVE RISKS.

Until recently, "Move fast and break things" was Facebook's famous motto. Yet rapid growth can cause nearly as many problems as it solves. As Mark Zuckerberg told me in an interview for my *Masters of Scale* podcast, "We got to a point where it was taking us more time to go back and fix the bugs and issues that we're creating than the speed that we were gaining by going faster." In one famous incident, a summer intern introduced a bug that brought down the entire Facebook site for thirty minutes.

There is a scientific term for out-of-control growth in the human body: "cancer." In this context, uncontrolled growth is clearly undesirable. The same is true for a business. Successful blitzscaling means that you're maintaining at least some level of control by rapidly fixing the things that will inevitably get broken so that the company can maintain its furious pace without flaming out or collapsing in on itself. Like an American football player streaking down the field for a game-winning touchdown, even a company that has achieved first-scaler advantage can lose the ball prior to crossing the goal line if it takes on a bigger risk than it can handle.

Blitzscaling is risky from a management perspective as well. Reinventing your leadership style, your product, and your organization at every new phase of scale won't be easy, but it is necessary. In the words of leadership guru Marshall Goldsmith, "What got you here won't get you there."

Market share and revenue growth earn headlines, but you can't achieve customer and revenue scale without scaling up your organization, in terms of the size and scope of your staff, as well as your financial, product, and technology strategy. If the organization doesn't grow in lockstep with its revenues and customer base, things can quickly spiral out of control.

For example, during a period of blitzscaling in the late 1980s and early 1990s, Oracle Corporation focused so single-mindedly on sales growth that its organization lagged badly on both technology (where it fell behind archrival Sybase's) and finance and nearly went bankrupt as a result. It took the turnaround efforts of Ray Lane and Jeff Henley to stave off disaster and reposition Oracle for its later success.

Blitzscaling your organization will require hard choices and sacrifices; for example, the people who are adept at launching a company aren't necessarily going to be the right people to scale it, as the Oracle example above demonstrates. Later in the book we'll discuss how successful blitzscalers consciously manage growth rather than letting it manage them.

THE FIVE STAGES OF BLITZSCALING

Blitzscaling a start-up isn't a linear process; a global giant isn't simply a start-up that's been multiplied by one thousand, working out of a gleaming high-rise headquarters instead of a grimy garage. Each major increment of growth represents a qualitative as well as quantitative change. Drew Houston of Dropbox expressed this well when he told me, "The chessboard keeps adding new pieces and new dimensions over time."

In the physical sciences, materials often undergo phase changes as their circumstances (e.g., temperature and pressure) change. Ice melts into water; water boils into steam. As a start-up scales up from one phase to the next, it undergoes fundamental changes as well.

And in the same way that ice skates are useless on water, and you can't skip rocks on water vapor, the approaches and processes that worked for one phase break down once the scale-up reaches the next phase.

This book is designed to help you successfully navigate the phase changes you'll face on the path to global dominance.

Throughout this book, we will refer to the five key stages of blitzscaling using the metaphor of a community. Since the most obvious, visible, and impactful change in a scale-up is the number of people it employs, we'll define the stages based on the number of employees in the company, or its organizational scale.

THE FIVE STAGES OF BLITZSCALING

Stage 1 (Family)	1–9 employees
Stage 2 (Tribe)	10s of employees
Stage 3 (Village)	100s of employees
Stage 4 (City)	1000s of employees
Stage 5 (Nation)	10000s of employees

Each stage has critical differences when it comes to management and leadership. When you're head of a nuclear Family, you have close relationships with all of your Family members. When you're the head of a whole Nation, you're responsible for the lives of a multitude of people, most of whom you'll never meet. (Later in the book we'll talk about how to optimize your people management strategy as your company grows.)

It's important to remember that while these powers of ten provide a clear and consistent set of categories, real life is often messier. For example, a start-up with a tight-knit team might feel and act like a Family even if it has nearly twenty employees. So these definitions are meant simply to offer a useful set of guidelines.

We also recognize that the number of employees is only one of several measures of an organization's scale. Some of the other measures of scale include the number of users (user scale), the number of customers (customer scale), and total annual revenues (business scale). These measures usually, but don't always, move in lockstep. While it's nearly impossible to achieve customer scale or business scale without organizational scale—customers require customer service representatives, and revenues typically require salespeople—it is possible to achieve user scale without organizational scale. Consider the example of Instagram: when that company was acquired by Facebook for $1 billion, it had over one hundred million users but just thirteen employees and no significant revenues.

The fact that the phases don't always move in lockstep is a *feature* of blitzscaling, not a bug. As we'll discuss, operational scalability is one of the primary growth limiters that scale-ups need to address. When a business can grow users, customers, and revenues faster than the number of employees without collapsing under the weight of its own growth, the business can achieve greater profitability and keep growing without being as tightly constrained by the need for financial or human capital. In contrast, when the number of employees grows faster than users, customers, and revenues, it's a major red flag that could indicate issues with the fundamental business model.

Nevertheless, for the sake of simplicity, this book will typically define the stage of a company by its organizational scale. A Family-stage company will have one to nine employees, a Tribe-stage company will have ten to ninety-nine employees, and so on.

When exceptions arise, we'll specifically call them out to avoid confusion.

THE THREE KEY TECHNIQUES OF BLITZSCALING

Through much study of, direct access to, and conversation with the leadership at companies such as Google, Amazon, and Facebook—and through my own experiences as an entrepreneur and an investor—we've been able to identify the three key techniques applied by entrepreneurs and investors to build dominant companies. These basic principles do not depend on geography and can be adapted to build great companies in any ecosystem, albeit with varying degrees of difficulty.

TECHNIQUE #1: BUSINESS MODEL INNOVATION

The first technique of blitzscaling is to design an innovative business model that can truly grow. This sounds like a Start-ups 101–level insight, but it's astounding how many founders miss this key element. A major mistake made by many start-ups around the world is focusing on the technology, the software, the product, and the design, but neglecting to ever figure out the business. And by "business" we simply mean how the company makes money by acquiring and serving its customers. In contrast, despite the popular "engineers are gods" narrative prevalent in Silicon Valley, the companies and founders we universally hail as geniuses aren't just technology nerds—they're almost always business nerds too. At Google, Larry Page and Sergey Brin built great search algorithms, but it was their innovations to the search engine *business model*—specifically, considering relevance and performance when displaying advertisements rather than simply renting space to the highest bidder—that drove their massive success.

As the world has gone digital, business model innovation has become even more important. So many technologies are available as services, which are on demand and built to be integrated, that technology is no longer as strong a differentiator, while figuring out the right combinations of services to bring together into a breakthrough product has become a major differentiator. Most of today's successful companies are more like Tesla, which combines a set of technologies that already existed, rather than SpaceX, which had to pioneer new ones.

Business model innovation is how start-ups are able to outcompete established competitors who typically hold a host of advantages over any upstarts. As a start-up, Dropbox competes with giants like Microsoft and Google, who ought to have major advantages in technology, finance, and market power. Dropbox founder and CEO Drew Houston knows that his company can't simply rely on better technology or outexecuting the competition: "If your playbook is the same as your competitor's, you are in trouble, because chances are they are just going to run your playbook with a lot more resources!"

Drew had to design a better business model, in which the focus on sharing files means that the number of files Dropbox has to store (or in the past, pay Amazon to store) increases far more slowly than the value created for the customer and thus the revenues Dropbox can collect from those customers. Uber and Airbnb also built large businesses at incredible speed based on novel business models rather than unprecedented new technologies. If technological innovation alone were enough, federal research labs would produce $100 billion companies on a regular basis. Spoiler alert: they don't.

This is not to say that technology innovation is unimportant. Technology innovation is the most common trigger for launching a new market or upending an existing one. Uber wasn't the first company to try to improve the experience of hailing a taxi. But prior to the technological innovation of the smartphone, complete with wireless Internet connection and GPS-enabled location-based services, Uber's business model simply wouldn't have worked. These innovations reduced the friction for both driver and rider, making Uber's core UberX ridesharing model a mass-market possibility for the first time.

Nor can companies afford to ignore technology innovation after they successfully blitzscale their way to City or Nation stage. Each and every one of the technology companies worth over $100 billion has used technology leadership to reinforce its competitive advantages. Amazon may have started as a simple online retailer with no unique technology, but today its technological prowess in cloud computing, automated logistics, and voice recognition help to maintain its dominance. In fact, the megacompanies built by blitzscaling are often the ones buying the technology innovators, much as Google bought DeepMind and Facebook bought Oculus.

Technology innovation is a key factor in retaining the gains produced by business model innovation. After all, if one technology innovation can create a new market, another technology innovation can render it obsolete, seemingly overnight. While Uber has achieved massive scale, the greatest threat to its future doesn't come in the form of direct competitors like Didi Chuxing, though these are formidable threats. The greatest threat to Uber's business is the technology innovation of autonomous vehicles, which could make obsolete one of Uber's biggest competitive advantages—its carefully cultivated network of drivers—essentially overnight.

The key is to combine new technologies with effective distribution to potential customers, a scalable and high-margin revenue model, and an approach that allows you to serve those customers given your probable resource constraints.

Ideally, you design your business model innovation before you start your company. This is what happened when I cofounded LinkedIn. The key business model innovations for LinkedIn, including the two-way nature of the relationships and filling professionals' need for a business-oriented online identity, didn't just happen organically. They were the result of much thought and reflection, and I drew on the experiences I had when founding SocialNet, one of the first online social networks, nearly a decade before the creation of LinkedIn. But life isn't always so neat. Many companies, even famous and successful ones, have to develop their business model innovation after they have already commenced operations.

PayPal didn't have a business model when it began operations (I was a key member of the PayPal executive team). We were growing exponentially, at 5 percent per day, and we were losing money on every single transaction we processed. The funny thing is that some of our critics called us insane for paying customers bonuses to refer their friends. Those referral bonuses were actually brilliant, because their cost was so much lower than the standard cost of acquiring new financial services customers via advertising. (We'll discuss the power and importance of this kind of viral marketing later on.)

The insanity, in fact, was that we were allowing our users to accept credit card payments, sticking PayPal with the cost of paying 3 percent of each transaction to the credit card processors, while charging our users nothing. I remember once telling my old college friend and PayPal cofounder/CEO Peter Thiel, "Peter, if you and I were standing on the roof of our office and throwing stacks of hundred-dollar bills off the edge as fast as our arms could go, we still wouldn't be losing money as quickly as we are right now." We ended up solving the problem by charging businesses to accept payments, much as the credit card processors did, but funding those payments using automated clearinghouse (ACH) bank transactions, which cost a fraction of the charges associated with the credit card networks. But if we had waited until we had solved this problem before blitzscaling, I suspect we wouldn't have become the market leader.

TECHNIQUE #2: STRATEGY INNOVATION

The most obvious element of blitzscaling is the pursuit of extreme growth, which, when combined with an innovative business model, can generate massive value and long-term competitive advantage. Many start-ups believe they are pursuing a strategy of extreme growth, when in fact they have the *goal* and the *wish* for extreme growth but no understanding of an actual strategy that will get them there. To achieve your goals, you have to know what you plan to do and, just as important, what you plan *not* to do. Also, growth doesn't create value in and of itself; for that, it has to be paired with a working business model. It's easy to achieve extreme customer and revenue growth if your company sells $20 bills for $1, but "we'll make it up in volume" won't allow you to build any sustainable value.

For successful blitzscaling, the competitive advantage comes from the growth factors built into the business model, such as network effects, whereby the first company to achieve critical scale triggers a feedback loop that allows it to dominate a winner-take-all or winner-take-most market and achieve a lasting first-scaler advantage. For example, Uber's strategy of aggressive city-by-city expansion allows its customers to hail rides with fewer delays than its competitors. Uber wants you to be able to get a ride faster with Uber than with anyone else. This attracts more customers, which attracts more drivers, which increases the liquidity of the marketplace, which allows customers to hail rides even more quickly, which attracts more customers, and so on. Early Uber investor Bill Gurley laid out Uber's strategy in his 2012 blog post "All Markets Are Not Created Equal."

> As the company grows, they are able to facilitate more cars on the road, and along with their investment in route and load optimization, this allows for shorter and shorter pickup times. The experience gets better and better the longer they are in the market.

Blitzscaling goes beyond just a strategy of aggressive growth because it involves doing things that don't make sense according to traditional business thinking, such as prioritizing speed over efficiency despite an uncertain environment. At the same time, blitzscaling also goes beyond just risk taking. It may be risky to bet the company, as Walt Disney did when he borrowed against his own life insurance to build Disneyland, but it's not blitzscaling. Blitzscaling would have involved inefficiencies like paying construction crews to work twenty-four hours a day in order to get Disneyland open a few months earlier, or reducing ticket prices 90 percent to get to one million visitors faster—knowing that those one million visitors were networked to ten million more.

Here is one of the ruthless practices that has helped make Silicon Valley so successful: Investors will look at a company that is on an upward trajectory but doesn't display the proverbial hockey stick of exponential growth and conclude that they need to either sell the business or take on additional risk that might increase the chances of achieving exponential growth. Achieving 20 percent annual growth, which would delight Wall Street analysts covering any other industry, simply isn't enough to transform a start-up into a multibillion-dollar company fast enough. Silicon Valley venture capitalists want entrepreneurs to pursue exponential growth even if doing so costs more money and increases the chances that the business could fail, resulting in a bigger loss. Dropping below even 40 percent annual growth is a warning sign for investors.

This mindset can be difficult for people to understand. "Why should I risk it all and potentially blow up what is a successful, growing business?" they might rightfully ask. The answer is that blitzscaling businesses tend to play in winner-take-most or winner-take-all markets. The greater risk for a successful, growing business is to move too slowly and allow its competitors to win market leadership and first-scaler advantage.

Nokia is a great example of the cost of caution. In 2007, Nokia was the world's largest and most successful maker of mobile phones, with a market capitalization of just under $99 billion. Then Apple and Samsung came blazing into the market. In 2013, Nokia sold its money-losing handset operations to Microsoft for $7 billion, and in 2016 Microsoft sold its feature phone assets and the Nokia handset brand to Foxconn and HMD for just $350 million. That's a drop in value for Nokia's mobile phone business from somewhere in the neighborhood of $99 billion to $350 million in less than a decade—a decline of over 99 percent.

At the time, Nokia's decisions may have seemed to make sense. Nokia actually continued growing even after the launch of the iPhone and Google's Android operating system. Nokia hit its peak in terms of unit volume when it shipped 104 million phones in 2010. But Nokia's sales declined after that, and were surpassed by Android in 2011 and iPhone in 2012. By the time Nokia's management realized the existential threat facing them, it was too late; even the desperation play of aligning themselves with Microsoft as its exclusive Windows Phone partner couldn't reverse the decline.

Because blitzscaling often requires spending significant amounts of capital in ways that traditional business wisdom would consider "wasteful," implementing a financial strategy that supports this aggressive spending is a critical part of blitz-scaling. For example, Uber often uses heavy subsidies on both sides of the marketplace when it launches in a new city, lowering fares to attract riders and boosting payments to attract drivers. By paying out more than it takes in on those early trips, Uber is able to reach critical scale faster than a more conservative competitor. Given the winner-take-most nature of the ridesharing market, that "wasteful" spending has helped Uber achieve a dominant market position in the cities in which it operates. Of course, that strategy isn't possible without the ability to raise massive amounts of capital on favorable terms. In Uber's case, it has been able to raise nearly $9 billion between its founding and the writing of this book. At some point, Uber will have to demonstrate the ability to significantly improve its unit economics, or its inves-tors will get very grumpy. This concern helps explain Uber's significant investments in autonomous vehicle technology, which could eliminate its biggest expense—driver payments—in one fell swoop.

The willingness to take on the risks of blitzscaling is one of the major reasons why Silicon Valley has produced such a dis-proportionate share of blockbuster companies in comparison to other geographies. To be fair, it has also produced a dispropor-tionate share of financial disasters—hence the word "risk" when talking about blitzscaling. But as the rise of juggernauts like Alibaba and Spotify illustrates, blitzscaling is also starting to take off around the world.

TECHNIQUE #3: MANAGEMENT INNOVATION

The final technique required for blitzscaling is management innovation. This is necessary because of the extreme strains placed on the organization and its employees by hypergrowth.

I am fond of pointing out to entrepreneurs and executives that "in theory, you don't need practice."

What I mean is that no matter how brilliant your business model and growth strategy, you won't be able to build a real-world (i.e., non-theoretical) blockbuster company without a lot of practice. But that problem is magnified when you're trying to blitzscale.

The kind of growth involved in blitzscaling typically means major human resources challenges. Tripling the number of employees each year isn't uncommon for a blitzscaling company. This requires a radically different approach to management than that of a typical growth company, which would be happy to grow 15 percent per year and can take time finding a few perfect hires and obsessing about corporate culture. As we will discuss in more detail later in the book, companies that blitzscale have to rapidly navigate a set of key transitions as their organizations grow, and have to embrace counterintuitive rules like hiring "good enough" people, launching flawed and imperfect products, letting fires burn, and ignoring angry customers.

Over the course of this book, we'll see how business model, growth strategy, and management innovation work together to form the high-risk, high-reward process of blitzscaling.

PART II

Business Model Innovation

Of the three core techniques of blitzscaling, the first and most foundational is to design an innovative business model capable of exponential growth.

The story of entrepreneurship in the Internet era is a story of this kind of business model innovation.

Think back to the dot-com era, which stretched roughly from the IPO of Netscape in 1995 until the NASDAQ began to crash in 2000. During this period, enormous numbers of start-ups and pretty much every established company tried to build great Internet businesses, yet nearly all of them failed. The problem was, most of them simply tried to cut and paste existing business models onto the new online medium. You can't transplant a heart from one species into another and expect it to thrive.

If you had asked stock market analysts in 1995 which companies were best positioned to dominate the Internet, most would have pointed to existing giants like Microsoft and Time Warner, which invested millions in Internet businesses like MSN and Pathfinder. Others would have mentioned "pure play" dot-com start-ups like eToys, which combined proven business models like the "category killer" store with the new online medium.

Yet when the wreckage of the dot-com crash cleared, the

most successful companies still charging full steam ahead were the few start-ups that were designed around totally new business models, such as Amazon, eBay, and Google.

Walmart should have dominated online retail, yet Amazon emerged and practically wrote the bible for e-commerce, including consumer reviews, shopping carts, and free shipping. Newspapers and phone book companies should have been able to transfer their information businesses to the online world, but Yahoo! and then Google stepped up to the plate. They built the search engines that indexed the world's information, and Google developed the business model that made it worth more than all traditional media companies combined.

In contrast, and much to their misfortune, start-ups that relied purely on technology innovation without any real business model innovation largely went bust. Companies like eToys that tried to "Amazon" various markets, but without Amazon's front- and back-office innovations, crashed and burned once the financial markets began to demand profits rather than just expensive revenue growth. Even Netscape, whose Netscape Navigator mainstreamed Web browsing, and whose IPO kicked off the dot-com boom, was forced to sell itself off to AOL. Netscape engineers invented JavaScript, SSL, and all kinds of cool technology for the Internet that are still used today, but Netscape accepted the status quo when it came to using tried-and-true business models rather than developing new ones that were enabled by its own technology innovation. Unfortunately for Netscape, its competitor Microsoft already understood those business models all too well and knew exactly how to use its economic might and resources to pull their levers. In the first "browser war," Microsoft preinstalled its Internet Explorer on all new Windows computers, then gave away its Web server software, Internet Information Server (IIS), which effectively destroyed Netscape's business model.

Could Netscape have succeeded with a different strategy? We believe so. Consider that one of the ways that Netscape monetized its Navigator browser was to sell the sponsorship of its Net Search button to the Excite search engine for $5 million. Netscape believed that the browser itself was the key, while search was simply a sideline. It was left to two pairs of Stanford graduate students, Jerry Yang and David Filo (Yahoo!) and Larry Page and Sergey Brin (Google), to prove that search was a much bigger business. Google's innovative model of selling text ads next to search results via an automated marketplace allowed it to build a franchise so dominant that it later withstood a series of frontal assaults by Microsoft, including a marketing program in which Microsoft essentially paid people to use its Bing search engine.

The same story has been repeated in multiple waves since. Facebook and LinkedIn dominate social networks even though AOL, Microsoft (Hotmail), and Yahoo! (Yahoo! Mail) controlled most consumer online identities when those social networks first emerged. Alibaba beat eBay in China. Uber outflanked the taxi companies. Airbnb has more room listings than any hotel company in the world.

These success stories are technology companies, sure. But as we've seen, technological innovation alone is insufficient—even when its impact on the future is huge. Services like Craigslist, Wikipedia, and IMDb (the Internet Movie Database) were early, influential Internet innovators, but they still never became massively (financially) valuable on their own.

The real value creation comes when innovative technology enables innovative products and services with innovative business models. Even though the business models of Google, Alibaba, and Facebook might seem obvious—even inevitable—after the fact, they weren't widely appreciated at the time they launched. How many people in 1999 would have realized that running tiny text ads next to the equivalent of an electronic card catalog would lead to the world's most valuable software company? Or that setting up an online shopping mall for China's emerging middle class would lead to a $100 billion business? Which of you in 2004 would have predicted that letting people see what their friends are talking about by staring at a tiny screen on a handheld computer would become the dominant form of media? Great companies and great businesses often seem to be bad ideas when they first appear because business model innovations—by their very definition—can't point to a proven business model to demonstrate why they'll work.

To really understand why these business models succeed, we need to clearly define what we mean by "business model" in the first place. Part of the problem is that the term can be interpreted in so many different ways. The great management thinker Peter Drucker wrote that business models are essentially theories composed of assumptions about the business, which circumstances might require to change over time. Harvard Business School professor and author Clay Christensen believes that you need to focus on the concept of the "job-to-be-done"; that is, when a customer buys a product, she is "hiring" it to do a particular job. Then there's Brian Chesky of Airbnb, who said simply, "Build a product people love. Hire amazing people. What else is there to do? Everything else is fake work."

As Andrea Ovans aptly put it in her January 2015 *Harvard Business Review* article, "What Is a Business Model?", it's enough to make your head swim! For the purposes of this book, we'll focus on the basic definition: a company's business model describes how it generates financial returns by producing, selling, and supporting its products.

What sets companies like Amazon, Google, and Facebook apart, even from other successful high-tech companies, is that they have consistently been able to design and execute business models with characteristics that allow them to quickly achieve massive scale and sustainable competitive advantage. Of course, there isn't a single perfect business model that works for every company, and trying to find one is a waste of time. But most great business models have certain characteristics in common. If you want to find *your* best business model, you should try to design one that maximizes four key growth factors and minimizes two key growth limiters.

DESIGNING TO MAXIMIZE GROWTH: THE FOUR GROWTH FACTORS

GROWTH FACTOR #1: MARKET SIZE

The most basic growth factor to consider for your business model is market size. This focus on market size may sound obvious, and it's right out of Pitch Deck 101 for start-ups, but if you want to build a massive company, you need to begin with the basics and eliminate ideas that serve too small of a market.

A big market has both a large number of potential customers and a variety of efficient channels for reaching those customers. That last point is important; a market consisting of "everyone in the world" might seem large, but it isn't reachable in any efficient way. We'll discuss this in greater depth when we look at distribution as a key growth factor.

It's not easy to judge the size of a market, or what pitch decks and venture capitalists often refer to as TAM (total available market). Predicting TAM and how it will grow in the future is one of the main sources of uncertainty in blitzscaling. But predicting it correctly and investing accordingly when others are still paralyzed by fear is also one of the main opportunities for unexpectedly high returns, as we'll see in the cases of Airbnb and Uber.

Ideally, the market itself is also growing quickly, which can make a smaller market attractive and a large market irresistible.

In Silicon Valley, the competition for venture capital exerts a strong pressure on entrepreneurs to focus on ideas that are going after big markets. Venture capital firms might raise hundreds of millions or even billions of dollars from their investors—limited partners like pension funds and university endowments—who are seeking above-market returns to compensate them for taking a chance on privately held companies rather than simply investing in the Coca-Colas of the world. To deliver these above-market returns, venture capital funds need to *at least* triple their investors' money. A $100 million venture capital fund would need to return $300 million over the typical seven- to ten-year life of a fund to achieve an above-market internal rate of return of 15 to 22 percent. A $1 billion fund would need to return $3 billion. Since most venture capital investments either lose money or barely break even, the only realistic way that venture capitalists can achieve these aggressive goals is to rely on a small number of incredibly successful investments. For example, Benchmark Capital invested $6.7 million in eBay in 1997. Less than two years later, eBay went public, and Benchmark's stake was worth $5 billion, which is a 745 times return. The specific fund that made that investment, Benchmark Capital Partners I, took $85 million from investors and returned $7.8 billion, for a 92 times return. (The initial investors in Facebook did even better, but were individuals rather than firms.)

Given the desire for home runs like eBay, most venture capitalists filter investment opportunities based on market size. If a company can't achieve "venture scale" (generally, a market of at least $1 billion in annual sales), then most VCs won't invest, even if it is a good business. It simply isn't large enough to help them achieve their goal of returning more than three times their investors' money.

When Brian Chesky was pitching venture capitalists to invest in Airbnb, one of the people he consulted was the entrepreneur and investor Sam Altman, who later became the president of the Y Combinator start-up accelerator. Altman saw Chesky's pitch deck and told him it was perfect, except that he needed to change the market-size slide from a modest $30 million to $30 billion. "Investors want B's, baby," Altman told Chesky. Of course, Altman wasn't telling Chesky to lie; rather, he argued that if the Airbnb team truly believed in their own assumptions, $30 million was a gross underestimate, and they should use a number that was true to their convictions. As it turns out, Airbnb's market was indeed closer to $30 billion.

When evaluating market size, it's also critical to try to account for how lower costs and product improvements can expand markets by appealing to new customers, in addition to seizing market share from existing players. In 2014, Aswath Damodaran, a professor of finance at NYU's Stern School of Business, estimated that Uber was probably worth roughly $6 billion, based on its ability to ultimately win 10 percent of the global taxi market of $100 billion, or $10 billion. According to Uber's own projections, in 2016 the company processed over $26 billion in payments. It's safe to say that the $10 billion market was a serious underestimate, as the ease of use and lower cost of Uber and its competitors expanded the market for transportation-as-a-service.

As Aaron Levie, the founder of the online file storage company Box noted in a tweet in 2014, "Sizing the market for a disruptor based on an incumbent's market is like sizing a car industry off how many horses there were in 1910."

The other factor that can lead to underestimating a market is neglecting to account for expanding into additional markets. Amazon began as Amazon Books, the "Earth's Biggest Bookstore." But Jeff Bezos always intended for bookselling to serve as a beachhead from which Amazon could expand outward to encompass his massive vision of "the everything store." Today, Amazon dominates the bookselling industry, but thanks to relentless market expansion, book sales represent less than 7 percent of Amazon's total sales.

The same effect can be seen in the financial results of Apple. In the first quarter of 2017, Apple generated $7.2 billion from the sale of personal computers, a category the company pioneered and once dominated. That's a great number to be sure, but, over that same financial quarter, Apple's total revenue was a whopping $78.4 billion, which meant that Apple's original market accounted for less than 10 percent of its total sales.

My Greylock colleague Jerry Chen, who helped Diane Greene scale VMware's virtualization software into a massive business, likes to point out, "Every billion-dollar business started as a ten-million-dollar business."

But whether you are creating a new market, expanding an existing market, or relying on adjacent markets to get to those "B's" that investors want (baby), you need to have a plausible path to get from here to there. This leads us to one of my favorite growth factors to discuss with entrepreneurs: distribution.

GROWTH FACTOR #2: DISTRIBUTION

The second growth factor needed for a strong, scalable business is distribution. Many people in Silicon Valley like to focus on building products that are, in the famous words of the late Steve Jobs, "insanely great." Great products are certainly a positive—we'll discuss the lack of product quality as a growth *limiter* later on—but the cold and unromantic fact is that a good product with great distribution will almost always beat a great product with poor distribution.

Dropbox is a company with a great product, but it succeeded because of its great distribution. In an interview for Reid's *Masters of Scale* podcast, founder and CEO Drew Houston said that he believes that too many start-ups overlook the importance of distribution:

> Most of the orthodoxy in Silicon Valley is about building a good product. I think that's because most companies in the Valley don't survive beyond the building-the-product phase. You have to be good at building a product, then you have to be just as good at getting users, then you have to be just as good at building a business model. If you're missing any of the links in the chain, the whole chain is broken.

The challenge of distribution has become even greater in the "mobile first" era. Unlike the Web, where search engine optimization and e-mail links were broadly applicable and successful distribution channels, mobile app stores offer little opportunity for serendipitous product discovery. When you go to Apple's or Google's app store, you're searching for a specific product. Few people install apps just for the hell of it. As a result, the business model innovators who have succeeded (e.g., Instagram, Whats-App, Snap) have had to find creative ways to get broad distribution for their product—without spending a lot of money. These distribution techniques fall into two general categories: leveraging existing networks and virality.

A) Leveraging Existing Networks

New companies rarely have the reach or resources to simply pour money into advertising campaigns. Instead, they have to find creative ways to tap into existing networks to distribute their products.

When I was at PayPal, one of the major vehicles for distribution of our payment service was settling purchases on eBay. At the time, eBay was already one of the largest players in e-commerce, and by the beginning of 2000 already had ten million registered users. We tapped into this user base by building software that made it extremely easy for eBay sellers to automatically add a "Pay with PayPal" button to all of their eBay listings. The amazing thing is that customers did so even though eBay had its own rival payments service, Billpoint! But sellers were required to add Billpoint manually to each of their listings; PayPal did it for them.

Many years later, Airbnb was able to perform a similar feat by leveraging the online classified service Craigslist. Based on a suggestion from Y Combinator's Michael Seibel, Airbnb built a system that allowed and encouraged its hosts to cross-post their listings to the much-larger Craigslist. Hosts were told, "Reposting your listing from Airbnb to Craigslist increases your earnings by $500 a month on average," and were allowed to do so by clicking a single button. This took serious technology skills—unlike many platforms, Craigslist doesn't have an application programming interface (API) that allows other software to interact with it—but it was technology innovation for the purposes of distribution innovation, not product innovation. "It was a kind of a novel approach," Airbnb founder Nathan Blecharczyk said of the integration. "No other site had that slick an integration. It was quite successful for us."

Leveraging an existing network can have downsides, of course. What the existing network gives (or unknowingly allows to be taken), the existing network can also take away. Zynga, the leading social games company, achieved great success leveraging Facebook for distribution, but had to dramatically reengineer its distribution model after Facebook decided to stop allowing people playing Zynga games to post their progress to their Facebook friends. (Disclosure: I am a member of Zynga's board of directors.) Zynga founder Mark Pincus was farsighted enough to build a strong enough franchise to survive the change.

In contrast, so-called content farms like Demand Media that leveraged Google's search platform to generate website traffic and advertising revenues never recovered after Google tuned its algorithms to deprioritize content from what it called "junk" websites.

Despite these dangers, leveraging existing networks can be a critical part of a business model, especially if these networks can provide a "booster rocket" that is later supplemented with virality or network effects.

B) Virality

"Viral" distribution occurs when the users of a product bring more users, and those users bring additional users, and so on, much like an infectious virus spreads from host to host. Virality can either be organic—occurring during the course of normal usage of the product—or incentivized by some kind of reward.

After launching LinkedIn, the team and I devoted significant time and energy to figuring out how to improve organic virality; that is, how to make it easier for existing users to invite friends to use the service. One way we did this was to refine what have become some of the standard tools of virality, such as address book importers. For example, we built software that allowed LinkedIn to connect to our users' Outlook contacts, which made it very easy for them to invite their most important connections.

But equally important was an unanticipated source of virality. As it turned out, users wanted to use their LinkedIn pages as their primary professional identity on the Internet. Having a page like this to point others to—with all the details of their professional life together in one place—generated value not only for the user, but for the people viewing the page, and it made viewers realize that they should get their own LinkedIn profile. As a result, we added public profiles as a systematic tool to boost both the member value proposition and our viral growth rate.

At PayPal, we combined organic and incentivized virality. The payment product was inherently viral; if someone e-mailed you money using PayPal, you had to set up an account to get paid. But we enhanced this organic virality with monetary incentives. If you referred a friend to PayPal, you got $10, and your friend got $10. This combination of organic and incentivized virality allowed PayPal to grow 7 to 10 percent per day. As the PayPal network grew, we reduced the incentives to $5 and $5, then finally eliminated them altogether.

Incentives don't have to be monetary; like PayPal, Dropbox used a similar combination of organic virality (as users share files with nonusers) and incentivized virality (Basic account holders get 500 MB of extra storage per user they refer; Pro account holders get 1 GB) to grow. Even though Dropbox invested in partnerships with leading PC makers like Dell, Drew Houston credits virality with driving the company's rapid growth, helping it double its one hundred thousand users at launch to two hundred thousand users just ten days later, then skyrocket to one million users just seven months after that.

If your distribution strategy focuses on virality, you also have to focus on retention. Bringing new users in through the front door doesn't help you grow if they immediately turn around and leave. According to Houston, Dropbox discovered this truth the hard way, when activation rates revealed that only 40 percent of the people signing up were actually putting files in their Dropbox and linking them to their computers. In an interview for my *Masters of Scale* podcast, Drew described a scene reminiscent of the television show *Silicon Valley* (but with a happier ending):

> What we did is we went on Craigslist and offered $40 to anyone who'd come in for half an hour—a poor man's usability test. We're like, "All right, sit down. This is an invitation to Dropbox in your e-mail. Go from here to sharing a file with this e-mail address." Zero of the five people we tested succeeded. Zero of the five even came close. This was just stunning. We're like, "Oh my God, this is the worst product ever created." So we made a list of like eighty things in this Excel spreadsheet, then just sanded down all these rough edges in the experience, and watched our activation rate climb.

Virality almost always requires a product that is either free or freemium (i.e., free up to a certain point, after which the user has to pay to upgrade—Dropbox, for example, offers 2 GB of free storage). We can't recall a single instance of a company that grew to a massive scale by leveraging the virality of a paid product.

One of the most powerful distribution innovations is to combine both strategies. Facebook was able to do this by harnessing the organic virality of a social network (where users invite other users to join them) and leveraging existing networks centered around campuses by rolling out the product on a college-by-college basis. We'll discuss Facebook's rollout strategy in greater depth when we consider network effects.

GROWTH FACTOR #3: HIGH GROSS MARGINS

One of the key growth factors that entrepreneurs often overlook is the power of high gross margins. Gross margins, which represent sales minus the cost of goods sold, are probably the best measure of long-term unit economics. The higher the gross margin, the more valuable each dollar of sales is to the company because it means that for each dollar of sales, the company has more cash available to fund growth and expansion. Many high-tech businesses have high gross margins by default, which is why this factor is often overlooked. Software businesses have high gross margins because the cost of duplicating software is essentially zero. Software-as-a-service (SaaS) businesses have a slightly higher cost of goods sold because they need to operate a service, but thanks to cloud providers like Amazon, this cost is becoming smaller all the time.

In contrast, "old economy" businesses often have low gross margins. Growing wheat is a low-margin business, as is selling goods in a store or serving food in a restaurant. One of the most amazing things about Amazon's success is that it has been able to build a massive business based on retailing, which is generally a low-margin industry. And even Amazon now relies heavily on its high-margin SaaS business, Amazon Web Services (AWS). In 2016, AWS accounted for 150 percent of Amazon's operating income, which means that the retail business actually lost money.

Most of the valuable companies we're focusing on in this book have gross margins of over 60, 70, or even 80 percent. In 2016, Google had a gross income of $54.6 billion on sales of $89.7 billion, for a gross margin of 61 percent. Facebook's gross income was $23.9 billion on sales of $27.6 billion, for a gross margin of 87 percent. In 2015, LinkedIn's gross margin was 86 percent. As we've already discussed, Amazon is the outlier, with a 2016 gross income of $47.7 billion on $136 billion in sales, for a gross margin of 35 percent. Yet even Amazon's gross margins are greater than those of a "high margin" traditional company like General Electric, which in 2016 had a gross income of $32.2 billion on sales of $119.7 billion, for a gross margin of 27 percent.

High gross margins are a powerful growth factor because, as noted below, not all revenue is created equal. The key insight here is that even though gross margins matter a great deal to the seller, they are irrelevant to the buyer. How often do you consider the gross margin involved when you make a purchase? Would you ever choose Burger King over McDonald's because Whoppers are lower margin than Big Macs? Typically, you focus solely on the cost to you, and the perceived benefits of the purchase. This means that it's not necessarily any easier to sell a low-margin product than a high-margin product. If possible then, a company should design a high-gross-margin business model.

Second, high-gross-margin businesses are attractive to investors, who will often pay a premium for the cash-generating power of such a business. As the prominent investor Bill Gurley wrote in his 2011 blog post, "All Revenue Is Not Created Equal," "Investors love companies where, all things being equal, higher revenues create higher profit margins. Selling more copies of the same piece of software (with zero incremental costs) is a business that scales nicely." Appealing to investors makes it easier to raise larger amounts of money at higher valuations when the company is privately held (we'll delve into the details of why this is so important later on), and lowers the cost of capital when the company is publicly traded. This access to capital is a key factor in being able to finance lightning-fast growth.

It's important to note the difference between potential gross margin and realized gross margin. Many blitzscalers, such as Amazon or the Chinese hardware makers Huawei and Xiaomi, deliberately price their products to maximize market share rather than gross margins. As Jeff Bezos is fond of saying, "Your margin is my opportunity." Xiaomi explicitly targets a net margin of 1 to 3 percent, a practice it credits Costco for inspiring. All other factors being equal, investors almost always place a much higher value on companies with higher potential gross margins than companies that have already maximized their realized gross margins.

Finally, most of a company's operational challenges scale based on revenues or unit sales volume, not gross margin. If you have a million customers who generate $100 million per year in sales, the cost to serve those customers doesn't change whether your gross margin is 10 percent or 80 percent; you still need to hire enough people to respond to their support requests. But it's a lot easier to afford good customer support when you have $80 million in gross margin to spend rather than $10 million.

Conversely, it's a lot easier to sell and service 125,000 customers who generate $12.5 million per year in sales and $10 million in gross margin than it is to have to sell and service a million customers who generate $100 million in sales to achieve that same $10 million in gross margin. That's eight times as many customers and eight times the revenues, which means eight times as many salespeople, customer service representatives, accountants, and so on.

Designing a high-gross-margin business model makes your chances of success greater *and* the rewards of success even greater. As we'll see in a later section, high gross margins have helped even nontech businesses, such as the Spanish clothing retailer Zara, grow into global giants.

GROWTH FACTOR #4: NETWORK EFFECTS

Market size, distribution, and gross margins are important factors in growing a company, but the final growth factor plays the key role in *sustaining* that growth long enough to build a massively valuable and lasting franchise. While the past twenty years have driven improvements in the first three growth factors, the rise in Internet usage around the world has pushed network effects to levels never before seen in our economy.

The increasing importance of network effects is one of the main reasons that technology has become a more dominant part of the economy.

At the end of 1996, the five most valuable companies in the world were General Electric, Royal Dutch Shell, the Coca-Cola Company, NTT (Nippon Telegraph and Telephone), and ExxonMobil—traditional industrial and consumer companies that relied on massive economies of scale and decades of branding to drive their value. Just twenty-one years later, in the fourth quarter of 2017, the list looked very different: Apple, Google, Microsoft, Amazon, and Facebook. That's a remarkable shift. Indeed, while Apple and Microsoft were already prominent companies at the end of 1996, Amazon was still a privately held start-up, Larry Page and Sergey Brin were still a pair of graduate students at Stanford who were two years away from founding

Google, and Mark Zuckerberg was still looking forward to his bar mitzvah.

So what happened? The Networked Age happened, that's what.

Technology now connects all of us in ways that were unthinkable to our ancestors. Over two billion people now carry smartphones (many of them made by Apple, or using Google's Android operating system) that keep them constantly connected to the global network of everything. At any time, those people can find almost any information in the world (Google), buy almost any product in the world (Amazon/Alibaba), or communicate with almost any other human in the world (Facebook/WhatsApp/Instagram/WeChat).

In this highly connected world, more companies than ever are able to tap into network effects to generate outsize growth and profits.

We'll use the simple layman's definition of network effects in this book:

> A product or service is subject to positive network effects when increased usage by any user increases the value of the product or service for other users.

Economists refer to these effects as "demand-side economies of scale" or, more generally, "positive externalities."

The magic of network effects is that they generate a positive feedback loop that results in superlinear growth and value creation. This superlinear effect makes it very difficult for any node in the network to switch from an incumbent to an alternative ("customer lock-in"), since it is almost impossible for any new entrant to match the value of plugging into the existing network. (Nodes in these networks are typically customers or users, as in the canonical example of the fax machine, or the more recent example of Facebook, but can also be data elements or other fundamental assets valuable in a business.)

The resulting phenomenon of "increasing returns to scale" often results in an ultimate equilibrium in which a single product or company dominates the market and collects the majority of its industry's profits. So it's no surprise that smart entrepreneurs strive to create (and smart investors want to invest in) these network effects start-ups.

Several generations of start-ups have tapped these dynamics to build dominant positions, from eBay to Facebook to Airbnb. To accomplish these goals, it's critical to develop a rigorous understanding of how network effects work. My Greylock colleague Simon Rothman is one of the world's premier experts on network effects from building eBay's $14 billion automotive marketplace. Simon warns, "A lot of people try to bolt on network effects by doing things like adding a profile. 'Marketplaces have profiles,' they reason, 'so if I add profiles, I'll be adding network effects.'" Yet the reality of building network effects is a bit more complicated. Rather than simply imitate specific features, the best blitzscalers study the different types of network effects and design them into their business models.

Five Categories of Network Effects

On his industrial organization of information technology website, the NYU professor Arun Sundararajan classifies network effects into five broad categories:

1) **Direct Network Effects:** Increases in usage lead to direct increases in value. (Examples: Facebook, messaging apps like WeChat and WhatsApp)

2) **Indirect Network Effects:** Increases in usage encourage consumption of complementary goods, which increases the value of the original product. (Example: Adoption of an operating system such as Microsoft Windows, iOS, or Android encourages third-party software developers to build applications, increasing the value of the platform.)

3) **Two-Sided Network Effects:** Increases in usage by one set of users increases the value to a different set of complementary users, and vice versa. (Example: Marketplaces such as eBay, Uber, and Airbnb)

4) **Local Network Effects:** Increases in usage by a small subset of users increases the value for a connected user. (Example: Back in the days of metered calls, certain wireless carriers allowed subscribers to specify a limited number of "favorites" whose calls didn't count against the monthly allotment of call minutes.)

5) **Compatibility and Standards:** The use of one technology product encourages the use of compatible products. (Example: within the Microsoft Office suite, Word's dominance meant that its document file format became the standard; this has allowed it to destroy competitors like WordPerfect and fend off open-source solutions like OpenDocument.)

Any of these different network effects can have a major impact; Microsoft's ability to tap into multiple network effects with Windows and Office contributed greatly to its unprecedentedly durable franchise. Even today, Windows and Office remain dominant in the PC market; it's simply that other platforms like mobile have achieved similar or greater importance.

Network Effects Both Produce and *Require Aggressive Growth*

A key element of leveraging network effects is the aggressive pursuit of network growth and adoption. Because the impact of network effects increases in a superlinear fashion, at lower levels of scale, network effects actually exert downward pressure on user adoption. Once all your friends are on Facebook, you have to be on Facebook too. But conversely, why would you join Facebook if none of your friends had joined yet? The same is true for the first user of marketplaces like eBay and Airbnb.

With network effects businesses, you can't start small and hope to grow slowly; until your product is widely adopted in a particular market, it offers little value to potential users. Economists would say that the business has to get past the "tipping point" where the demand curve intersects with the supply curve. Companies like Uber subsidize their customers in an attempt to manipulate the demand curve to reach that tipping point faster; the bet is that losing money in the short term may allow you to make money in the long term, once you're past the tipping point.

One challenge that this approach produces is the (eventual) need to eliminate the subsidies in order to make the unit economics work. When I was at PayPal, one of the things we did to encourage adoption was to proclaim that the service would always be free. This meant eating the transaction costs of accepting credit card payments. I wish I could say we had a grand plan. We had hoped that we could make up for the credit card transaction fee subsidy by making money off the float—the funds being kept in PayPal. Unfortunately, this came nowhere close to offsetting the fee subsidies, and the company was hemorrhaging money. So we switched PayPal from "always free" to "ACH always free" and started charging fees to accept credit card payments. Fortunately, we already had a loyal following, and our customers accepted the change.

When the business can't change the economics of the product (free services like Facebook can't lower their prices), it can instead sway the expectations of potential users. The value users place on the service when deciding whether or not to adopt it depends on both the current level of adoption *and* their expectations for future adoption. If they think others are going to jump on board, the perceived value of the service increases, and they become more likely to adopt it.

This technique is reflected in one of the most influential business books of all time, Geoffrey Moore's *Crossing the Chasm*. Moore argues that technology companies often run into problems when they try to transition from a market of early adopters to the mainstream—the proverbial "chasm." He recommends that companies focus on niche beachhead markets, from which the company can expand outward using a "bowling pin" strategy in which these markets help to open up adjacent markets. This strategy is even more important for network effects businesses.

A company can also reshape the demand curve by designing the product to be valuable to the individual user regardless of network adoption. At LinkedIn, for example, we discovered that public LinkedIn profiles had some value independent of the user's network, since they served as an online professional identity. This gave people a reason to join LinkedIn even if their friends and colleagues hadn't done so yet.

Connectivity Enables Network Effects Businesses

In addition to supporting network effects, the high connectivity of the world we live in today also makes it easier to reach the tipping point where network effects kick in, and to sustain those network effects and the market dominance they produce.

First, the Internet has driven the cost of discovery for products and services lower than ever. Unlike in the past, when companies needed to offer goods in retail stores or broadcast advertising in order to be visible to customers, today buyers can find whatever they're looking for on Amazon or other online marketplaces like Alibaba, in app stores, or, when all else fails, by Googling. Because products and services that are already popular will almost always come up first in search results, companies with a competitive advantage can quickly grow to the point where the increasing returns of network effects produce a winner-take-most or winner-take-all market. This also explains why the growth factor of distribution is as or more important to company success as the product itself—without distribution, it is difficult to reach the tipping point.

After network effects take hold, the efficiencies enabled by the Networked Age make it easier to sustain the pace of rapid growth. In the past, rapid customer growth inevitably led to rapid organizational growth and to dramatic increases in the overhead required to coordinate a large number of employees and teams. Today's networks allow companies to sidestep these traditional growth limiters, such as when Apple used Foxconn to get around the potential limitation of its manufacturing infrastructure (more on this in the next section). The more you can remove those limiters, the more dominant a network effects–driven business can grow. This is why companies like Google that have surpassed the $100 billion mark in annual revenues are still growing at over 20 percent per year.

Finally, the remarkable profitability of these companies gives them the financial resources to expand into new fields and invest in the future. The S-curve of innovation argues that the rate of adoption of every innovation eventually slows as the market saturates. However, companies like Apple have mastered the strategy of investing in new products that let them hop onto additional S-curves. Apple hopped from music players to smartphones to tablets, and it is no doubt spending some of its vast profits chasing the next S-curve. The premium that the public markets grant these companies also helps them use mergers and acquisitions (M&A) to jump these curves, much as Facebook did with Instagram, WhatsApp, and Oculus, and Google did with DeepMind.

Of course, network effects don't apply to every company or market, even if they are superficially similar—as many companies and their investors discovered to their chagrin during the dot-com bust, the Great Recession, and the funding slowdown of 2016. This is why the best entrepreneurs try to design innovative business models that leverage network effects. One of the reasons that Google is Google and Yahoo! is now part of AOL (which in turn is owned by Verizon) is that Google focused on AdWords (a marketplace with strong network effects) while Yahoo! tried to become a media company (a traditional model based on economies of scale).

Much of Silicon Valley's historical success in building giant companies can be traced to its cultural emphasis on business model innovation, which results in the creation of network effects–driven businesses. The irony is that many people in Silicon Valley couldn't define a network effect or what caused it if asked. Yet simply because so many entrepreneurs are trying so many different business models, they can end up stumbling into powerful network effects. Craig Newmark simply started e-mailing his friends about local events in 1995; almost twenty-two years later, network effects have kept Craigslist a dominant player in online classifieds despite operating with a skeleton crew and making seemingly no changes to the website design during that entire period!

This is where an emphasis on speed also plays an important role. Because Silicon Valley's entrepreneurs focus on designing business models that can get big fast, they are more likely to incorporate network effects. And because the fierce local competition forces start-ups to grow so aggressively (i.e., blitzscale), Silicon Valley start-ups are more likely to reach the tipping point of network effects before start-ups from less aggressive geographies.

One of the motivations for this book is to help entrepreneurs from around the world emulate these successes by teaching them how to systematically design their businesses for blitzscaling. When you design your business model to leverage network effects, you can succeed anywhere.

DESIGNING TO MAXIMIZE GROWTH: THE TWO GROWTH LIMITERS

Building key growth factors into your innovative business model is only half the battle. It is fiendishly difficult to grow an amazing business, in part because it is fiendishly easy to run smack into obstacles that *limit* your growth. A key component of business model innovation is designing around these growth limiters.

GROWTH LIMITER #1: LACK OF PRODUCT/MARKET FIT

Product/market fit enables rapid growth, while the lack of it makes growth expensive and difficult. The concept of product/market fit originates in Marc Andreessen's seminal blog post

"The Only Thing That Matters." In his essay, Andreessen argues that the most important factor in successful start-ups is the combination of market and product.

His definition couldn't be simpler: "Product/market fit means being in a good market with a product that can satisfy that market."

Without product/market fit, it's impossible to grow a start-up into a successful business. As Andreessen notes,

> You see a surprising number of really well-run start-ups that have all aspects of operations completely buttoned down, HR policies in place, great sales model, thoroughly thought-through marketing plan, great interview processes, outstanding catered food, 30" monitors for all the programmers, top tier VCs on the board—heading straight off a cliff due to not ever finding product/market fit.

Unfortunately, it's far easier to define product/market fit than it is to establish it!

When you start a new company, the key product/market fit question you need to answer is whether you have discovered a nonobvious market opportunity where you have a unique advantage or approach, and one that competing players won't see until you've had a chance to build a healthy lead. It's usually difficult to find such an opportunity in a "hot" space; if an opportunity is obvious to everyone, the chance that you'll be the one who succeeds is exceedingly low.

Most nonobvious opportunities arise from a change in the market that the incumbents aren't willing or able to adapt to. In many cases, this can be a disruptive technological innovation, but it can also be a change in the law or financial regulations, the rise of a new group of customers, or any other major shift. For example, Charles Schwab was able to build his eponymous financial empire by leveraging the deregulation of brokerage commissions to launch a discount brokerage.

Frequently, you won't be able to fully validate product/market fit before you commit to building a company. But you should try. As authors and entrepreneurs, we're huge fans of Eric Ries and his lean start-up methodology. It is an excellent process for systematically tackling risk. But the fact is that most start-ups don't follow that process; instead, their chosen experiment is "Do we succeed or run out of money?"

The best way for a small, resource-strapped team to assess potential strategies is to leverage what we dubbed "network intelligence" in our previous book, *The Alliance*. Even a small group of founders is likely to have a huge collective personal network of smart people with relevant knowledge or experience. Initiate a conversation, inviting them to challenge your idea and tell you what else you should consider.

Of course, even the best network intelligence won't guarantee that you've actually found product/market fit during this design phase. The only way to truly prove product/market fit is to get the product into the hands of real users. But entrepreneurs can and should do their research, and try to design their business model to maximize their chances of achieving product/market fit as quickly as possible.

GROWTH LIMITER #2: OPERATIONAL SCALABILITY

Designing a scalable economic model isn't enough if you can't scale up your operations to meet demand. Too often, entrepreneurs dismiss the challenges of operational scalability by saying, "Managing explosive growth is a high-class problem." High-class problems are still problems; it may feel better for your ego to be wrestling with the issues of growth rather than simply trying to avoid missing payroll, but both can still kill your company. Rather than dismiss these challenges, the wisest innovators design operational scalability into their models.

A) Human Limitations on Operational Scalability

A significant number of operational issues arise simply because of human limitations. As much as we might wish that we and our colleagues could work tirelessly and seamlessly, regardless of the scale of the organization, the fact is that growth causes us to trip over a wide array of issues.

If you are leading a small founding team with four members, you have to worry about your direct relationship with the three other cofounders, plus their direct relationships with one another. Combinatorial mathematics tells us that this means you need to manage the relationships between six pairs of individuals ([4*3] / 2). Now imagine that you hire two employees, for a total team size of six. Now you need to manage the relationships between fifteen pairs ([6*5] / 2). You increased the team size by 50 percent, but the number of relationships you need to manage went up by 150 percent. The math just gets more daunting from there. And that only considers the relationships of individual pairs of team members, not the relationships between any three members, any four members, and so on.

One approach is to design a business model that requires as few human beings as possible. Some software companies employ business models that allow them to achieve massive success with minimal numbers of employees. The founders of WhatsApp, Jan Koum and Brian Acton, designed a clever business model that addressed some of the key growth factors (their messaging service leveraged both classic network effects and the existing distribution network of telephone address books to grow faster) but also managed to skirt around issues of operational scalability. WhatsApp had a freemium business model; the service was free for a year, after which it cost $1 per year. This low-friction model essentially eliminated the need for people working in functions like sales, marketing, and customer service, allowing WhatsApp to grow to five hundred million monthly active users by the time of its acquisition by Facebook, with a staff of just forty-three employees, a ratio of over ten million active users per employee!

Another approach is to find ways to outsource work to contractors or suppliers. Airbnb's strategy for photographing its hosts' rooms offers an instructive example. Early on, Airbnb's founders discovered that one of the key factors that increased the chances of renting a room on Airbnb was the quality of the photographs of that room. It turns out that most of us aren't professional photographers, and our poorly composed, poorly shot cell phone pictures don't do a good job of conveying the awesomeness of our living spaces. So the founders took to the road, visiting hosts and taking photographs for them. Obviously, personally visiting every host was hardly a scalable solution, so the the task was soon outsourced to freelance photographers. As Airbnb grew, the strategy shifted from the founders managing a short list of photographers, to an employee managing a large group of photographers, to an automated system managing a global network of photographers. Founder Brian Chesky describes this strategy succinctly: "Do everything by hand until it's too painful, then automate it."

Ultimately, even with clever business models and automation, nearly every massively successful company requires thousands or even tens of thousands of employees. Smart techniques can delay the reckoning, but not forever. Later on, we'll discuss some of the management innovations that allow companies to handle this kind of organizational growth and scale.

B) Infrastructure Limitations on Operational Scalability

The other main challenge of operational scalability comes from the strain of scaling up the nonhuman infrastructure of the business. It doesn't matter how much demand you generate if your infrastructure can't handle it. Infrastructure limitations can even be fatal to a company's ambitions. Consider the examples of the social networks Friendster and Twitter.

While many have forgotten it now, Friendster was the first (pre-Facebook) online social network to break through into the mainstream (disclosure: I was an early investor in Friendster). Launched in March 2003, Friendster rode viral growth to millions of users within months. Before the year was out, Friendster-mania was such a cultural phenomenon that founder Jonathan Abrams appeared on the late-night television program *Jimmy Kimmel Live!* But Friendster's massive growth brought massive headaches, especially on the infrastructure side. Despite a talented technology team, Friendster's servers couldn't handle the growth, and it became common for Friendster profiles to take up to forty seconds to load. By the beginning of 2005, a faster new entrant, MySpace, was generating more than ten times the number of pageviews as Friendster, which never recovered. MySpace, of course, ultimately lost the consumer social networking war to Facebook, which is a story we'll discuss in detail later in this book.

Twitter came close to melting down in the same way, but managed to recover in time to build a massive business. When Twitter began its rise in the late 2000s, it became infamous for its "Fail Whale," a whimsical error message that appeared whenever its servers couldn't handle the load. Unfortunately for Twitter, the Fail Whale made fairly regular appearances, especially when big news hit, such as the death of the recording artist Michael Jackson in 2009 (to be fair, Twitter was hardly the only website that had these issues when the King of Pop passed away) or the 2010 World Cup. Twitter invested serious resources into rearchitecting both its systems and its engineering processes to be more efficient. Even with this strenuous effort, it took several years to "tame" the Fail Whale; it wasn't until after Twitter made it through the 2012 US presidential election night without melting down that the company's then–creative director Doug Bowman announced that the Great Blue Whale had been put to death.

One of the main reasons for the very large increase in the growth of valuable Web companies that we've seen in recent years is Amazon's cloud offering, Amazon Web Services (AWS), which has helped many such businesses navigate around infrastructure limitations. Dropbox, for example, was able to scale up its storage infrastructure much more quickly and easily because it used AWS storage, eliminating the need to build and maintain its own arrays of hard disks.

AWS reflects one of the ways that Amazon has made operational scalability a competitive advantage. Web services like AWS tap into what Harvard Business School professor Carliss Baldwin and former Harvard Business School professor Kim Clark refer to as "the power of modularity." As Baldwin and Clark describe in their book, *Design Rules, Vol 1: The Power of Modularity,* this principle makes it possible for a company like Amazon and its customers to build complex products out of smaller, standardized subsystems. But the power of modularity goes beyond just software development and engineering. By building easy-to-integrate subsystems like payments and logistics, Amazon makes its entire business more flexible and rapidly adaptable.

The equivalent to AWS on the hardware side is China. Hardware start-ups are able to manage infrastructure limitations and scale much more quickly by tapping into Chinese manufacturing capabilities, either directly or by working with companies like the custom manufacturing design firm PCH. The smart thermostat maker Nest, for example, had only 130 employees when it was acquired by Google for $3 billion, largely because it had outsourced all of its manufacturing to China.

In contrast, Tesla Motors has seen its growth held back by infrastructure limitations. Due to the complexities of its manufacturing process, Tesla's production rates have lagged behind those of other automakers, the result being that its award-winning vehicles are almost always sold out, with back orders measured in months and even years. Demand generation is not a problem for Tesla; meeting that demand is.

PROVEN BUSINESS MODEL PATTERNS

Whether by design or not, the business models of rapidly growing companies often follow proven patterns that tap into growth factors and bypass growth limiters. These patterns will be described in more detail below, but here it bears noting that these high-level patterns are principles rather than exact recipes. Simply adopting any of these particular patterns isn't enough to ensure an innovative business model, but understanding them does provide an entrepreneur with a set of good role models.

It is also worth mentioning that not all patterns are created equal. Some common business models follow proven patterns, but nonetheless don't seem to produce $100 billion businesses or even $10 billion businesses. Take open-source software, which has been wildly successful as a pattern for spreading software products like Linux. Open source, which means offering free, community-created software that users can modify, arose to prominence during the dot-com era and has been an integral part of the world's technology stack ever since.

The story of open-source software fits the pattern of business model innovation. Open-source software serves a large market, has powerful distribution via open-source software code repositories, benefits from the network effects of standards and compatibility, and neatly avoids many of the human limitations on operational scalability by tapping into a distributed community of volunteer contributors rather than building a large organization of employees.

Yet even the most successful open-source business, Red Hat, has a market capitalization of "only" about $15 billion, and that's after being in business for two decades. The empirical evidence suggests that open source is a pattern that is valuable for engagement but not for building a massively profitable business.

In order for a pattern to be proven, it must be able to demonstrate that multiple massively valuable businesses follow it. Based on that criterion, we've assembled the following list of proven patterns to help inspire your own business model innovation.

PROVEN PATTERN #1: BITS RATHER THAN ATOMS

Google and Facebook are largely software businesses that focus on electronic bits rather than material atoms. Bits-based businesses have a much easier time serving a global market, which in turn makes it easier to achieve a large market size. Bits are also far easier to move around than atoms, so bits-based businesses can more easily tap into distribution techniques like virality, and their ability to be highly networked provides more opportunities to leverage network effects. Bits-based businesses tend to be high-gross-margin businesses because they have fewer variable costs.

Bits also make it easier to design around growth limiters. You can iterate more quickly on software products (many Internet companies release new software daily) than on physical products, making it faster and cheaper to achieve product/market fit. And bits-based businesses, as we saw with WhatsApp, can get away with far fewer employees than most of their atom-based counterparts.

Back in 1990, the futurist George Gilder demonstrated his prescience when he wrote in his book *Microcosm,* "The central event of the twentieth century is the overthrow of matter. In technology, economics, and the politics of nations, wealth in the form of physical resources is steadily declining in value and significance. The powers of mind are everywhere ascendant over the brute force of things."

Just over twenty years later, in 2011, the venture capitalist (and Netscape cofounder) Marc Andreessen validated Gilder's thesis in his *Wall Street Journal* op-ed "Why Software Is Eating the World." Andreessen pointed out that the world's largest bookstore (Amazon), video provider (Netflix), recruiter (LinkedIn), and music companies (Apple/Spotify/Pandora) were software companies, and that even "old economy" stalwarts like Walmart and FedEx used software (rather than "things") to drive their businesses.

Despite—or perhaps because of—the growing dominance of bits, the power of software has also made it easier to scale up atom-based businesses as well. Amazon's retail business is heavily based in atoms—just think of all those Amazon shipping boxes piled up in your recycling bin! Amazon originally outsourced its logistics to Ingram Book Company, but its heavy investment in inventory management systems and warehouses as it grew turned infrastructure limitations from a growth limiter to a growth factor. On the retail side, merchants pay Amazon to manage their inventories and logistics for them, while the massive computer systems that Amazon built to operate its retail business gave it the capabilities to launch its AWS business (which is a high-margin, bits-based business!).

PROVEN PATTERN #2: PLATFORMS

Platform economics predates the Networked Age, and even the Industrial Age. Trade-oriented principalities like the Republic of Venice provided a welcoming ecosystem for merchants, complete with currency and the rule of law, as well as taxes to harvest the value of the platform. Technology platforms like Microsoft Windows demonstrated the power of being the chosen platform on which businesses were built back when the World Wide Web was still a glimmer in Tim Berners-Lee's eye (Sir Berners-Lee wrote his proposal for a global hypertext system in 1989). Yet despite the proven value of platforms in the pre-Internet era, the Networked Age has made them vastly more powerful and valuable.

Rather than being limited like the Republic of Venice to a specific geography, today's software-based platforms can achieve global distribution almost immediately. And since transactions on today's platforms are conducted through application programming interfaces (APIs) rather than person-to-person negotiations, they proceed swiftly, seamlessly, and in incredible volumes, all with barely any human intervention.

If a platform achieves scale and becomes the de facto standard for its industry, the network effects of compatibility and standards (combined with the ability to rapidly iterate and optimize the platform) create a significant and lasting competitive advantage that can be nearly unassailable. This dominance lets the market leader "tax" all the participants who want to use the platform, much as levies were imposed in the bygone Republic of Venice. For example, the iTunes store takes a 30 percent share of the proceeds whenever a song, a movie, a book, or an app is sold on that platform. These platform revenues tend to have very high gross margins, which generate cash that can be plowed back into making the platform even better. Amazon's merchant platform, Facebook's social graph, and, of course, Apple's iOS ecosystem are great examples of the power of platforms.

PROVEN PATTERN #3: FREE OR FREEMIUM

"Free" has an incredible power that no other pricing does. The Duke behavioral economist Dan Ariely wrote about the power of free in his excellent book *Predictably Irrational,* describing an experiment in which he offered research subjects the choice of a Lindt chocolate truffle for 15 cents or a Hershey's Kiss for a mere penny. Nearly three-fourths of the subjects chose the premium truffle rather than the humble Kiss. But when Ariely changed the pricing so that the truffle cost 14 cents and the Kiss was free—the same price differential—more than two-thirds of the subjects chose the inferior (but free) Kisses.

The incredible power of free makes it a valuable tool for distribution and virality. It also plays an important role in jump-starting network effects by helping a product achieve the critical mass of users that is required for those effects to kick in. At LinkedIn, we knew that our basic accounts had to be free if we wanted to get to the million users we theorized represented critical mass.

Sometimes you can offer a product for free and still be profitable; in the advertising-driven business model, a large enough mass of free users can be valuable even if they never pay for your service. Facebook, for example, doesn't charge its users a dime, but it is able to generate large amounts of high-gross-margin revenue by selling targeted advertising. But sometimes a product doesn't lend itself to the advertising model, as is the case with many services used by students and educators. Without third-party revenue, the problem with offering your product to users for free is that you can't offset your lack of sales by "making it up in volume."

Here is where the innovation of freemium comes in. The venture capitalist Fred Wilson coined the term in a 2006 blog post (based on a suggestion from Jarid Lukin), but the business model itself predates the term, having its origin in the "shareware" model for selling software in the 1980s. The free product was a tool for discovery and gaining a critical mass of users, while the paid version of the software allows the business to extract value from those users once its value is clear. Dropbox is one of the premier examples of a successful freemium business—by giving away 2 GB of storage, Dropbox attracted a massive user base, a reasonable percentage of which decides to pay for the value and convenience of additional storage.

PROVEN PATTERN #4: MARKETPLACES

Marketplaces represent one of the most successful business model patterns, with the dot-com era's Google and eBay and today's Alibaba and Airbnb standing out as examples of important, valuable companies that follow this pattern. One reason marketplaces are powerful is because they often tap into two-sided network effects. While it is difficult to create a successful marketplace from a cold start, the first marketplace that does manage to achieve liquidity—the ability for buyers and sellers to quickly and efficiently find a counterparty to conduct a transaction—becomes very attractive to both sides of the market. As buyers and sellers pour in, the marketplace becomes even more attractive to both parties, triggering a positive feedback loop that makes it very hard for new entrants to win any market share.

Marketplaces also offer key advantages beyond the obvious network effects. By creating a liquid market where buyers and sellers both participate, the dynamic forces of supply and demand price their transactions better than any human judgment could. The more efficient the prices in a marketplace, the more value it creates, because that means more transactions that *might* create value actually occur. In contrast, in illiquid markets, sellers often misprice their products, resulting in fewer sales and less value creation than optimal.

The best example of the benefits of efficient market pricing is probably Google's AdWords advertising marketplace. AdWords allows anyone to bid on targeted keywords, in any quantity, so even the smallest businesses can tap into global distribution. Contrast this to the traditional advertising market, in which large clients spend millions of dollars paying advertising agencies to run expensive thirty-second television ads during coveted programming like the Super Bowl broadcast. Google's system also measures advertising quality; ads targeted at its audience to generate the most paid click-throughs are favored. The net effect is that consumers are shown the most effectively targeted ads, without the overhead of a middleman like Don Draper and his three-martini lunch. Google also increases its own gross margin, because, unlike commercials during a television broadcast, search-based ad space is virtually unlimited and costs Google next to nothing.

Although marketplaces, even local ones, have always been a powerful business model, the changes ushered in by the Networked Age have made them potentially more valuable than ever. But unlike a local market with its size constraints—think of an old-fashioned bazaar in the center of a populous city—online marketplaces tap a global market. And by connecting buyers and sellers instead of holding inventory or managing logistics (and thus dealing in bits rather than atoms), online marketplaces avoid many of the growth limits of human or infrastructure scalability.

PROVEN PATTERN #5: SUBSCRIPTIONS

When Salesforce.com first launched its on-demand customer relationship management product, there were many legitimate questions about this new software-as-a-service (SaaS) model. Selling software as a subscription, delivered via the Internet, represented a major departure for enterprise software vendors. The previous model of selling permanent licenses for on-premise software and charging for maintenance provided more cash up front than monthly or annual subscriptions. The personnel required to support the model were also different; selling and supporting on-premise software required field salespeople and sales engineers to install pilot deployments, while the new SaaS model required additional staff to provide 24/7 data center coverage and support.

As it turns out, of course, SaaS eventually became the dominant business model for enterprise software. The cash flow disadvantages and required personnel shifts were real concerns, but mainly for existing players in the market. New SaaS businesses like Salesforce.com and Workday were designed and built around the new model, giving them a major advantage over existing players who tried to convert their on-premise software businesses to subscription ones.

Subscription Internet services have been successful because the sales and delivery model provides a larger market size and better distribution than traditional packaged software. Due to the cost and overhead of the extensive field operations required to support on-premise software, traditional enterprise software licenses had to be in the six- or seven-figure range simply to make the model work. This meant that software vendors focused on the needs of only the largest customers.

In contrast, Salesforce.com and other SaaS vendors can sell software licenses in any quantity, not only to Fortune 500 companies, but also to midmarket and small to medium-sized businesses, significantly enlarging their potential market. Internet delivery and self-service allow new forms of distribution that weren't possible in the packaged software world, such as Dropbox's viral incentive of additional free storage for referring new customers.

Nor is the pattern of Internet subscriptions limited to enterprise software. The dominant players in both music (Spotify, Pandora) and video (Netflix, Hulu, Amazon) also enjoy lower overhead and greater distribution by using the subscription business model.

Another, less obvious benefit to this model is that once a subscription business achieves scale, the predictability of its revenue streams allows it to be more aggressive with long-term investments, since it isn't obliged to maintain large cash balances to weather short-term variations in the business. This financial firepower can represent a major competitive advantage. For example, Netflix, which announced plans to invest $6 billion in original content for its streaming service in 2017, has exploited its direct subscription model to outspend classic television networks, which have to rely on less robust revenue streams like payments from cable providers and advertising sales.

PROVEN PATTERN #6: DIGITAL GOODS

One of the emerging patterns that build on new platforms and services is the business of selling digital goods. Sitting at the intersection of "bits rather than atoms" and platforms, digital goods are intangible products that, arguably, have no intrinsic value—but they can still make for a profitable and scalable business. For example, the messaging service LINE derives significant revenues by selling "stickers": images that are incorporated into the text of smartphone messages. In 2014, its first year of operation, LINE's sticker business generated $75 million in revenue. That figure grew to $270 million in 2015, which represented over a quarter of LINE's total revenues. Not bad for an intangible product with no intrinsic value!

Digital goods have also become a key business model in the video game industry, with in-game purchases of digital items that can help players advance in the game or advertise their status. Market-wide revenue from in-app purchases are projected to outstrip paid-app downloads in 2017, $37 billion to $29 billion.

In addition to enjoying the advantages of any bits-based business, digital goods tend to have nearly 100 percent gross margins, since they are purely digital and usually do not add significantly to infrastructure or overhead costs.

PROVEN PATTERN #7: FEEDS

One of the most underrated and underappreciated proven patterns is the news feed. Facebook's powerful network effects allow the site to attract its users, but its innovation of the news feed has made it a world-class business. Yet Facebook is hardly the only feed-centric success story. Companies like Twitter, Instagram, and Slack have all built multibillion-dollar market values around the news feed pattern.

The power of the news feed comes from its ability to drive user engagement, which in turn drives both advertising revenue and long-term retention. As Facebook has demonstrated, a news feed with sponsored updates is the most effective way to monetize proverbial Internet "eyeballs." Facebook's News Feed's dominance of the online advertising market is only exceeded by Google's AdWords, and AdWords starts with the significant built-in advantage of capturing active consumer intent rather than simply the desire to be amused. For example, how many people visit Facebook with the intention of going shopping? The magic of the news feed model has been its ability to monetize bored people catching up on what their friends are doing.

Of course, effective use of the news feed model requires a lot of sophisticated technology. Facebook doesn't just insert sponsored updates at random. The company knows your interests better than you do, based on all the items you've ever clicked on, liked, or otherwise engaged with. It can carefully target the advertisements it shows you based on your individual habits and the context of what surrounds them in your feed. This targeting ability explains why Facebook succeeded in monetizing this model when other feed-based products like RSS readers failed.

This pattern is so powerful that Twitter, whose product is essentially one long news feed, is still an important Internet company despite barely changing its product in nearly a decade (going from 140 characters to 280 characters doesn't count). Twitter is a business that scaled massively because of the power of business model innovation, not product or technology innovation.

THE UNDERLYING PRINCIPLES OF BUSINESS MODEL INNOVATION

Underlying the proven patterns of business model innovation are larger principles that can help refine those patterns or even create new ones. These principles aren't themselves business models, but they often power the technological innovation that enables business model innovation.

UNDERLYING PRINCIPLE #1: MOORE'S LAW

Moore's Law is the fundamental principle that puts the "Silicon" in Silicon Valley, and has powered the worldwide ascent of the technology industry. Moore's Law is named after its codifier, Intel cofounder Gordon Moore, who coined the term in a paper he wrote in 1965, observing that the number of transistors that could be crammed onto the surface of a silicon chip appeared to double each year. While Moore revised his eponymous law in 1975 to a doubling of transistors every twenty-four months, the industry has since settled on a broad consensus of eighteen months. Today, Moore's Law no longer refers specifically to transistor density; rather, it predicts that computing power tends to double every eighteen months. In recent years, this growth in computing power has been driven by the transition to multicore, multithreaded computing. Perhaps in the future, Moore's Law will be met by quantum computing, optical chips, the use of DNA, or something even more impossible to foresee. The point is, it appears that the true limit to Moore's Law is human engineering ingenuity, not solid-state physics.

Moore's Law matters because the relentless increase in computing power that it predicts acts as a constant source of technological innovation, which, as we have seen, can help enable business model innovation. For many years, the power of Intel's central processing units (CPUs) was measured by their "clock rate"—the number of times per second that the CPU could perform an operation. While clock rate is no longer a good measure of computing power, it is still a good metaphor for how Moore's Law drives the world of computer technology: each tick of the clock enables new technologies, driving faster and faster innovations.

Increasing computing power allowed the shift from gigantic mainframes to smaller minicomputers to personal computers, all the way to today's smartphones and wearables. We've seen similar increases in things like network bandwidth, allowing the Web to shift from text to images to audio to video, and in the future, 3-D and virtual reality (VR). Yet today's smartphones aren't simply smaller versions of IBM mainframes—remember, technology innovation enables business model innovation.

The best entrepreneurs don't just follow Moore's Law; they anticipate it. Consider Reed Hastings, the cofounder and CEO of Netflix. When he started Netflix, his long-term vision was to provide television on demand, delivered via the Internet. But back in 1997, the technology simply wasn't ready for his vision— remember, this was during the era of dial-up Internet access. One hour of high-definition video requires transmitting 40 GB of compressed data (over 400 GB without compression). A standard 28.8K modem from that era would have taken over four months to transmit a single episode of *Stranger Things*. However, there was a technological innovation that would allow Netflix to get partway to Hastings's ultimate vision—the DVD.

Hastings realized that movie DVDs, then selling for around $20, were both compact and durable. This made them perfect for running a movie-rental-by-mail business. Hastings has said that he got the idea from a computer science class in which one of the assignments was to calculate the bandwidth of a station wagon full of backup tapes driving across the country! This was truly a case of technological innovation enabling business model innovation. Blockbuster Video had built a successful business around buying VHS tapes for around $100 and renting them out from physical stores, but the bulky, expensive, fragile tapes would never have supported a rental-by-mail business.

(As hard as it may be for some readers to comprehend, when we were in college, we would often drive to a Blockbuster Video store on a Friday or Saturday night, pay a couple of bucks to rent a VHS tape of a movie, and use a landline telephone to call Domino's to order a pizza before popping the videotape into a VCR that was connected to a twenty-five-inch standard-definition cathode-ray tube.)

DVD technology allowed Netflix to create a completely new business model. Rather than renting out individual movies and being charged exorbitant late fees if they failed to return the VHS tape in time, Netflix customers paid $20 per month for a subscription to "unlimited" movies—provided they checked out just one movie at a time. This allowed Netflix to eliminate Blockbuster's widely loathed late fees and capture the powerful and certain revenue stream from the proven model of a subscription service. Netflix took off, and even went public as a DVD-by-mail service.

But Hastings never lost sight of his ultimate vision for Netflix—

on-demand television delivered via the Internet. And as Moore's Law continued to work its magic, making computers ever more powerful and Internet bandwidth ever greater and cheaper, Netflix bided its time, waiting for streaming video to become viable.

"When we first started raising money in 1997, we thought we'd be mostly streaming in 5 years," Hastings told us when he visited our Blitzscaling class at Stanford. "In 2002, we had no streaming. So we thought that by 2007, it would be half our business. In 2007, we were still nowhere. So we made the same prediction. And this time we were wrong the other way—by 2012, streaming was 60% of our business." It may have taken longer than Hastings expected, but Moore's Law eventually came through for him.

Today, Netflix is synonymous with television on demand delivered via the Internet, and it has created an entirely new category of "binge watching." As of 2017, 53 percent of American adults say that their household has access to Netflix, and the service is growing rapidly across the rest of the world. Netflix has used the financial power of its subscription model to become one of the premier sources of original video content, from television shows like *Stranger Things,* to movies like *Beasts of No Nation,* to events like comedian Dave Chappelle's comeback stand-up comedy specials.

Traditional television commissions large numbers of pilot episodes, the majority of which never make it to series, trying to produce optimistically named "Must See TV" to appeal to a broad audience, which has to be convinced to tune in every single week. In contrast, the on-demand model allows Netflix to cater to many different audiences rather than program a small number of thematic channels, as cable television does. Broadcast television succeeded by providing the same thing to all its viewers—a model driven by the technological innovation of broadcasting content via wireless signals and later coaxial cable. Netflix succeeds by providing a carefully personalized experience to each of its many viewers, giving it a huge advantage over its traditional television competitors. Moreover, Netflix produces exactly what it knows its customers want based on their past viewing habits, eliminating the waste of all those pilots, and only loses customers when they make a proactive decision to cancel their subscription. The more a person uses Netflix, the better Netflix gets at providing exactly what that person wants. And increasingly, what people want is the original content that is exclusive to Netflix. The legendary screenwriter William Goldman famously wrote of Hollywood, "Nobody knows anything." To which Reed Hastings replies, "Netflix does." And all this came about because Hastings had the insight and persistence to wait nearly a decade for Moore's Law to turn his long-term vision from an impossible pipe dream into one of the most successful media companies in history.

Moore's Law has worked its magic many other times, enabling new technologies ranging from computer animation (Pixar) to online file storage (Dropbox) to smartphones (Apple). Each of those technologies followed the same path from pipe dream to world-conquering reality, all driven by Gordon Moore's 1965 insight.

UNDERLYING PRINCIPLE #2: AUTOMATION

Blitzscaling companies use automation. If they have the ability to perform a task (which is a big if), computers are almost always faster, cheaper, and more reliable than human beings. Furthermore, computers continue to get faster and cheaper, doubling in power every eighteen months according to Moore's Law, as opposed to human beings, who evolve over the course of millions of years according to Darwin's principle of natural selection.

In 2014, the journalist Jan Vermeulen compared the original Apple II (introduced in 1977) with the then state-of-the-art iPhone 5S. He found that in the intervening thirty-seven years, Apple's products had become 2,600 times faster in terms of clock speed (from a 1 MHz single-core CPU to a 1.3 GHz dual-core CPU) and had 16,384 times the amount of RAM. That's three to four orders of magnitude of improvement in the span of a single human generation. And that massive delta doesn't even take into account that the Apple II was a desktop computer with a bulky cathode-ray tube monitor, and the iPhone 5S was a portable supercomputer that people carried in their pockets.

The same year that the Apple II was introduced, Joe Bottom set a world record by swimming the 50-meter freestyle in 23.74 seconds, for a brisk pace of just under 7.6 km/h (4.7 mph). If human swimming speed had increased as quickly as the computing speed in Apple's products, the world record in 2014 would have been 19,700 km/h (12,250 mph)—not quite enough to achieve orbital velocity, but about twenty-five times the speed of the average commercial jetliner. The actual human world record for the 50-meter freestyle in 2014 was 20.91 seconds, for a more modest 11 percent improvement.

That's the power that automation taps into.

The power of automation applies not just to direct-to-consumer products like the iPhone but also to internal processes and capabilities. Think of the value that automation creates by increasing the productivity in Amazon's warehouses, or by making it easier to keep Google's server farms running 24/7.

UNDERLYING PRINCIPLE #3: ADAPTATION, NOT OPTIMIZATION

At a higher level of abstraction, successful scale-ups place more emphasis on adaptation than optimization. Rather than the giant assembly lines of Detroit automakers, which trace their origins to Henry Ford's Model T, the current generation of Silicon Valley companies practice continuous improvement, whether through an emphasis on speed or the constant experiments and A/B testing of growth hacking. This emphasis makes sense in an environment where companies need to seek product/market fit for new and rapidly changing products and markets. Consider how Amazon expanded into new markets like AWS rather than simply honing its retail capabilities, or how Facebook has been able to adapt to the shift from a text-based social network accessed via desktop Web browsers to an image- and video-based social network accessed via smartphones (and soon, perhaps, VR).

UNDERLYING PRINCIPLE #4: THE CONTRARIAN PRINCIPLE

My friend Peter Thiel has written eloquently about the power of being a contrarian in his book *Zero to One*.

> Whenever I interview someone for a job, I like to ask this question: "What important truth do very few people agree with you on?"
>
> This question sounds easy because it's straightforward. Actually, it's very hard to answer. It's intellectually difficult because the knowledge that everyone is taught in school is by definition agreed upon. And it's psychologically difficult because anyone trying to answer must say something she knows to be unpopular. Brilliant thinking is rare, but courage is in even shorter supply than genius.

Being contrarian is often critical to the process of creating a massively valuable technology company. As we've discussed, key growth factors like distribution and network effects tend to provide disproportionate rewards to a company that is the first in its space to achieve critical scale. Being contrarian and right gives you a huge advantage because you get a head start on achieving scale.

If your company is pursuing an opportunity that nearly everyone agrees is very attractive, you're likely to have a difficult time distancing yourself from your army of competitors. But if your company is pursuing an opportunity that conventional wisdom ignores or disdains, you will probably have the time you need to refine your business model innovation into a well-oiled machine. Amazon pursued e-commerce when most people didn't think consumers would feel comfortable using credit cards online. Google launched its search engine when most people thought search was a mature commodity. And Facebook built its social network when most people believed social networking to be either useless, a market dominated by MySpace, or both.

As we've already seen, most great ideas look dumb at first. Being contrarian doesn't mean that dumb people disagree with you; it means that smart people disagree with you! Remember what happened when Brian Chesky, Joe Gebbia, and Nathan Blecharcyzk tried to pitch Airbnb? Investors like Paul Graham literally couldn't imagine why people would ever use the service. This doesn't happen because investors are dumb; most venture capitalists and angel investors are smart, and most smart, successful people would probably agree that investing in proven ideas is better than investing in unproven ones.

The problem is that, by definition, business model innovation involves trying something that is new, and thus unproven!

In this book, we've tried to lay out a set of tools, principles, and patterns that you can use to design, invest in, or evaluate an innovative business model. Many venture capitalists like to brag that they are masters of "pattern matching"—but here we must caution not all pattern matching is helpful. The bad kind of pattern matching is what B- and C-grade investors love—the Hollywood high-concept pitch. The movie *Speed* was famous for its high-concept pitch: "*Die Hard* on a bus." And if you're the first person to make the connection, you might succeed. *Speed* was in fact a commercial success, mostly because it did in fact live up to its description. But the success of *Speed* led to a raft of derivative and inferior movies, ranging from Steven Seagal's *Under Siege* ("*Die Hard* on a ship") to Steven Seagal's *Executive Decision* ("*Die Hard* on a plane"). When an investor funds "Uber for Pets," that's bad pattern matching.

The good kind of pattern matching involves understanding what medical science terms "the mechanism of action." *Speed* works because confining the action to a bus that has to stay at a certain speed or higher to avoid setting off a bomb creates built-in dramatic tension—especially given the famously bad traffic in Los Angeles. Airbnb works because it has a large market, because travelers spreading awareness from city to city creates virality, and because it follows the proven pattern of an online marketplace.

To help you get a feel for applying our principles of business model innovation, let's practice by analyzing some of today's great businesses and how they follow those principles.

ANALYZING A FEW BILLION-DOLLAR BUSINESS MODELS

CASE #1: LINKEDIN

When we started LinkedIn in 2002, the recent dot-com bust had led most people to consider the consumer Internet industry to be dead. The last thing venture capitalists were willing to do was provide millions of dollars to fund rapid growth. Despite this fact, I thought there was a big opportunity available, and was able to guide LinkedIn through the start-up growth phase until we could raise the capital to really blitzscale.

This is the story of how it happened.

Market Size

The key insight behind LinkedIn was that the Internet was shifting from anonymous cyberspace to an extension of the real world, and thus your online identity was an extension of your real identity. Readers of my generation might remember the famous *New Yorker* cartoon with the caption "On the Internet, nobody knows you're a dog." I didn't think this kind of anonymity would work in a professional context, hence the need for a professional online identity. And though our thesis was contrarian at the time, my cofounders and I were fairly confident that the market of "all white-collar professionals" was sufficiently large to represent a major opportunity.

Distribution

In order to raise money to scale LinkedIn, we had to find a way to prove our distribution strategy. Unfortunately, investors thought of us as "Friendster for business relationships," which was bad pattern matching and made about as much sense to them as "Tinder for business relationships" would to today's VCs. Instead, we had to find a way to use the money and reputation I had acquired by helping build PayPal to get LinkedIn to the point where people would invest.

The first step was to assemble a small, super-scrappy team. We got our first office by squatting in the building of a friend's failing start-up. "Just clean up after yourselves so we can get the lease deposit back, and you can use it for three months," he told me. I leveraged my reputation to secure a small investment, but I knew we needed to show significant progress in distribution before we could raise our next round. Since we didn't have the capital to pay for traditional marketing, we implemented a number of techniques similar to what people today call "growth hacking" to get to one million users, which allowed us to raise money from Greylock.

Our core distribution strategy was organic virality, much as it had been at PayPal. Our users would invite their contacts via e-mail because it helped them build their networks and keep track of their key connections. But the initial level of virality simply wasn't enough. We couldn't offer PayPal's kind of financial incentives, so instead we built things like the e-mail address book importer so that we could increase the number of invitations and let our users know when their contacts joined the service.

Gross Margins

Gross margins were important because it became apparent that our user growth was always going to be surpassed by that of the leading consumer social networks. At this point, MySpace had eclipsed Friendster, and Facebook was quickly gaining on MySpace—and all of them had far more users than LinkedIn.

Our argument was that our professional users were far more valuable, but to prove that argument we had to demonstrate our ability to earn significant high-margin revenues.

The first business model pattern we tried was a freemium subscription service. The free LinkedIn.com service limited the number of requests a user could send to friends of friends (In-Mails), and when users hit those limits, they would be offered the chance to upgrade to a premium subscription. This subscription revenue was enough to get us to cash-flow profitability, but it wasn't growing fast enough to be truly compelling.

The key inflection point came when we discovered that companies were willing to pay for the ability to scan LinkedIn profiles to find the best job candidates. So we offered it to companies as an enterprise subscription product, and once we proved that this new model was a source of significant high-gross-margin revenues, we had the confidence to blitzscale.

Network Effects

The long-term value of LinkedIn was always intended to come from network effects. As a professional social network, LinkedIn leveraged both direct and two-sided network effects, as well as becoming a standard format for presenting one's professional identity. The direct network effects come from the fact that each additional LinkedIn user makes the network slightly more valuable to all other LinkedIn users. The two-sided network effects occur because more users attract more corporate employers, while more employers increase the value of LinkedIn as a passive job-hunting tool. Finally, by becoming an integral part of most people's professional online identities, LinkedIn has become a standard that has largely replaced the traditional résumé. Just one of these network effects would probably be enough to create first-scaler advantage; all three working together built a massive strategic moat that protected the LinkedIn business from any new entrants, and even from attempts by consumer networks like Facebook to take away the professional market.

Product/Market Fit

Finding product/market fit for our enterprise product was the key inflection point in the business. How did we do it? We focused on getting market feedback as quickly as possible. We hired a salesperson, gave him some mock-ups of an enterprise product, and sent him to visit potential customers. It turned out that they all wanted to buy it!

Operational Scalability

Blitzscaling LinkedIn presented two major operational scalability challenges, beyond the obvious one of supporting a global social network with hundreds of millions of users. First, to support the business, we actually had to develop, maintain, and update two different products. Without the consumer product, companies wouldn't see the value of our enterprise product. Without the enterprise product, we couldn't make enough money to build a great business. We had to do both. It's hard to find an engineering expert who would recommend fracturing your product and engineering group to work on two largely separate products, but that's precisely what we did, despite the inefficiency and messiness.

Second, we had to rapidly scale a salesforce while we were still developing the product they were selling. This took a lot of hard work on the part of LinkedIn's CEOs, Dan Nye and then Jeff Weiner, and their teams. But where we could, we also used technology to help alleviate scaling constraints. Our "Merlin" tool helped make our salespeople more productive (and thus scalable) by automating much of their manual work. Merlin would analyze usage patterns and tell each salesperson which companies to call, how they were already using LinkedIn, and even create a personalized sales deck for each individual prospect!

CASE #2: AMAZON

Market Size

Jeff Bezos's original vision for Amazon was to take advantage of unlimited digital shelf space to run a store where a customer could buy literally anything. Amazon began with books because this represented a large enough market with a product amenable to e-commerce (durable, fairly standard sizes, readily available through wholesale distributors). Since then, Amazon has steadily expanded from books into many other verticals, and today very nearly lives up to Bezos's vision of an "everything store" (though you still can't buy automobiles on Amazon . . . yet). Retail is a truly gargantuan market and Amazon has captured an almost unthinkable portion of it and even made its market much bigger by launching Amazon Web Services. Now, in addition to being "the everything store," Amazon also provides much of the Internet's computing power, bandwidth, and storage (including for other dominant companies like Netflix).

Distribution

Amazon was one of the first companies to fully grasp the possibilities of the Internet as a distribution platform in creating the first successful affiliate program, Amazon Associates, which incentivizes individuals and owners of other websites to refer customers to Amazon in exchange for a share of the revenues generated. This allows Amazon to turn everyone else's websites and online communications into a powerful distribution channel. Even today, if you see a book title on the Internet, or in a tweet or an e-mail signature, and you follow that link, you'll probably find yourself on Amazon's website via an affiliate link.

Gross Margins

Amazon actually scores fairly poorly on this growth factor, though this is largely a function of the industry rather than being specific to Amazon. Retail is a relatively low-margin business, and Amazon's devotion to offering low prices further hurts margins. Even today, Amazon's retail business isn't profitable (though it probably could be if the health of the company required it; for example, Amazon's core North American operations are profitable—it's just that its profits are outweighed by the losses generated by Amazon's efforts in Asia).

Yet even within Amazon's retail business, we detect signs that these low gross margins are actually part of a long-term strategy that can generate high gross margins, even on retail sales. It's no secret that Amazon dominates e-commerce; in 2017, analysts like Slice Intelligence reported that Amazon accounted for 44 percent of US e-commerce sales in 2016, and predicted the figure would be even higher in the future. But what is often overlooked is that Amazon's retail business consists of two very different units. The first is Amazon's traditional retail operation, in which Amazon buys products from suppliers and sells them to its customers. The second, far less well-known unit is Amazon's marketplace, which lets third-party sellers sell their products on Amazon. Those third-party sellers store their inventory in Amazon warehouses and pay Amazon to deliver their products to their customers. If you've ever shopped on Amazon, you've probably bought a product from a third-party seller; Jeff Bezos has said that almost 50 percent of units purchased on Amazon come from them. Because this marketplace business doesn't require tying up Amazon's capital in inventory (it ties up the third-party sellers' capital instead), its gross margins likely resemble high-margin eBay's more than it does low-margin Walmart's. As Benchmark's Matt Cohler notes, "I sometimes wonder if Amazon's owned-inventory business is just a marketing loss leader and a capital-intensive competitive moat."

Where Amazon is already tapping into high gross margins is with its AWS business. Remember, 150 percent of its operating margins in 2016 came from AWS, which accounted for $12.2 billion in revenue and over $3 billion in operating income. The high gross margins of AWS allow Amazon to invest heavily in maintaining its lead over its competitors. Indeed, AWS is estimated to hold over 40 percent of the market for cloud computing infrastructure, more than its three biggest rivals—Microsoft, Google, and IBM—put together!

Network Effects

Amazon is relatively weak on network effects. One customer's use of Amazon doesn't make it more valuable for another customer, with the possible exception of Amazon's product reviews. Yet whatever direct network effects exist because of product reviews pales in comparison to the impact of network effects on something like Facebook. Amazon technically is a marketplace with two-sided network effects, thanks to its third-party sellers, but one side is largely missing: Amazon sellers are attracted by

Amazon's massive customer base, but Amazon's customer base is largely indifferent to those sellers. Amazon does benefit from scale effects, and explicitly uses the "flywheel" framework of author and strategy guru Jim Collins. Brad Stone summarized this approach in his book on Amazon, *The Everything Store*:

> Lower prices led to more customer visits. More customers increased the volume of sales and attracted more commission-paying third-party sellers to the site. That allowed Amazon to get more out of fixed costs like the fulfillment centers and the servers needed to run the website. This greater efficiency then enabled it to lower prices further. Feed any part of this flywheel, they reasoned, and it should accelerate the loop.

Yet as impressive as Amazon's flywheel is, when compared with the powerful superlinear effect of most network effects, it is merely linear or sublinear. Fortunately, Amazon does benefit from strong network effects in one of its units.

Most of Amazon's network effects, like most of its gross margins, come from its AWS business. The AWS platform benefits from both indirect network effects and compatibility and standards. The success of AWS encourages developers and development products like Docker to rely on it as their infrastructure of choice, which makes AWS even more successful (while the emergence of AWS as a standard makes it easier for services built on the platform to connect via API).

Product/Market Fit

Amazon has rarely struggled with product/market fit in its core business. For the most part, because it was tapping into an existing—and thriving—retail market, Amazon was able to leap into hypergrowth almost immediately. Even AWS met with rapid uptake, helped by Amazon's savvy decision to lead with its simplest product, S3 (Simple Storage Service), before expanding to more complicated ones. It is important to remember that Amazon has had many failures outside its core business. Amazon's powerful core retail operations didn't allow it to take over auctions or payments from eBay or PayPal, and its Fire Phone was a costly and fruitless attempt to take on Apple and Android.

Operational Scalability

Amazon has managed operational scalability so well that it might be the best in the world at this task.

On the human side, Jeff Bezos has been able to guide Amazon with a strong and steady hand while allowing business leaders like Andy Jassy, the CEO of AWS, or Jeff Wilke, the global head of the consumer business, to run large portions of the company. This delegation has allowed Amazon to grow to over 541,900 employees as of 2017, making it one of the ten largest employers in the United States.

On the infrastructure side, Amazon has deftly shifted from minimizing infrastructure spending, as it did during its early years by using techniques such as outsourcing logistics to book distributors like Ingram, to becoming one of the world's great infrastructure companies. Amazon is so good at infrastructure that its fastest-growing and most profitable business (AWS) is all about allowing other companies to leverage Amazon's computing infrastructure. Amazon also makes money by offering Fulfillment by Amazon to other merchants who envy its mastery of logistics, which ought to strike fear into the hearts of frenemies like UPS and FedEx. In addition to its eighty-six gigantic fulfillment centers, Amazon also has at least fifty-eight Prime Now hubs in major markets, allowing it to beat UPS and FedEx on performance by offering same-day delivery of purchases in less than two hours. Amazon has also built out "sortation" centers that let it beat UPS and FedEx on price by shipping small packages via the United States Postal Service for about $1 rather than paying FedEx or UPS around $4.50.

CASE #3: GOOGLE

Market Size

Google's market size was dramatically underestimated at the outset. When Google came on the scene, many considered it "yet another search engine" in a market that was already dominated by companies like Yahoo! and Lycos. Even in the unlikely event that Google was able to capture a significant share of the search market, it would still be a niche player in comparison to, say, Yahoo!, which was a portal with major properties like Yahoo! Mail and Yahoo! Finance.

Observers failed to realize two things. First, Google's business model innovation—the relevance-based, revenue-maximizing, self-service advertising system of AdWords—allowed it to generate far more revenue per search than its predecessors. Second, the importance of search was growing at a faster rate than the Internet as a whole. As the Internet grew and the amount of content increased at a superlinear rate, so did the difficulty of filtering and finding relevant information, making search increasingly important. Combine that effect with the rapid growth of the Internet itself, and the result was a massive market.

Google has astutely expanded the market since then by leveraging the power of its business model to make and monetize key acquisitions like Android, Google Maps, and YouTube.

Distribution

Google's technology receives most of the credit for the company's success, and it is impressive. However, this means that Google's skillful use of the distribution growth factor is often overlooked.

To go from "yet another search engine" to "the last search engine" (as my old friend Peter Thiel put it in his 2014 Stanford lecture "Competition Is for Losers"), Google had to leverage a series of existing networks and partners. For example, Google's bold deal to power AOL's search results helped the company grow its search business by orders of magnitude. Later, other distribution bets like the Firefox partnership, the acquisition of Android, and the creation of the Chrome browser all paid off and helped maintain Google's distribution dominance.

Google also found ways to leverage small partners as well, with its AdSense program for Web publishers feeding more raw traffic into the AdWords machine.

Gross Margins

Google is a phenomenally profitable company, with an enviable margin of 61 percent in 2016. But this profitability didn't happen by accident or luck; the credit belongs to Google's AdWords business model. As we discussed in our section on business model patterns, the advertising-supported media model hasn't worked for the Internet. Yet when Google first emerged, this was the dominant business model being pursued by major players like Yahoo! and Lycos. Google adopted the self-service advertising auction model of Overture, added its own refinement of selecting ads based on considerations of relevance and quality as well as bid prices, and pursued a business model of capturing purchase intent rather than just gathering eyeballs. This purchase intent proved to be far more valuable per unit of traffic, enabling Google to earn fat margins.

Google has since used the financial power of its gross margins to place big bets that other companies might shy away from, such as investing in Android and Chrome, two products that were going up against dominant competitors (Apple's iOS in mobile phone software and Microsoft and Firefox in Web browsers). Google has also used its margins to fund radical experiments like X (formerly Google X) and Waymo (self-driving cars). These bets may or may not pay off, but even if they fail, Google's margins give it the ability to recover quickly and keep going.

Network Effects

Google has leveraged network effects quite a bit in its major business lines, though not, ironically enough, in its core search product!

The mobile traffic app Waze is a classic example of a direct network effect. Waze harnesses each user's location to create a more accurate model of traffic conditions, while also letting drivers easily report events such as traffic accidents, speed traps, and stopped cars on the side of the road. Then Waze makes all that data public to everyone using the app. In other words, the more Wazers on the road, the more accurate that road information becomes. Each additional user creates value for all the previous users.

The Android mobile operating system is a classic example of indirect network effects. Its broad adoption by end users increases the incentives for developers to create Android versions of their applications. The increased availability of useful apps encourages more people to use devices that run on the plaftorm.

YouTube is a classic example of two-sided network effects. YouTube brings together video creators and consumers—the more content is created, the more people show up to consume it. The more consumers who show up, the more incentive there is to create content.

Finally, Google's G Suite provides a great example of the power of compatibility and standards (ironically enough, much like Microsoft Office, its archrival) as well as local network effects. When users share Google Docs or Google Sheets with others, they lock in anyone who wants to collaborate on those documents to do the same. This is especially common in individual networks like a project team or school. Once some of the school's teachers start using Google Docs for homework assignments, the pressure builds for all of them to standardize on Google Docs, and for children and parents to adopt it as well. Chris speaks from experience here.

Product/Market Fit

Google got the product/market fit for its core search and AdWords product incredibly right. Even from the start, Google's search results were better than those of its competitors. But many people don't realize that it actually took Google a long time to find the right product for the right market. Google started off trying to sell enterprise search appliances, a tool that sits inside a corporate data center, indexing content stored on a company's servers, then offering a Google search box to find items within that content. Next, Google tried the advertising-supported model by running DoubleClick ads; ironically enough, Google would later buy DoubleClick. Fortunately, Google found product/market fit by refining Overture's advertising auction model. Google's AdWords product was so much better at monetizing search through its self-service, relevance-driven, auction system that by the time those competitors managed to play catch-up, Google had amassed the financial resources that allowed it to invest whatever was necessary to maintain product superiority.

Google doesn't always get product/market fit right (and if it had run out of money before hitting upon AdWords, the search business might have died before ever achieving that fit). This is a reflection of its very intentional product management philosophy, which relies on bottom-up innovation and a high tolerance for failure. When it works, as in Gmail, which was a bottom-up project launched by Paul Buchheit, it can produce killer products. But when it fails, it results in *killed* products, as demonstrated by projects like Buzz, Wave, and Glass. To overcome this risk of failure, Google relies on both its financial strength (which comes from its high gross margins, among other things) and a willingness to decisively cut its losses. For example, when Google bought YouTube (which had clearly achieved product/market fit), it was willing to abandon its own Google Video service, even though it had invested heavily in that product.

Other massively successful companies take a very different approach. In contrast to Google, where new ideas can come from anywhere in the company and there are always many parallel projects going on at the same time, Apple takes a top-down approach that puts more wood behind fewer arrows. Apple keeps its product lines small and tends to work on a single major product at a time. One philosophy isn't necessarily better than the other; the important thing is simply to find that product/market fit quickly, before your competition does.

Operational Scalability

Unsurprisingly for an engineering-driven organization, Google excels in operational scalability. For one thing, its heavy investment in its own tools and infrastructure has allowed its engineering organization to fine-tune its infrastructure for high performance as the company has grown.

Google has innovated in people scalability as well. While most of Google's people management practices are smart but relatively straightforward—for example, Google uses smaller teams to work on new products and larger teams to sustain and grow existing products—Google has invested heavily in people analytics and data to determine things like the optimum number of interviews per candidate (no more than five) and to improve practices for recruitment, performance reviews, and so on.

CASE #4: FACEBOOK

Market Size

Market size is one of the key reasons that many failed to appreciate the potential value of Facebook in its early days. At the time, the elevator pitch for Facebook would have been "social network for college students." This description, which combined a new and unproven product category with a specific (and narrow) audience, made Facebook sound like a niche product. But by the time I invested in Facebook, Mark Zuckerberg's vision was far broader and more valuable. Mark wanted Facebook to be the default way that people stayed in touch with their friends, which was and is an enormous market. Of course, even when Mark pitched his broader vision, many investors didn't believe him, much to their later regret.

Distribution

Facebook excelled at distribution. As noted earlier, Facebook's early focus on college students, which caused some to dismiss it as a niche product, was actually part of an extremely successful distribution strategy. To achieve incredible virality, Facebook would deliberately delay launching at a college campus until over 50 percent of the students had requested it so that local critical mass was reached almost immediately.

Facebook further benefited from leveraging existing friend networks to expand outward from its original college user base. As users experienced the benefits of staying connected via Facebook, they naturally wanted to add their off-line friends to the network.

Gross Margins

Like Google, Facebook started its life without an effective revenue model. But once it discovered the value of sponsored posts within a news feed, Facebook was able to become wildly profitable. About 90 percent of Facebook's revenue today comes from advertising sales, and the company achieves an astounding 87 percent gross margin.

This gross margin allows Facebook to invest heavily in talent and technology. It has also allowed Mark Zuckerberg to make canny (and expensive) acquisitions, like Instagram and Whats-App, to become a dominant player in mobile as well as desktop social networks, and also long-term future bets like Oculus.

Network Effects

We've already talked about how Facebook leverages classic direct network effects (the more users that join the platform, the greater the value of Facebook to every other Facebook user) and local network effects (once it becomes the dominant social network at a college, it becomes extremely difficult for any other player to pry away Facebook's users).

Facebook also experiences some helpful indirect network effects thanks to its platform services, such as the Graph API (which allows developers to leverage the Facebook social graph of users and their relationships) and Facebook Connect (which allows users to log in to a Web service using Facebook rather than create a new account for that service).

Product/Market Fit

Facebook achieved product/market fit for its core consumer experience almost immediately, hence its rapid growth. However, part of what makes Facebook a great company and Mark Zuckerberg a great CEO is that Facebook has been able to achieve product/market fit in additional and less obvious areas at other points in the company's history.

Many people forget how Facebook struggled with the transition from desktop to mobile. Facebook's initial mobile product provided a slow, suboptimal experience, and adoption of that product was accordingly slow. Fortunately for Facebook, Mark Zuckerberg saw that the market was going mobile and put a moratorium on new feature development in order to focus the entire team on building a new, far superior mobile product. In parallel, he also moved quickly and decisively to acquire Instagram and WhatsApp; when they were announced, both acquisitions were considered pricey, but in hindsight they were clearly bargains. Today, Facebook has over 1.7 billion active mobile users each month, and mobile advertising accounts for 81 percent of the company's advertising revenue. Over 56 percent of Facebook users access the service exclusively via mobile.

Equally important was Facebook's ability to achieve product/ market fit for its advertisers. When Facebook began, the conventional wisdom was that user-generated content like Facebook would never be able to attract advertisers, who would not want their brands appearing with poor-quality or even inappropriate content. Google's search model was what worked in online advertising. Facebook was able to overturn the conventional wisdom by developing algorithms to block inappropriate content, and by learning from Twitter's sponsored update model and incorporating ads into the Facebook News Feed. The news feed model has been especially effective for monetizing mobile usage. In a return to what worked in the print world, advertisements are intermixed with content, and as you page through the magazine or scroll through the feed, you encounter advertisements as part of your normal flow, as opposed to the interruptions of pop-up or takeover ads, or the easily ignored static placement of the traditional banner ad. Yet Facebook's News Feed is even better for advertisers than a magazine, because Facebook's core social actions (clicking, liking, sharing) train users to engage with whatever appears in the News Feed, including advertisements!

Operational Scalability

How did Facebook successfully overcome the growth limiter of operational scalability? On the technology side, one of the philosophies that helped Facebook become successful was its famous motto "Move fast and break things." This emphasis on speed, which came directly from Mark Zuckerberg, allowed Facebook to achieve rapid product development and continuous product improvement. Even today, every new software engineer who joins Facebook is asked to make a revision to the Facebook codebase (potentially affecting millions or even billions of users) on his or her first day of work. However, as Facebook's user base and engineering team grew to a massive size, Mark had to change the philosophy to "Move fast and break things with stable infrastructure."

While this new motto might seem self-contradictory, Mark explains that it focuses on a higher-level goal. "The goal is to move fast," Mark told me. "When we were smaller, being willing to break things allowed us to move faster. But as we grew, the willingness to break things actually started slowing us down, because increasing complexity made it harder and harder to fix things once they broke. By taking the extra time to focus on stable infrastructure, we reduce the impact and time to recover from breaking things, so that we can actually move faster."

WHAT COMES AFTER A STRONG, PROVEN BUSINESS MODEL?

If you believe you've designed a business model that can support massive growth and value creation, the next step is to decide on your strategy. That's where strategy innovation comes in.

PART III

Strategy Innovation

While blitzscaling is the main topic of this book and the secret weapon behind the staggering growth and market domination of hundreds of the world's most valuable companies, it is also a strategy innovation. It is in fact *the* strategy innovation that supports its own ecosystem of rapid growth in the face of risk and uncertainty. To blitzscale or not to blitzscale is a strategic (and difficult) choice, and because of this we want to take a look at when and how founders and CEOs approach that decision, and how it changes their companies and even their own roles in their businesses.

WHEN SHOULD I *START* TO BLITZSCALE?

Here is the question we are most often asked by founders of start-ups when we talk about blitzscaling: When should I start to blitzscale my company?

One of the reasons you might find it challenging to grasp and apply the principles of blitzscaling, especially if you're an experienced executive, is that doing so requires you to throw out many of the normal rules of business. It basically takes everything you thought you knew from years of hard-won experience or from business school or from obsessing about staying lean during your early start-up phase . . . and hurls it out the window. Careful planning, cautious investment, courteous service, and a tightly controlled "burn rate" (the amount of cash the company consumes each month to make payroll, pay the rent, and so on) may end up being tossed aside in favor of rapid guesstimates, ignoring angry customers, and inefficient capital expenditures. Why would you ever want to pursue such a risky and unintuitive course of action? In a word, speed.

Remember, the objective of blitzscaling is to achieve "lightning" growth despite the increased risks and costs. The only time that it makes sense to blitzscale is when (whether for offensive or defensive reasons) you have determined that speed into the market is *the* critical strategy to achieve massive outcomes.

You don't necessarily need to have solved your revenue model before deciding to blitzscale. In fact, a key element of blitzscaling is often the willingness of investors to fund growth before the revenue model is proven—after all, it's pretty easy to fund growth *after* the revenue model is proven.

Slack had spent nearly five years and $17 million on development prior to its public launch in February 2014. Just two months later, before the end of April, it had raised another $43 million. Both of these investments took place before Slack had proven its revenue model and started generating significant sales. Slack's freemium business model (offering a free service and encouraging users to upgrade later to becoming paying customers) meant that even after two months of rapid user growth, the company hadn't proven its ability to make money. Fortunately for Slack and its investors, this aggressiveness paid off. As the initial wave of free users started converting to paid, Slack was able to raise an additional $120 million six months later to accelerate its growth even further.

Every $100 billion scale-up blitzscaled to get there, but that doesn't mean every start-up can or should blitzscale. If your product/market fit isn't right, or your business model doesn't work yet, or if the market conditions aren't right for hypergrowth, then premature blitzscaling can lead oh so painfully (and rapidly!) to "blitzfailing."

Sadly, premature blitzscaling can sometimes kill a nascent market by "poisoning the well" so dramatically that investors and entrepreneurs avoid the space. For example, Webvan's notorious failure kept most players out of the grocery delivery space for over a decade.

Here are a few factors to look for if you are wondering whether the time is right for your company to blitzscale.

A BIG NEW OPPORTUNITY

To achieve massive success, you need to have a big new opportunity—one where the market size and gross margins intersect to create enormous potential value, and there isn't a dominant market leader or oligopoly. A big new opportunity often arises because a technological innovation creates a new market or scrambles an existing one. Shishir Mehrotra, the former general manager of YouTube, visited our Blitzscaling class at Stanford and explained how technological changes created a big new opportunity for YouTube to exploit:

> Why was YouTube at the right time? Networks were finally big enough to stream video. Cell phone cameras allowed everyone to record videos. And the investment environment allowed a very capital-intensive bet.

If the gross margins of this new opportunity are low, the market size has to be even bigger to make it a big opportunity. You have to know that the ultimate size of the prize is worth it.

The cost of blitzscaling, even when successful, is usually quite high. It simply isn't worth the risk and pain to use blitzscaling to pursue a small opportunity. The good news is that in the Networked Age, the ability to rapidly expand products and services into a truly global market means that there are more big opportunities than ever before.

Consider the rise of Alibaba. Jack Ma realized that the opportunity for e-commerce in China and other Asian markets was an even bigger long-term opportunity than e-commerce in the US market. When Jack founded Alibaba in 1999, the e-commerce market in China was negligible and lacked key complementary resources like the equivalent of FedEx, UPS, Visa, and Mastercard (and PayPal). Yet he knew that the ultimate prize was as big as they come. The Organization for Economic Cooperation and Development (OECD) has predicted that China's middle class (defined as a household income of between $20,000 and $160,000 per year) will reach 73 percent of its population by 2030, making its market size nearly triple the entire population of the United States. Such a prize justifies an extremely high level of investment. Jack raised $25 million from SoftBank, Goldman Sachs, and Fidelity to grow the business, and another $75 million in growth equity from General Atlantic in 2009. Today, Alibaba controls an estimated 80 percent of the e-commerce market in China (the same figure for Amazon in the United States is 44 percent), and its 2014 IPO on the New York Stock Exchange became the largest in history, raising $25 billion for the company. In July 2017, Alibaba became the first Asian company to surpass $400 billion in market value.

Some big opportunities are so enormous that they spawn secondary opportunities for blitzscaling. For example, Alibaba's Taobao Marketplace supports countless merchants, Facebook's rise created the platform for Zynga's initial growth, and Apple's iOS devices created a big opportunity for game developers like Rovio and Supercell.

FIRST-SCALER ADVANTAGE

The most frequent offensive reason for blitzscaling is to achieve a critical mass that confers a lasting competitive advantage. Sometimes this is simply a matter of capturing economies of scale, as with Amazon or Walmart, but most often critical mass triggers network effects, as with Uber or Airbnb.

Blitzscaling is unlikely to prove successful if another company has already achieved first-scaler advantage. During the dot-com era, both Amazon and Yahoo! attempted frontal assaults on eBay's auction business, but the network effects of eBay's two-sided marketplace of buyers and sellers meant that its first-scaler advantage was too strong to overcome. In contrast, when Amazon entered the business of selling music CDs—yes, once upon a time music was sold on physical disks—which lacked network effects, it quickly destroyed the incumbent market leader, CDNow.

First-scaler advantage can also be specific to a particular market or set of customers. Latin American e-commerce giant MercadoLibre was founded in 1999, when Amazon was already generating billions in revenue, and eBay was already aggressively expanding overseas. Yet despite not being the global e-commerce first scaler, MercadoLibre was still able to build a vital business by being the first scaler in Latin America. In an interview for

Reid's *Masters of Scale* podcast, MercadoLibre's founder and CEO, Marcos Galperin, explained why he was able to achieve first-scaler advantage:

> Before I started MercadoLibre, I actually did a survey with twenty Latin American students that were colleagues of mine at the Stanford Graduate School of Business, and they all said that this [an eBay for Latin America] would never work in Latin America. At that time, eBay was basically successful and operational in the US, Germany, and Japan.

By jumping into a market where even other Latin American entrepreneurs feared to tread, MercadoLibre was able to gain a head start on the competition and achieve first-scaler advantage.

It's important not to confuse critical mass with *first-mover* advantage. Being first to launch in a market might earn you congratulations on being a product visionary, but if you aren't also the first to scale, you'll end up as a footnote in a Wikipedia article about your competitor who did.

Furthermore, sometimes there is no first-scaler advantage to be won. If you can't identify any network effects or customer lock-in, scaling might not confer sufficient advantage to warrant blitzscaling. For example, we suspect that the market for food delivery from existing restaurants—a pure commodity business—is unlikely to offer any lasting competitive advantages that would justify an expensive blitzscaling campaign.

LEARNING CURVE

Another way to use blitzscaling to create a lasting competitive advantage is to be the first to climb a steep learning curve. Some opportunities, such as self-driving cars, require you to solve hard, complex problems. The more rapidly you scale, the more data you have to drive learning (or train machine learning), which improves your product, making it easier to scale further in the market while your competitors who have just begun to learn lag far behind.

Netflix is the leader in streaming video entertainment, but it only achieved this status by being willing to climb a series of steep learning curves. Remember the situation Reed Hastings faced when he started Netflix in 1997: the dial-up modems that connected most consumers to the Internet were far too slow to stream high-quality video content. So Netflix decided to compete with video stores like Blockbuster by offering a subscription service (with no hated late fees!) to mail movie DVDs to consumers' homes. This meant that Netflix had to climb a steep learning curve in terms of both DVD-specific tasks, such as negotiating with the studios for access to movie DVDs and coordinating the logistics required to ship them to and from consumers, and developing new features like the ability to recommend movies based on past selections. Climbing the learning curve for these tasks was painful and expensive, but it gave Netflix a competitive advantage over its competitors.

Later, as broadband connections became more widespread, Netflix had to climb the learning curve when building out its massive streaming infrastructure while continuing to improve its consumer recommendation engine. That was when Netflix began running into a major strategic issue. Netflix relied on the studios for its content (movies and TV shows), but the studios now saw online video companies like YouTube and Netflix as a threat. In response, they began to increase the price they demanded from Netflix for licensing their content and held back some of their "crown jewels" (e.g., massively popular content like *Saturday Night Live*) for themselves and Hulu (an industry joint venture).

The logical conclusion was clear but daunting. Netflix needed to develop its own original content. Now the company had to climb what was perhaps its steepest learning curve yet, since it would be competing with Hollywood studios that had nearly a century of experience in their field. Netflix hired Ted Sarandos as its head of content, and successfully climbed this learning curve, just as it had climbed so many others in the past. Today, Netflix might very well be the leader in original video content, and even traditional Hollywood power players, such as superproducer Shonda Rhimes (*Grey's Anatomy, Scandal, How to Get Away with Murder*) and comedian Adam Sandler (*Happy Gilmore, Grown Ups*), have switched from traditional studios to Netflix. What's more, the other learning curves that Netflix climbed along the way actually helped it beat the studios at their own game. The consumer recommendation engine gives Netflix an unprecedented ability to predict what content its users want to watch, which allows it to work with creators to produce that content (such as the popular drama *Stranger Things*). And because Netflix has greater confidence in its own predictions than its competitors have in theirs, it can outbid them for content when they go head-to-head.

COMPETITION

Yet despite these offensive reasons to scale, the most common driver of blitzscaling is the threat of competition. Even without competition, you would still want to achieve first-scaler advantage and climb the learning curve, but you might prefer the less risky fastscaling approach to growth. Ask yourself, "Can some-body else realize this opportunity before me?" If the answer is yes, moving faster probably reduces the risk of competition more than it raises the risk of failure. The more intense the competition, the faster you should try to move.

Remember the situation that faced Brian Chesky and Airbnb in the spring of 2011? Just as the business began to take off, the company faced a terrifying competitor in the form of the Samwer brothers of Germany and their rapidly growing European Airbnb clone, Wimdu. Chesky and his cofounders were forced to make a hard decision: stick to business as usual in San Francisco and risk being trounced by Wimdu ... or blitzscale and win. Looking back a few years later, Chesky admitted that the competition forced his hand for the better.

The Airbnb/Wimdu story is becoming more common in the Networked Age. The world used to have a lot more businesses that were protected from competition by geographic fragmentation—such as regional newspapers and physical bookstores—much like Darwin's finches on the Galápagos Islands. The rise of both the Internet and the Networked Age has connected those "islands" into a single, hypercompetitive market, with fierce competition for a few disproportionately valuable leadership positions. Because person-to-person information exchange occurs so quickly and seamlessly today, our communications networks have accelerated the process by which individual market preferences result in dominant suppliers. Today, we buy our books from Amazon, and its founder, Jeff Bezos, owns the *Washington Post*.

One of the reasons businesses tend to rely on blitzscaling is that speed is one of the primary advantages they hold vis-à-vis large companies. Start-ups can act quickly to capitalize on the new opportunities created by technological advances. If they dawdle and proceed at the same pace as a big company, they're fighting on an even playing field, which means that the big company's resources will likely confer massive advantage.

GOOD TIMES, BAD TIMES

While it may seem like blitzscaling is a strategy that only works in "hot" markets, it can be successful under any market conditions. The key nuance is that a company's rate of growth needs to be measured on a relative rather than absolute scale. In a rapidly growing market, a company that grows 100 percent per year might be losing share; during turbulent times, a company that grows 50 percent per year might be gaining enough share to achieve market dominance. You can successfully blitzscale in good times, and you can successfully blitzscale in bad times, though market conditions can and should affect your strategy.

Hot markets make it easier to attract the capital and talent (especially capital) to plow into blitzscaling. Uber is a clear example of how access to capital can fund aggressive and inefficient growth that may confer long-term strategic benefits. Uber's ability to raise billions of dollars has allowed it to subsidize its service to attract more drivers and passengers, reinforcing the network effects of its two-sided marketplace. Plentiful capital has also allowed it to expand aggressively into other markets in an attempt to beat its competition to critical scale. Even after a scandal-plagued 2017, Uber still dwarfs its US archrival Lyft. In July 2017, Lyft announced that it had reached one million rides per day, a milestone that Uber achieved at the end of *2014*.

During the dismal days of the dot-com bust, Google followed the blitzscaling playbook by using a distribution deal with AOL to dramatically expand its AdWords business. The deal, first announced in May 2002, gave AOL an 85 percent share of the revenue generated by AOL searches powered by Google, with a guaranteed minimum of $150 million per year. At the time, Google had less than one-tenth that amount in the bank. This may have seemed risky, given that the NASDAQ had fallen nearly 80 percent from its high two years earlier, but it is precisely this perceived risk that probably allowed Google to outbid the incumbent providers, the publicly-traded Overture and Inktomi. Yet while both the revenue share and guarantee were highly aggressive, Google's improved AdWords algorithms made the deal highly profitable for both parties, and the move allowed Google to increase its revenues from roughly $19 million pre-AOL in 2001 to $347 million post-AOL in 2003, a nearly twentyfold jump.

No one truly knows whether the markets will go up or down in any particular year. But regardless of which direction they move, blitzscaling can be a key strategy for capitalizing on the biggest opportunities.

GOING FASTER

Once you decide to blitzscale, the key question you need to ask and answer is "How can we move faster?" This isn't simply a matter of working harder or smarter with the same resources. It's doing things that other companies normally don't do, or choosing not to do things that they do because you're willing to tolerate greater uncertainty or lesser efficiency.

For example, in 2015, Payal Kadakia, the founder of ClassPass (a monthly subscription service for fitness classes) decided that she needed to double the size of her staff in just three months so that ClassPass would be able expand into more cities. To achieve this kind of speed, Kadakia and her team abandoned traditional hiring processes and followed two simple rules. First, they hired people from their personal networks, with an emphasis on "branded" talent. For example, if an employee had a friend, and that friend worked for the management consulting firm Bain & Company, that friend got hired because ClassPass could assume that the person was smart and would get along with people. Second, some of the time saved by not interviewing for skills allowed the team to interview for alignment with the company's mission. Crazy? Perhaps. But ClassPass was in a crowded, emerging market, and being able to hire faster than the competition helped it maintain and increase its leadership position.

Blitzscaling also requires a strong focus on risk management. While blitzscaling requires risk taking, it doesn't require *unnecessary* risk taking. Indeed, the higher level of risk associated with blitzscaling makes risk management even more valuable and important. As Yahoo! cofounder Jerry Yang told us in an interview for Reid's *Masters of Scale* podcast, "All bold strategies have a risk. If you don't see it, you're flying risk-blind."

A final word of caution—just because you *can* blitzscale doesn't mean that you *should*. Throwing out the rules of business doesn't guarantee success any more than following the rules does.

In the early days of LinkedIn, we knew that achieving a critical mass of users was going to be a challenge. We had to do a lot of education to get professionals to understand our value proposition. Most didn't realize the power of their networks, and how technology could help them enhance, extend, and leverage them better. One approach, which quite a number of people recommended we follow, was to raise a large amount of venture capital and embark on an aggressive advertising campaign to accelerate user growth. This would be a classic example of blitzscaling—sacrificing efficiency for growth against a backdrop of uncertainty. But we decided against this strategy; we believed that the competition wasn't as urgent as many thought, and keeping our burn rate lower would allow us to wait for the market to catch up to our point of view. As we pursued our "slow and steady" start-up growth strategy, the people who recommended investing in inefficient growth warned us that our competitors would leave us behind. We weren't worried, since our reading of the market was that competitors like Plaxo didn't truly understand the power of a professional social network (instead, they were treating their product like an address book) and thus weren't competing for the same market. This hypothesis ended up being proven by later events.

If taking on additional cost and uncertainty doesn't actually confer an advantage, it's better to follow the traditional rules of business (at least for the time being) so that when blitzscaling does become appropriate, your organization can be efficient, well maintained, and more ready to scale. When LinkedIn finally did identify the opportunity to grow a major business by selling an enterprise product to recruiters, we were a more mature company that could blitzscale with confidence in our ability to make these judgment calls.

WHEN SHOULD I *STOP* BLITZSCALING?

While blitzscaling is a powerful strategy, it is not a permanent one. No business can grow forever, simply because no market is infinite. You blitzscale when your market is big or growing fast—or preferably both. If your market stops growing or reaches its upper limit, you should stop blitzscaling.

Because blitzscaling is—by definition—an inefficient use of capital, it only makes sense when speed and momentum are important. Blitzscaling is like the afterburners on a fighter jet that allow you to fly at double or triple normal speed but consume fuel at a shockingly high rate. You don't just switch on the afterburners and never turn them off.

One of the major challenges of blitzscaling is knowing when your business is outgrowing your current strategy, and when you need to change course. It's unwise to wait until you stop growing to make the transition. Instead, you should pay attention to some of the leading indicators that can act as an early-warning sign that you've outgrown your strategy:

- Declining rate of growth (relative to the market and competition)

- Worsening unit economics

- Decreasing per-employee productivity

- Increasing management overhead

When these leading indicators begin to appear, it is probably a sign that your current strategy won't scale further, and it's time to begin the cycle anew. For example, Yahoo! was able to ride its core strategy of being the leading online media company for a decade, with revenues growing briskly (albeit with a downdraft during the dot-com bust) through 2005. At that point, however, Yahoo!'s revenues stopped growing (and indeed began to decline in 2007, even before the global recession hit). Google had just passed Yahoo! in annual revenues in 2005 ($6.1 billion for Google, $5.3 billion for Yahoo!), and after that the fates of the companies diverged dramatically. Yahoo!'s revenue was roughly flat in 2006, while Google's nearly doubled again.

Blitzscaling can actually be dangerous when you reach the limits of your market. If you run out of market headroom, all that speed and momentum will come to a crashing halt as you slam into your market's ceiling.

The usual symptom of running out of headroom, besides a sudden slowdown in growth, is internal conflict. Managers and investors who have gotten used to continuing growth start asking questions like "What went wrong?" and "Who's responsible?" If the company doesn't realize the root cause, the most common (and unhelpful) response is to call for changing the CEO or the executive team—the VP of sales is particularly vulnerable because he or she often takes the blame for the slowdown—or both. How many times does replacing the CEO actually reignite massive growth? The only good example we can think of is what Steve Jobs did at Apple. So if you have a Steve Jobs waiting in the wings, go ahead and switch CEOs. Otherwise, it probably won't help.

Consider what happened to two blitzscalers who ran out of headroom—Groupon and Twitter. Groupon was one of the fastest-growing companies of all time, thanks to its leadership position in the rapidly-emerging daily deals market. Unfortunately, the daily deals market suddenly stopped growing. The problem was actually an ironic echo of bad blitzscaling—Groupon merchants used Groupon's daily deals as an inefficient way to generate rapid revenue growth, only to discover that the promotions didn't lead to repeat business or any other long-term competitive advantage or value.

Groupon began suffering from internal turmoil, and, sure enough, Andrew Mason was replaced as CEO. It didn't help.

What Groupon should have done is to stop blitzscaling. The pursuit of inefficient growth was overheating the market and making it unsustainable. If Groupon had reduced the discounts it required of merchants, growth would have declined, but the business generated by those smaller discounts would have been more sustainable.

Twitter ran into a similar problem. At the end of 2014, its user growth slowed to a crawl. This was the signal for Twitter to ease off the gas and focus on efficiency. In the period from 2011 to 2014, Twitter had increased its employee base by more than a factor of ten, anticipating continued growth. Twitter continued to hire in 2015, adding nearly three hundred employees despite the lack of user growth. Twitter may have been "head faked" because revenue continued to grow as the advertising market matured. Revenues more than doubled over the course of 2015, then stopped growing.

Twitter is beginning to shrink its number of employees today, but probably should have been even more aggressive in doing so once it became apparent that its blitzscaling period was over.

Naturally, it was during this period that Twitter decided to change CEOs again, with Dick Costolo (who had replaced founder Ev Williams) departing and Jack Dorsey assuming the role of interim CEO. Both Costolo and Dorsey are incredibly talented executives, but even great talent can't blitzscale in a market that has hit its ceiling.

CAN I CHOOSE NOT TO BLITZSCALE?

First, as we've discussed above, blitzscaling is not for everyone. For example, in 1994, the same year that Jeff Bezos founded Amazon, the restaurateur Thomas Keller bought The French Laundry in Yountville, California, and turned it into one of the world's greatest restaurants, winning a coveted three-star rating from the *Michelin Guide*. Today, Amazon has over 541,900 employees and is the market leader in online retail, ebooks, cloud computing, and more, while The French Laundry, with less than fifty staff members, in a single location, serving just sixty customers per day, is still one of the world's most famous restaurants.

Both Amazon and The French Laundry are great businesses, but they exist in fundamentally different worlds. Amazon's business relies on massive scale and billions of dollars of infrastructure; The French Laundry relies on local ingredients of the highest quality, prepared by some of the most skilled cooks in the world. Scale is critical to e-commerce and cloud computing; scale is antithetical to world-class fine dining. It is as impossible to imagine Amazon as a small, independent bookstore as it is to imagine The French Laundry as a global restaurant chain, vying with McDonald's for franchise supremacy.

But if the conditions are ripe for blitzscaling, competitors may choose to take on the risks you're reluctant to assume in exchange for a chance at reaping the potential rewards. That's what Airbnb learned when Wimdu entered its market.

Blitzscaling requires capital—whether from investors or from cash flow—to fund relatively inefficient growth. If investors are willing to act quickly and provide large amounts of capital, the risk that a competitor decides to blitzscale is higher. The same is true when a business model provides a lot of high-margin revenue to fund growth. So the safest time to choose not to blitzscale is when you're pursuing a relatively low-margin business model that investors are unwilling to fund at all, unwilling to fund at scale, or unwilling to fund quickly—like, say, a fine-dining restaurant.

Many small or "lifestyle" businesses fall into this category, which makes their decision to avoid blitzscaling perfectly rational. However, markets can change quickly. Let's return to 1994 and the founding of Amazon. For many years, independent bookstores had carved out a market niche by positioning themselves relative to competition from chain stores such as Barnes & Noble and Borders. The rise of Amazon and its pursuit of a blitzscaling strategy significantly changed the competitive landscape for those bookstores, forcing them to respond. In 1994, the American Booksellers Association had over 8,000 members; by 2009, that number had declined to 1,651, down nearly 80 percent.

Shockingly, that number has grown every year since 2009, rebounding to 2,321 in 2017. We'll delve more into how independent bookstores managed to survive in the age of Amazon when we examine how to defend your business against blitzscaling competitors.

Even if you don't face such a competitor, blitzscaling still makes major waves that can impact your business. Here in Silicon Valley, blitzscaling has caused higher property values, a higher cost of living, and a tight labor market that has affected nearly every business within its boundaries, regardless of industry. Even if you don't compete with blitzscalers for customers, you probably compete with them for office space and employees.

BLITZSCALING IS ITERATIVE

Successful blitzscaling is an exercise in serial problem solving. Each of the five stages requires different solutions to the same basic problems of people, product, finance, and so on. Each time you manage to solve a problem, the problem is never solved forever, it's only solved for now. As the company continues to grow, you have to solve the same problem again, under a new and potentially radically different set of circumstances.

In 2013, Paul Graham, the cofounder of Y Combinator, wrote a famous essay titled "Do Things That Don't Scale," in which he argues that start-ups are like old-fashioned cars with engine cranks. To get them started, founders need to engage in a separate and laborious process that couldn't possibly work at scale, such as personally recruiting a product's first users. This essay is a classic, but it may give some readers the mistaken impression that once the "engine" starts, all you need to do is keep doing things that scale.

In other words, the conventional (and erroneous) wisdom says:

Step 1: Do things that don't scale.
Step 2: Achieve scale.
Step 3: Do things that scale.

But when you're blitzscaling, the things you do to help you scale up to the next stage probably won't allow you to scale up to the stage after that. To build a true scale-up, almost everything you do has to change with each stage. Blitzscaling extends the simple three-step process of "Do Things That Don't Scale" as follows:

Step 1: Do things that don't scale.
Step 2: Reach the next stage of blitzscaling.
Step 3: Figure out how to do one set of things that scale, while somehow also finding a way to do a completely different set of things that don't scale.
Step 4: Reach the next stage of blitzscaling.
Step 5: Repeat over and over until you reach complete market dominance.

This doesn't mean that you don't need to plan ahead. Although you will often need to do things that don't scale, at the same time you will have to make choices that permit the possibility (though not the certainty) of massive scale. For example, if your core business model lacks scale advantages and network effects, and the only possible go-to-market strategy consists of door-to-door sales, it's unlikely that you'll ever be able to build a massively important business, whether or not you attempt to blitzscale.

HOW BLITZSCALING STRATEGY CHANGES IN EACH STAGE

As we saw in our discussion of blitzscaling in different economic environments, speed is always relative. What represents hypergrowth speed at one stage might be only average during another. For example, nearly every start-up tries to move quickly. This means that during the Family and Tribe stages of blitzscaling (up to one hundred employees), it can be challenging to move at a speed that is clearly faster than the average start-up. There are only three ways to accomplish this.

First, you might be the only competent player in your market space. This is extremely rare, because any attractive market space tends to draw in smart, aggressive entrepreneurs.

Second, you might be the first player in your market to have figured out a brilliant growth strategy (wonderful if you can manage it but also somewhat rare). For example, PayPal wasn't the only payments start-up trying to attack the market, but it was the first to tap into viral marketing for extremely rapid and cost-effective user acquisition.

Third, you can distinguish yourself from your peers by pursuing scale more resolutely. Start-ups that assume success and make commitments and investments accordingly can get a jump on their rivals—provided the market plays out as they anticipate. This kind of confidence manifests itself in being more aggressive about fund-raising, hiring, and infrastructure investment—incurring current expenses that hopefully will allow your company to move much faster in the future. Throughout its history, Amazon has been more aggressive than its competitors, and that aggressiveness has paid huge dividends. Of course, it helps that Jeff Bezos and his team are world-class at executing against this strategy.

The downside, of course, is that the cost of failure is much higher than if you proceeded with deliberate caution and waited for proof before making commitments. But this additional cost can be dwarfed by the potential benefits of achieving first-scaler advantage in a valuable winner-take-most or winner-take-all market.

At the Village (hundreds of employees) and City (thousands of employees) stages, the speeds of competing organizations become much more varied. Some will be content with focusing on optimizing for efficiency (scale-up growth), while others will focus on speed (fastscaling) or speed in the face of uncertainty (blitzscaling). At this stage, blitzscaling is less about raw aggression and more about pursuing a differentiated (but still aggressive) strategy.

For example, one of the signature strategies for blitzscaling is rapid, parallel market development. When Airbnb made the decision to blitzscale, its chosen strategy was to rapidly expand from a single office in the United States to a score of offices around the world, especially in Europe. This kind of growth is highly inefficient—think of all the new knowledge and infrastructure and personnel an organization has to acquire to successfully open offices around the world—but it can allow a company to stand out from its competitors. It would have been more efficient for Airbnb to expand one country and one office at a time, refining its approach based on the lessons of each rollout, but that would have allowed its competitor Wimdu to be the faster mover. In other words, when it needed to grow from a forty-person company to a global company in a single year, Airbnb couldn't afford to be cautious with its capital and focus on efficiency. We'll see this pattern of simultaneous market development in later examples and across multiple industries.

At the Nation stage (tens of thousands of employees), the strategy shifts again. Companies get to massive scale by dominating an industry until they become mature and mainstream. As described in Geoffrey Moore's *Crossing the Chasm,* Nation-stage companies have succeeded in crossing the chasm between a customer base of early adopters and "Main Street." Market dominance makes it difficult to grow much faster than the overall market, while market maturity reduces the number of opportunities for organic growth. As a result, scaling at this stage is about incubating and growing a major new business.

In 2007, Apple had over twenty thousand employees, was the dominant company in the online music business, and was a successful player in the personal computer business. Meanwhile, Google had over ten thousand employees and was the dominant company in search. Nokia, the dominant mobile phone handset maker, had over seventy thousand employees. These Nation-stage companies were all starting out with roughly the same share of the market for the newfangled "smartphones."

In 2007, Apple introduced the iPhone and Google introduced the Android operating system. Three years later, they dominated the mobile phone market, while Nokia was in disarray, eventually selling its handset business to Microsoft in 2013. The ability to blitzscale new businesses in a new market is what separated Apple and Google from Nokia, and it's what has powered their ascent to the number one and number two most valuable companies in the world (as of 2017).

HOW THE ROLE OF THE FOUNDER CHANGES IN EACH STAGE

The role a founder plays in the blitzscaling process changes in each stage (and an employee's role relative to the founder will likely also change). As the organization grows, the specific skills required to lead it evolve as well.

Stage 1 (Family): The Founder Personally Pulls the Levers of Hypergrowth

In the very early days of a company, a founder has to do everything, including implementing the techniques of blitzscaling. For example, if your business relies on viral marketing for distribution, you probably will do everything from writing the copy for the invitation e-mails to segmenting the data on open and conversion rates.

Stage 2 (Tribe): The Founder Manages the People Who Are Pulling the Levers

As the organization grows, a founder probably starts to manage a team of employees. Even if you retain some individual responsibilities, the bulk of your value creation comes from working with the team members and helping them be more productive. For example, if you now run the engineering team, you might still be doing some work to maintain the earlier code you wrote, but your focus should be on managing the other engineers and letting them build new features.

Stage 3 (Village): The Founder Designs an Organization That Pulls the Levers

The Village-stage transition can be difficult for you as a founder, because it is at this phase that it becomes harder to see the immediate impact of your work. While you might know and interact with frontline employees, you're not likely to be their direct manager anymore. Now you need to take a big-picture view and focus on designing the organization. Founders who don't find this interesting or appealing may choose to remain individual contributors or team managers. This is also the stage at which organizations hire executives from the outside; we'll discuss this further in the next part.

Stage 4 (City): The Founder Makes High-Level Decisions About Goals and Strategies

When the company reaches the City stage, the founder's role is to make the big strategic decisions. These decisions may very well have tactical implications, but now it's someone else's job to work those out. At Facebook, one of the key high-level decisions that Mark Zuckerberg made was to halt new feature development for nearly two years to focus on Facebook's mobile product. When he made this gutsy decision in early 2012, Facebook was deep into the City stage, with over four thousand employees. He didn't personally hire the developers who joined the mobile team, or design the new mobile app, but he made the tough call, then held accountable those who were pulling the levers directly.

Stage 5 (Nation): The Founder Figures Out How to Pull the Organization Back from Blitzscaling and Start Blitzscaling New Product Lines and Business Units

Even though managing a Nation-stage company has some things in common with managing a traditional business, it's critical to keep blitzscaling, even as you implement some traditional management practices. When Steve Jobs returned to Apple, for example, he both focused on traditional measures of operational effectiveness and invested in building new, insanely great products. On the traditional management side, he slashed inventories and improved Apple's financial management, but he also launched major new products, such as the iPod, iTunes, the iPhone, and the iPad.

FROM STRATEGY TO MANAGEMENT

When a company is blitzscaling, the constant doubling or even tripling of its size makes it difficult to apply traditional management techniques designed for environments in which 15 percent represents brisk annual growth. As a result, successful blitzscalers have to implement management innovations to steer their burgeoning organizations through their growing pains. The upcoming sections will discuss how.

PART IV

Management Innovation

One of the key features that sets global giants apart from those companies that flame out or implode before they can reach market dominance is an ability to evolve and optimize their management practices at each stage of growth. The proven techniques we'll describe in this part fall into two main categories: eight key transitions, which help guide the company through the stages of blitzscaling, and nine counterintuitive rules, which turn the conventional wisdom of traditional management on its head in order to cope with blitzscaling's frenzied pace of growth.

Whether you are at the helm of a company, run a specific division, or lead a smaller team, each of the following techniques can offer you guidance on how to manage growth as your organization progresses from start-up to scale-up.

EIGHT KEY TRANSITIONS

TRANSITION #1: SMALL TEAMS TO LARGE TEAMS

The first and most obvious management challenge for blitzscaling organizations to navigate is the shift from small teams to large teams. Even if a rapidly growing company tries to organize itself as a collection of small teams, it still requires a very differ-ent approach to pursue its corporate goals and initiatives. Nor is growth simply a matter of turning a crank. Every aspect of people management, from recruiting to coaching to communica-tions, has to adapt to the different stages of blitzscaling.

Small teams, which are especially common in the Family and Tribe stages of blitzscaling, can operate spontaneously and infor-mally thanks to the personal relationships and frequent contact between team members. This flexibility allows these teams to be extremely adaptable and to change directions quickly as the company learns new information and has to adjust its strategy and tactics.

During the Family and Tribe stages of PayPal, having a small, nimble team allowed us to execute four hard pivots dur-ing the first year of the company's existence. When Peter Thiel, Max Levchin, and Luke Nosek founded PayPal (then known as Confinity) in December 1998, Confinity was intended to be a mobile phone encryption company using Max's highly efficient encryption technology. From there, the company pivoted first to mobile phone cash (pivot #1) and then to PalmPilot payments via infrared beaming (pivot #2). Unfortunately, the network of PalmPilot users who wanted to beam money to each other sim-ply wasn't that robust, so we pivoted again and added e-mail payments (pivot #3). By the end of the year, we saw an emerg-ing market in settling eBay transactions and pivoted our product development efforts to serve that market (pivot #4).

In just twelve months, we had launched a company, built a product, and pivoted four times! This was possible only because between eight and forty people worked for the company when each of the pivots took place, allowing us to easily shift the entire business focus and tactics quickly with each pivot.

As the business grows into the Village stage and beyond, its organization necessarily includes larger teams, such as departments with tens of employees often dispersed across various offices and places. These larger teams cannot operate spontaneously and informally; an individual employee might only see certain team members a few times a year, if ever. Coordinating the efforts of tens or hundreds of individuals—and ensuring alignment with the goals of the entire organization as a whole—requires planning and formal processes, often to the chagrin of an idealistic founder more interested in long-term vision than the minutiae of day-to-day management.

Wendy Kopp, the founder of Teach for America, learned this lesson the hard way. In an interview for Reid's *Masters of Scale* podcast, she told us, "I started out twenty-eight years ago with a total disdain for organizational matters. I just thought everyone who comes to this should be mission-driven, and we're not going to have any hierarchy, and we're going to pay everyone the same thing. About five years into this, I realized if I didn't become obsessed with the very mundane matter of how to manage effectively, we'd never get there!"

Yet beyond simple organizational logistics, one of the major challenges that leaders of blitzscaling organizations need to overcome is the psychological effect that this transition has on early employees and even founders.

At the Family stage, it's often the case that every member of the team is involved in every major decision. At the Village stage and beyond, this is nearly impossible. Employees are busy enough simply keeping up with the activities of their immediate team or area; the operations of other departments are largely a mystery. For new employees, this state of affairs will seem normal, but for early employees, this shift can be disconcerting, leaving them feeling like they used to be insiders but are now treated like outsiders. The answer is not to involve those employees in every decision—that would be inappropriate and logistically impossible. Rather, create other systems to help them feel connected to the company's mission. For example, *The Alliance* outlines how tours of duty keep employees engaged. Visit alliedtalent.com for more information and resources.

You're also adding qualitatively different kinds of people to the team. One metaphor I use to explain this shift is to take yet another analogy from military history: the marines take the beach, the army takes the country, and the police govern the country. Marines are *start-up people* who are used to dealing with chaos and improvising solutions on the spot. Army soldiers are *scale-up people,* who know how to rapidly seize and secure territory once your forces make it off the beach. And police officers are *stability people,* whose job is to sustain rather than disrupt. The marines and the army can usually work together, and the army and the police can usually work together, but the marines and the police rarely work well together. As you blitzscale, you may need to find new beaches for your marines to take rather than ask them to help patrol the existing ones.

The expansion of the organization may also create issues around career expectations. One of the topics we'll discuss later is the need to swap in key executives as the company grows. Most people have skills and experiences that optimize them for a particular stage, and not every person can effectively grow in lockstep with the company. Simon Rothman saw this firsthand when he was helping eBay to blitzscale. "People have elastic limits," he told us. "Of the first hundred people, only a few scaled to a ten-thousand-person organization. It was hard to predict who would scale. People who were smarter than me didn't always scale."

Here in Silicon Valley, it's quite common for an executive to specialize in getting a company from zero to $1 million, and for another to specialize in getting it from $1 million to $10 million.

This can cause frustration among early employees, especially if they were leading a specific function and now an outside executive is being hired above them to be their boss. That's why it's important to set correct expectations up front. Be clear that employees will get opportunities to grow and advance their careers, but this doesn't necessarily mean that if they're running engineering now, they'll be VP of engineering when the company has ten thousand employees and is planning its IPO. Focus on responsibility instead of the specific title. An employee who runs the engineering "department" at the Family stage might consider it a demotion to be one of several directors of engineering at the City or Nation stage, but you can point out that at the Family stage she was managing a team of three engineers and now she oversees a team of one hundred. Encourage employees to focus less on their job titles and more on how each tour of duty's activities and experiences prepare them for greater responsibilities in the future.

This facet of the transition to larger teams can be the most difficult to manage, but it is crucial to blitzscaling success. No one likes firing employees who have been there from the beginning, but think of it this way: if your executives can't scale, your business won't scale either. The ideal solution is to retain early employees in new roles that advance their careers and help the company, but if you have to choose between losing a cherished employee and allowing him to flounder in a role for which he isn't suited, it is better to have an honest conversation and an amicable parting than it is to allow both the employee and ultimately the company to fail.

TRANSITION #2: GENERALISTS TO SPECIALISTS

Another important organizational arc is moving from generalists to specialists. During the early stages of blitzscaling, the need for speed and adaptability places a hefty premium on hiring smart generalists who can get many different things done in an uncertain and rapidly changing environment. But as the company grows, it needs to shift to hiring specialists who are less fungible but have expertise in an area that is crucial to scaling the organization.

This isn't to say there is no place for generalists at blitzscaling organizations. In fact, one of the main benefits of bringing on specialists is that it allows you to redeploy capable generalists to attack your most pressing challenges.

For example, when LinkedIn was still in the Tribe stage, one of the early employees I hired was Matt Cohler. Fresh out of McKinsey, Matt was a brilliant young man who wanted to get into the start-up world. I explicitly hired him as a generalist and, once he was on board, used him as a firefighter to tackle the most urgent problems. At the time, our biggest area of need was recruiting, so Matt's first job was to lead the recruiting function. It wasn't something that his prior education or work experience had prepared him for, but I knew he was smart and scrappy, and I counted on him figuring it out. He performed admirably in the role, then moved on to tackle other fires, both for me and for Mark Zuckerberg at Facebook later on. (Today, Matt is a general partner at Benchmark, a venture capital firm.)

Google even codified the value of generalists in its Associate Product Manager (APM) program, an initiative Marissa Mayer founded because she believed that hiring technical people straight out of college as product generalists would result in flexible, adaptable employees who could fill a lot of needs. Today, distinguished APM alumni include Quip founder/CEO (and former Facebook CTO) Bret Taylor, Asana cofounder Justin Rosenstein, and Optimizely cofounders Dan Siroker and Pete Koomen.

Specialists also play a key role. Consider Pat Wadors, LinkedIn's former chief human resources officer. Pat joined us in 2013, during the City stage of our growth, and helped lead us into Nationhood (she recently left LinkedIn to join my friend John Donahoe, former eBay CEO, at ServiceNow—a return to the City stage). Like Matt, Pat is brilliant and talented, but also a specialist who has held HR roles at leading companies such as Viacom, Merck, Yahoo!, and Plantronics. Running a major function for a City- or Nation-stage company requires deep domain expertise and isn't something that a smart generalist can just "figure out" in a matter of weeks.

While hiring specialists is an incredibly powerful tool to help you scale, it is dangerous to do so prematurely. Specialists are just that—specialized. While they are talented enough to be able to do things outside their specialty, redeploying them seldom allows them to generate anywhere near the value they can provide within their specialty. For example, I have no doubt that Pat is smart enough to learn JavaScript programming, but I would question the wisdom of asking her to give up her role to go through a coding boot camp and join ServiceNow's engineering team as an entry-level software engineer. It would be a criminal waste of Pat's talent and likely a bad financial move for the company.

In addition, the transition that occurs when you bring in specialists to manage or replace generalists can strain the morale of the organization. "Demands for functional expertise often outstrip early employees' abilities to keep up through organic learning," wrote Harvard Business School's Ranjay Gulati and Alicia DeSantola in "Start-Ups That Last: How to Scale Your Business," which appeared in the March 2016 issue of the *Harvard Business Review*. "As a consequence, functional leadership titles increasingly go to outsiders, and the legacy folks may grow resentful. Early employees may also chafe against the narrowing confines of their changing roles. Not every generalist can or even wants to become a specialist. Often people get frustrated and leave, taking their valuable relationships and their tacit understanding of the firm's mission and culture with them."

In many cases, you should work to retain your generalists, both for their cultural and institutional knowledge, and for their ability to tackle new problems. But if you are unable to do so, and early generalists decide to leave the organization, you should try to maintain a positive relationship with them as members of your corporate alumni network. You can read much more about this topic in our previous book, *The Alliance*.

In the Family stage, you should hire only generalists. You can certainly follow the traditional approach of recruiting from elite colleges or hiring ex-McKinsey analysts, but you should also try to focus on people with prior experience at early-stage start-ups who list a broad range of responsibilities and accomplishments. They may not have the pedigree, but they are great at learning new things and at charging hard to execute on them. Plus, the early business is in too much flux to effectively leverage the finely tuned capabilities of a true specialist. Even at the Tribe stage, hiring a specialist should be considered a major exception—for example, if you need an engineer with a very specialized area of expertise, such as data science or machine learning. The Village stage is where it becomes prudent to hire specialists, as both executives and key contributors. At the Tribe stage you want employees with skill sets flexible enough to pivot along with the company, but if you have hundreds of employees, you better have some pretty well-developed theories about your business and where it is going! Almost any executive hire at the City or Nation stage is going to be a specialist. But even at these largest, latest stages, you should still mix in some number of generalists.

Think of generalists as the "stem cells" of your organization. Your body has a small number of stem cells that have the capability to morph into various other types of cells as needed. In a large organization, you may need a small number of people who can perform various functions as needed, whether exploring new products and technologies or tackling issues that lack a well-defined solution.

TRANSITION #3: CONTRIBUTORS TO MANAGERS TO EXECUTIVES

The terms "manager" and "executive" are often used interchangeably. We believe that managers and executives play very different roles. Most of the confusion probably comes from the tendency in early-stage start-ups for the same person to play the role of manager and executive. These are separate roles, even when the same person plays them.

Managers are frontline leaders who worry about day-to-day tactics: they create, implement, and execute detailed plans that allow the organization to either do new things or do existing things more efficiently.

By contrast, the role of the executive is to lead managers. For the most part, executives don't manage individual contributors. Instead, they focus on vision and strategy. Yet they are still connected to the frontline employees because they are also responsible for the "fighting spirit" of their organizations; they need to be role models who help people persist through inevitable adversity.

Both executives and managers are necessary for successful blitzscaling, but they play different roles at different stages. When a company is in the Family stage, it may not need any formal managers. And even if it does, that role is generally filled by the founder/CEO. As the company grows into a Tribe, it will need managers to run the various functional departments, such as engineering and sales. These managers may be the founders, or they may be outside hires. Their key objective is to make a small team productive on a day-to-day basis.

When the company reaches the Village stage, it will need executives. It simply isn't possible to coordinate a company with hundreds of employees without executives to manage and lead multiple managers. Let's imagine a company with six departments: engineering, sales, marketing, product, support, and administration. If each department head managed ten direct reports, and each manager reported directly to the CEO, the maximum number of employees under this executive-less arrangement would be sixty-seven (eleven in each of six departments, plus a founder/CEO). This is still small enough as to be manageable, but were the company to grow beyond that, it would become important to build in an executive layer to keep things running smoothly.

A company in the Village stage might have hundreds of employees. The engineering department alone would require multiple teams and team leaders who would report to a VP of engineering charged with coordinating the teams and architecting the overall organization of the department.

One of the typical challenges we discussed in the section on the transition from small teams to large teams is the need to recruit executives from outside the organization. This represents a major change in approach for a company that probably promoted from within to this point, rewarding early employees who emerged as natural leaders. However, the transition from manager to executive is generally far more difficult in these organizations than that from contributor to manager. Every employee

has likely reported to managers with varying styles and quali-
ties; when promoted to a first-time manager, they can draw on
these experiences to help develop their own management style.
But when an organization needs executives for the first time, internally promoted managers can't draw on the experience working with executives at that company—because there weren't any.
There are no role models to provide guidance.

We call this situation the "Standard Start-up Leadership Vac-
uum," and the result is that inexperienced founders find themselves having to hire and integrate experienced executives from
the outside. The situation is made worse when those founders
wait until the strain on the organization has become unbear-
able before making the new hires, meaning that all the leaders
are new to the company precisely at the time when tension and
uncertainty are running high. The key to navigating this transition is open-mindedness: insiders need to be open to the outside
ideas of the new executives, while the outsiders need to be open
to learning from what happened before they arrived.

No one is born an executive, and very few make the transition from manager to executive without stumbling along the
way. Hiring outside executives lets you offload that often painful and expensive education to those executives' prior employers.
However, a blitzscaling organization can't simply hire anyone
with executive experience at another company of similar or
slightly larger size. An executive at a larger company may not
have any experience with blitzscaling or even start-ups. Running
a hundred-person department at a hundred-year-old company
that grows at 5 percent a year does practically nothing to prepare
you for running a hundred-person department at a company that
is tripling in size every year! At the same time, you don't want to
hire someone whose experience with blitzscaling is at a company
much larger than yours. As we'll discuss a little later, instead of

hiring for the skills you think you might need in the future, you should be hiring for the skills you need right now.

The ideal, of course, is to hire an executive with past experience at a blitzscaling start-up that has already dealt with the challenges your company currently faces. This is why investors have more confidence in serial entrepreneurs. One of the major advantages that companies in Silicon Valley enjoy is generations of rapidly scaling companies that have produced a rich supply of executives with blitzscaling experience. Yet even if you can't land an ideal candidate, second best is to hire a manager who has previously worked with successful executives in a very rapidly growing company, or an executive who earned her executive experience at a larger or more traditional business but who also worked at a blitzscaling start-up at another time in her career.

Consider the case of Facebook. Mark Zuckerberg hired Sheryl Sandberg in part because she had experience blitzscaling as an executive, having helped her group within Google grow from a handful of people to over four thousand employees. And one of the key things Sheryl did that helped Facebook scale up to the Village, City, and Nation stages was to fill critical leadership positions with other experienced scale executives, such as Mike "Schrep" Schroepfer as VP of engineering and David Ebersman as CFO. Schrep had learned how to scale engineering organizations at Mozilla, where he oversaw massive growth, and had also founded his own start-up, CenterRun, before that. David had previously worked as CFO of the biotech leader Genentech and had firsthand experience with the rapid growth associated with blockbuster drugs such as Herceptin and Avastin.

Martin Lau played a similar role for Pony Ma (Ma Huateng) and the rest of the founding team at Tencent. Ma and his co-founders were smart technologists but lacked business experience, especially outside China. Lau had the international business experience from his work with Goldman Sachs but, crucially, also had a strong engineering background and could relate to the team. Lau was able to bring much-needed organizational best practices to Tencent, such as revenue goals and long-term plans. "This was a discipline that was urgently needed for a young company growing extremely fast," said Hans Tung, a partner at the venture capital firm GGV Capital, who coinvested with Tencent in Didi Chuxing.

Another helpful strategy for hiring outside executives is to be strategic about how you blend those outside hires with inside promotions. Mariam Naficy of the online art and graphic design marketplace Minted realized that she could combine the strengths of both groups to create a more effective management team. "It takes years and years to grow candidates from within," she told our Blitzscaling class at Stanford. "We take disciplines where we aren't strong, like finance and HR, and hire in experts from the outside. When it comes to our secret sauce, like crowd-sourcing, we grow people from the inside. Our VP Art and Stationery grew internally, while our VP Finance and Chief People Officer are outside hires."

Even if an outside executive has the requisite blitzscaling experience, though, he or she could still fail because of poor cultural fit—the "transplant rejection" phenomenon. When hiring an executive from another company, there are things you can and should take into account to help ensure the graft "takes" to the host culture.

One master of these techniques is John Lilly, a venture capitalist at Greylock Partners and the former CEO of Mozilla. When he was CEO at Mozilla, John oversaw incredibly rapid growth; during his first six months at the organization, the number of employees tripled. Given Mozilla's small initial size, this growth necessitated hiring executives from the outside ("the graft"), which was particularly challenging because of the company's strong engineering-driven culture ("the host") that was already skeptical about outsiders. John was able to do this successfully by following the same three-step process that was used to hire him.

1. *Hire someone who is already a known quantity to at least one member of the team.* John was hired by Mitchell Baker, his predecessor as CEO of Mozilla. The two had gotten to know each other by serving on a board together, and Mitchell's personal endorsement of John carried weight with the team at Mozilla. Similarly, John had known Schrep at Stanford and worked with him at John's own start-up, Reactivity, before he hired Schrep at Mozilla.

2. *Bring the new executive in at a lower level initially and let the executive prove himself or herself.* John gave himself the title "Director of Business Development and Operations" and only took on bigger titles after he had demonstrated his ability and value to existing teams. He employed the same technique when he hired Schrep, bringing him in as "Director of Engineering." Once Schrep had a chance to prove himself, John noted, "It became pretty clear to everyone pretty quickly that Schrep was incredibly confident, and improved everything he touched." This visible success made promoting him to VP of engineering both obvious and uncontroversial.

3. *Once the executive has earned the team's trust and credibility, consider promoting him or her.* Another executive that John hired, Dan Portillo, was brought in to run recruiting but proved so valuable that he was promoted to VP of people and

asked to run HR as well. Today, Dan serves in a similar role at Greylock.

As your company progresses from a Village to a City or even a Nation, you'll continue to need to hire executives, both because the growth in size will require you to add layers above your frontline managers, and because your executives won't always have what it takes to scale to the next stage. But once your organization has successful executives who can serve as role models and mentors, you will be able to start promoting promising managers with personal experience working with those successful executives from within. When Facebook was growing, it was critically important to bring in experienced executives like Sheryl Sandberg, but almost all of Facebook's key product leaders today were trained internally.

While entrepreneurs often resist creating a hierarchy by classifying their people into executives, managers, and contributors, this kind of formal structure is essential to growth, according to Ranjay Gulati and Alicia DeSantola, who wrote in the *Harvard Business Review* in 2016:

> When launching their start-ups, many founders eschew hierarchy because of their egalitarian ideals. But as their firms scale, a growing number of people report to a handful of leaders. Founders may think this allows them to remain in command, because all decisions pass through them. But ironically, their organizations spin out of control as centralized authority becomes a bottleneck that hinders information flow, decision making, and execution. A couple of people at the top can't effectively supervise everyone's increasingly specialized day-to-day work; in such a system, accountability for organizational goals gets lost.

Gulati and DeSantola cite the example of Cloudflare, whose founders publicly committed to building a completely flat organization without hierarchy or job titles. While the founders made this decision for a commendable reason—CEO Matthew Prince felt that eliminating job titles would prevent early employees from feeling "demoted" if the company later hired more experienced people—the results, as documented in a Harvard Business School case study by Tom Eisenmann and Alex Godden, were poor: "In the three months ending in July 2012, five of the firm's thirty-five employees quit, some citing the lack of a clear midlevel reporting structure and the nonexistent HR practices. They described situations in which they had no one to turn to (short of pestering the founders) if they thought certain practices, such as activities related to software or coding standards, needed to change."

Blitzscaling organizations need organization, not just to coordinate their many resources and activities, but in order to maximize speed. The organization's collective learning rate—especially within its leadership team—determines its ability to anticipate future trends, while the strength of its internal structure—especially in terms of its frontline teams—determines its ability to act quickly on those key insights and seize the competitive advantage.

TRANSITION #4: DIALOGUE TO BROADCASTING

One area that undergoes the most change during blitzscaling is the internal communications process. As the company grows, you have to shift from informal, in-person, individual conversations to formal, electronic, "push" broadcasting and online "pull" resources. You also have to shift from sharing all information by default to deciding on what is secret and what is shareable. If you don't manage to develop an effective internal communications strategy, your organization will become disjointed and start to fall apart.

In the Family stage, the entire organization is typically under the same roof, possibly even all working in the same room. As a result, information spreads quite naturally without any additional intervention—possibly more than you'd like. When you have a question or need feedback, you can simply pop up from your chair (or balancing ball or treadmill desk) and say, "Hey! Does anyone know . . . ?"

This "prairie dog" style of communication is organic, quick, and effective. Everyone is still working on the same initiative, so the interruption is likely relevant and/or productive (or easily ignored by wearing headphones if necessary). The biggest challenge you likely face at this stage is keeping the rare virtual employee in the loop. Because it is so easy for the rest of the team to communicate with one another, you have to make an effort to constantly communicate with any remote members to keep them on the same page as the rest of the team. Communications tools like Slack not only provide a medium where all teammates participate on the same terms but also allow for asynchronous communication, which helps overcome time zone differences. Another approach some companies take is to set up a 24/7 video-conference using tools like Skype or Google Hangouts to simulate being in the same room.

These informal bonds remain a critical part of the communications process, even as your firm grows into a global giant. Human beings are social animals, and the bonds between co-workers and teammates require regular dialogue.

However, as early as the Tribe stage, you will need to begin implementing processes to supplement the one-to-one dialogue. For example, nearly every Tribe-size start-up holds a weekly company meeting, though with wildly varying degrees of effectiveness. The weekly meeting is most effective when it serves as a mechanism to bring together the entire company, and for company leaders to convey key messages to employees with whom they don't work directly.

A Tribal meeting should be well organized, with an agenda and other materials provided in advance so that participants can engage in an interactive discussion rather than simply listen to senior leaders talking or, worse, suffer through text-dense PowerPoint presentations. The goal shouldn't be to make decisions in these meetings (unless the topic is one on which everyone can and should have input, like where to hold the holiday party); rather, it's to maximize input from smart people and make sure that everyone feels heard. As a leader, you should seek out opinions from across the organization on important issues, but you can't abdicate your responsibility and rely only on group consensus to make tough decisions.

The best Tribal meetings include rituals that go beyond the cut-and-dried business of the company and help the employees get to know one another better as people, not just workers. For example, one rapidly growing start-up that Chris was involved with reserved a portion of each company meeting for one employee to give a "get to know me" presentation. This allowed everyone to get to know the "new kid on the block" on a level well beyond the typical welcome e-mail. Obviously, this is the kind of activity that only works at the Tribe stage—in a Family it isn't necessary, and a larger company would never have time to introduce every employee in this fashion.

When a company grows to the Village stage, simple logistics can make it difficult to hold a company meeting (often called an "all-hands" meeting). Even if the company hasn't already grown to the point where it occupies multiple offices, it may be difficult to find a physical space where hundreds of employees can gather. Renting an off-site auditorium for a weekly company meeting is both expensive and impractical. The right thing is generally to shift the cadence of such meetings to a lower frequency, such as monthly or quarterly, and to leverage technology like videoconferencing to bring the various offices together.

One interesting approach is to have *all* employees use a teleconferencing service rather than allow headquarters employees to have a better in-person experience than the rest of the company. For example, at the asset management company BlackRock, certain meetings are held by teleconference, even for the subset of employees who could gather in a single conference room so that all employees are on an equal footing.

With technology eliminating the logistical challenges, the company all-hands is highly scalable; these broadcast techniques can work for organizations even as they scale through the City and Nation stages. At LinkedIn, you could trace the growth of the company over time by observing its all-hands meetings. As the business grew, these meetings moved from the company cafeteria to an auditorium, and today they involve live video broadcasts across the globe. The all-hands needs to have a formal questions period so that employees can request needed information and feel part of the decision-making process. At LinkedIn we have moderators in each office gather questions for management.

It's also at this point that the founder/CEO needs to make a conscious effort to develop broadcast channels to reach far-flung employees who might not otherwise feel a personal connection with the company's leader. Of course, at the Village stage, the company likely exceeds Dunbar's number (the number of individuals with whom any one person can maintain stable relationships), and the founder simply won't have time to meet one on one with every employee with any reasonable frequency. For example, even if you made time in your schedule for two one-to-one employee meetings each day, and spent time in every one of the company's offices, you would still only touch each member of a five-hundred-person company once every eight months—not enough to build a strong relationship.

Switching to "one-to-many" communications doesn't always feel comfortable for founders and CEOs. Patrick Collison, the cofounder and CEO of the fast-growing payment company Stripe, described how he overcame these feelings when he visited our Blitzscaling class at Stanford:

> The big change is the need for formal, explicit, broadcast communication. It feels unnatural, especially for me for some reason. Part of the way to rationalize it is to realize that a start-up is not a natural environment. The optimal things to do don't always feel natural. The social groups you belong to don't typically grow 100 percent per year. The new people weren't there for all the tortured discussions of the past. That can be good, but they also don't have the context, so it is a delicate balancing act.

Brian Chesky addresses this need at Airbnb by sending a long e-mail to every employee each Sunday night. Chesky's e-mail isn't simply a recitation of key performance indicators, which could be just as easily accessed on a dashboard somewhere; rather, Chesky shares his thinking on a topic he considers important to the company. This broadcast communication's length, specificity, and authenticity transmit to every Airbnb employee an understanding of who Chesky is and what matters to him.

Regular e-mails to all employees are a common best practice. Blitzscaling masters Patrick Collison and YouTube's Shishir

Mehrotra also employed this technique to manage their rapidly growing organizations. "I was a big believer in writing a weekly email," Shishir told our Blitzscaling class at Stanford. "Leaders [who] write things down tend to deal with [fewer] communications issues. You have to clarify your thought processes in a completely different way. If you just have a meeting and say, 'Okay, so we've all decided,' then people play telephone."

If you can't overcome your discomfort with writing, you can record and distribute regular voicemails or short videos. These broadcasts can be supplemented with smaller one-to-many events, such as Q&A sessions when the CEO visits a local office, or a breakfast with that month's newly hired employees. For example, Mark Pincus of Zynga holds Monday morning coffee talks with all new employees joining that week. Electronic communications are great for establishing regular contact, but face-to-face interaction is still important for establishing a deeper, more emotionally resonant relationship. Reed Hastings meets this need by not having an office at all, and wandering the halls and conference rooms of Netflix.

As your company grows and plays an increasingly important role in your industry, you will likely experience a need to make more of your organization's sensitive information secret. You probably won't share the bank balance with all employees, or keep people up to speed on the twists and turns of the latest fund-raising effort. More secretive cultures might make this move in the Tribe or Village stages, but as a company gets closer to being publicly traded, even the most open cultures have to make moves in this direction.

"What is the role of data in scaling your company?" In an interview with Reid, Jeff Bezos of Amazon discussed how he makes data a critical part of his management process. "If this is a decision based on opinions, then my opinion wins," said Jeff. "However, data beats opinion. So bring data." Jeff follows this policy faithfully; on one occasion, he argued that Amazon customers would never answer questions from potential customers about a product. Just too much friction, he thought. The product team didn't try to change Jeff's opinion with rhetoric and argument; instead, they e-mailed product questions to a thousand Amazon customers who had recently purchased a product and tracked the responses. The data their simple experiment produced changed Jeff's mind, and the "Customer Questions & Answers" section that resulted has added billions of dollars in incremental sales by increasing conversion rates.

Data is the lifeblood of decision making for any company, but it is particularly fundamental if it informs the design of your product, or if acquisition marketing is your key distribution strategy. For example, when he was at Twitter, my Greylock colleague Josh Elman needed to figure out how to keep Twitter users actively using the service. By analyzing the data, he was able to determine that the "core users" who were 90 percent likely to be active month after month were using Twitter on at least seven different days per month. Further analysis showed that what set these users apart from the less active users was that they followed over thirty other Twitter users. Once Elman understood these figures, Twitter was able to encourage new users to follow more accounts, and, within sixty days, Twitter was able to get its ratio of daily active users to monthly active users above its 50 percent target.

Most companies start with relatively little in the way of analytics during the Family and Tribe stages (they might have performed an analysis to estimate market size, but they rarely have much data from actual customers). At this stage you're introducing a new product, not fine-tuning an existing process. You don't need an analytics dashboard to know if people are using your product or not. And if customers aren't using your product, a dashboard isn't going to tell you how to change course. In other words, if you don't have customers to listen to, the best you can do is listen to your gut.

But as Harvard Business School's Ranjay Gulati and Alicia DeSantola noted in "Start-Ups That Last," this approach doesn't scale: "Improvisation is integral to young ventures; it's how they make discoveries. However, as firms grow they need a framework of plans and goals to guide them. That way they can keep trying new things and reacting to dynamic markets, but with an eye toward larger objectives and sustaining the business. Otherwise improvisation essentially amounts to aimless riffing."

You're already dealing with your fair share of unknowns as your company grows at a breakneck pace, so it makes sense to seek certainty wherever you can. To make the transition from inspiration (or improvisation) to data more easily, it helps to start with the basics. Track a few key stats, such as the number of users (registered users, application downloads, retail buyers, etc.), churn, and raw engagement. When Selina Tobaccowala joined SurveyMonkey in 2009, she had to build up the company's data infrastructure quickly. "There were no analytics before 2009," Selina told our Blitzscaling class at Stanford. "There was a daily cash report and that was it. I strongly believe that as a whole company, you can't get behind more than three to five metrics. The key metrics we picked were free users, free users that become paid users, and then user engagement metrics—number of surveys, and return rate."

Sometimes even a single metric can tell you a lot. At You-Tube, Shishir Mehrotra decided that their single clarifying metric would be watch time. "Our goal was to get to one billion hours per day of watch time," he said. "At the time, we were doing 100 million hours per day. Facebook had about double that. Television as a whole was 5.5 billion hours per day. . . . Picking a single clarifying metric is very hard, but it clarifies decision-making and what constitutes success."

Whatever metric(s) you select, that information must be easy to access and provide clear context. Particularly when your company is still small and lean with limited manpower, it pays to invest in the infrastructure necessary to support fast, data-driven decision making. A text-based log file might technically provide all the data you need, but anyone who has to manually process that data into a user-friendly graph each time will rapidly stop using that data to drive decisions. What matters isn't what you collect but what you convey to decision makers.

The key stats will evolve as your company grows. You can't simply "set it and forget it" when it comes to data. The critical metrics for predicting the long-term viability of your business may be very different as you achieve scale, particularly if the environment is changing rapidly. For that matter, your definition of "long-term" will change a great deal. In the Family stage, next month often counts as "long-term," whereas a Nation-stage company might have multiyear plans. At LinkedIn, we began with a laser focus on the number of user registrations as our key stat, but the long-term engagement of our users and a number of other stats are more important today.

This doesn't mean that you should throw out all your old

metrics; there can be a lot of value to continuity. For example, Mariam Naficy of Minted told me, "The key is to create consistent questions from the beginning and to not change them over time, because that's the only way to compare metrics over time. We've been using Net Promoter Score [a customer-loyalty metric that measures how likely customers would be to recommend a product or service to others] from the beginning."

Watch out for what Eric Ries dubbed "vanity metrics"—numbers that present a rosy picture of the business but don't actually reflect its key drivers of growth. Note that one company's vanity metric might be another's key driver. For example, pageviews are a vanity metric for most start-ups, but the key driver for a media company. In an interview for Reid's *Masters of Scale* podcast, Ev Williams, founder of Blogger, Twitter, and Medium, reported that in the early days of Twitter, his team got caught up in a particularly harmful vanity metric. Twitter was being praised in the press for encouraging developers to build on top of its API, and Ev's team celebrated the rapid rise in the volume of API calls Twitter was handling each day. Unfortunately, they discovered that API call volume didn't actually correlate with business success. In fact, the opposite was true; the large number of API calls were overwhelming Twitter's infrastructure and causing scalability and performance issues. "We discovered that a lot of the developers who built on top of our API were very inefficient," he recalled. "There was one Mexican radio station that had a particularly bad JavaScript on their Web page—just that one Web page was bringing us down!" Twitter had to tighten its API access rules to reduce the call volume.

Whatever metrics you choose, when the organization is still small, the data can generally spread via osmosis between individual employees, supplemented by a regular review during weekly company meetings. You don't need fancy business intelligence (BI) tools or a dedicated team.

Once your organization reaches the Village stage, however, osmosis won't work. Your people are working on multiple threads, and the organization (which has exceeded Dunbar's number) is now too big for everyone to know one another. Using a common dashboard will allow you not only to see how the threads interlock but also to coordinate the work of different groups. Through the dashboard each group can tell the others, "This is what we're working on; this is how we're doing it; and this is how we're working together with the rest of you."

Almost all quality Village-size businesses will use a dashboard to assess the daily health of their companies. Your organization's dashboard will tell you what you want to track and ensure that you're keenly aware of sudden changes so that you can quickly investigate any surprises and assign actions to the responsible person or group.

At the City and Nation stages, you'll almost certainly need a dedicated BI team to ensure that the necessary data is getting to the people who need to support and carry out key decisions. The stakes are so high, and the cost of bad decisions so great, that the expense of a dedicated team is small in comparison.

Mark Pincus invested heavily in his BI team at Zynga, which allowed the company to track every click in their games rather than rely on Google Analytics like most of his competitors. "People would say, Zynga has fifty people working on analytics, this other company only has ten," Mark recalled during an interview for Reid's *Masters of Scale* podcast. "Zynga must be dumb. Actually, collecting that data let us make and evaluate our bets faster."

In addition to simply supplying data and insights to existing business units, many of the top-performing companies create a dedicated growth team, which combines marketing, product, and engineering to drive and coordinate the response to these insights. Most companies, even in the highly competitive world of the consumer Internet, still think it's sufficient to conduct a lot of A/B tests and iterate accordingly. This is an effective tactic but poor strategy, since local optimizations do not necessarily lead to a globally optimal result. A dedicated growth team can look at the big picture and see how product and marketing decisions interact to produce (or not produce) the desired results. According to Greylock's Josh Elman, "The best growth teams identify the core insights that get users from 'curious' to 'activated habitual' users and build every feature and program in the product— including the nonsoftware features that are a part of the whole product—to get users through this hurdle faster."

A growth team also helps by making growth a number one priority rather than a second- or third-class citizen. Elman likes to compare a typical marketing team to a Dickensian orphan, pleading with the product and engineering teams for resources: "Please, sir, may I have another landing page?" Any product changes or engineering infrastructure needed to drive growth, no matter how potentially valuable, typically end up taking a back seat to the product or engineering team's own road maps. In contrast, a growth team's engineers can move far faster because building scalable and extensible testing infrastructure is a core part of their jobs.

One of the challenges you face as you build up your data capabilities is that your strategy can disappear behind the numbers. The numbers might not measure the real health of the business or reveal the real major threats you face. For example, if LinkedIn were to e-mail all of its members every week to remind them to update their LinkedIn profiles, the initiative would result in a short-term boost to profile edits. It would also be a horrible strategy, because it would annoy the users and degrade the user experience.

Jonathan Rosenberg of Google has told the story of how blindly managing to the numbers led Excite@Home astray. Excite@Home measured the click-throughs on every element of its home page. If an element didn't look like it would hit its click-through target, Excite@Home would make the element more visually prominent. In other words, in attempting to hit its numbers, the home page team was emphasizing the least compelling elements and de-emphasizing the most compelling ones!

This is why you may need to blend quantitative and qualitative analysis. Our friend John Lilly likes to distinguish between "genius-driven design" (e.g., Apple) and "data-driven design" (e.g., Google). Both approaches have their strengths and weaknesses. Data-driven design is great at optimizing products with incremental changes, but it could steer you to the top of a local hill rather than the highest peak. Genius-driven design may be the only way to build a revolutionary product, but it usually needs to be supplemented with data-driven refinement.

TRANSITION #6: SINGLE FOCUS TO MULTITHREADING

As the company grows, the product focus will also undergo a major change, from a single-threading to a multithreading approach. What we mean by this is that start-ups in the early stages of blitzscaling are generally single-product companies that focus on doing one thing extremely well. But to keep the company growing in the later stages, scale-ups need to manage multiple product lines or even business units.

We don't know of a single start-up that succeeded without starting out as single-threaded. That focus is the key to beating larger competitors in the early stages of a company's existence.

For years, Drew Houston of Dropbox was told that Google would kill his company because of its secretive "Project Platypus" (which eventually launched as Google Drive). Houston found these proclamations more annoying than frightening, because he knew the power of singular focus. In an interview for Reid's *Masters of Scale* podcast, he explained:

> For a company like Google that's doing a hundred different things, there's a very long breadline to get the next good engineer. And if you're project #35, which is about where Google Drive was on their list, it's going to take a long time before that team gets fed with any amazing people. When you consider the eleven players you put on the field versus your counterpart at a big company, you can actually have a massive talent advantage. Not because Google doesn't have great engineers; they probably have better engineers than you. But the leader of the project is a midlevel product manager for whom it's just the next rung on the ladder. As a founder, you're just so much more committed, and your team is so much more committed.

Today, years after the launch of Google Drive, Dropbox continues to grow in terms of both users and paying customers—so much for the "Dropbox killer."

Even companies that pivot several times, as PayPal did in its first year, need to stay focused, especially as they shift their attention and effort from one initiative to another. My Greylock colleague Joseph Ansanelli, the cofounder and CEO of the customer service software start-up Gladly, tells entrepreneurs, "Don't try a second channel until you have your main flywheel working. Most successful companies dominate one channel."

The shift to multithreading usually occurs during the City

stage of blitzscaling. Once the company has more than a thousand employees, the organization is large enough to support the creation of multiple divisions or business units. While moving to a decentralized organization makes it harder to coordinate the different divisions or business units, the key motivation for the change is how it allows each group to focus on its specific thread. Your teams need the ability—and the manpower—to relentlessly pursue a specific objective; asking a team to split its time between two different business lines is likely to result in the failure of both.

This is especially true when the main thread is a business line that has matured. In their *Harvard Business Review* article "The Ambidextrous Organization," Charles A. O'Reilly III and Michael L. Tushman draw the distinction between "exploiting" and "exploring." Mature business lines focus on incremental innovations that help them exploit a well-known market, whereas new threads focus on more radical innovations and exploring a new market opportunity. They examined thirty-five attempts to spin up new threads, across nine different industries. What they found was that these efforts were most likely to be successful in "ambidextrous" organizations, where the new threads were organized as structurally independent units but integrated into the existing management structure. In other words, the leaders of the new threads not only have the freedom to innovate but also the ability to coordinate with senior leadership to leverage existing resources and expertise from more mature threads.

Multithreading your organization allows you to tackle problems that might not be vulnerable to a single-threaded approach. At LinkedIn, for example, we knew that we needed to address the issue of user engagement. LinkedIn is enormously valuable as a database of résumés, but it is even more valuable as the leading community for professionals. The challenge was figuring out how to develop a daily use case that helped LinkedIn users with their professional lives and encouraged them to use the service continuously rather than just when they were looking to switch jobs or hire a new employee.

We tried a number of single-threaded efforts to meet the challenge. We rolled out features one after another, such as a recommendation engine for people that our users should meet and a professional Q&A service. None of them worked well enough to solve the problem. We concluded that the problem might require a Swiss Army knife approach with multiple use cases for multiple groups of users. After all, some people might want a news feed, some might want to track their career progress, and some might be keen on continuing education. Fortunately, LinkedIn had grown to the point where the organization could support multiple threads. We reorganized the product team so that each director of product could focus on a different approach to address engagement. Even though none of those efforts alone proved a silver bullet, the overall combination of them significantly improved user engagement.

Multithreading comes with a definite cost. Some people are eager to jump to multithreading as quickly as possible because they think it increases their competitive bandwidth. In reality, you should be thoughtful and careful about making this decision. Companies like Google grant a great deal of freedom to individual units, and, as a result, the different products and services do not fit together seamlessly. Many of Google's services are strong enough to succeed on their own, but this means that they are succeeding in spite of, rather than because of, multithreading.

In contrast, Apple's highly centralized approach allows it to produce highly integrated and polished products, but, as a result, it restricts itself to a much smaller product line. Of course, this is intentional; Steve Jobs always wanted to run as close to single-threaded as possible to maintain Apple's unity of purpose. One of the first things Steve did when he returned to Apple as CEO in 1997 was to reduce the company's product line from dozens to a simple two-by-two matrix: consumer desktop, pro desktop, consumer laptop, and pro laptop. "Deciding what not to do is as important as deciding what to do," he told his biographer Walter Isaacson. Another famous Steve story involves an Apple strategy off-site where Apple's top one hundred people worked for a day to reduce Apple's strategy to ten key priorities, at which point Steve crossed off the bottom seven items and said, "We can only do three."

Generally, you should start adding threads when it's strategically necessary, and with a realistic assessment of the negative impact that multithreading will have on organizational focus, resource efficiency, and so on.

At LinkedIn, we made an explicit strategy decision to multi-thread our revenue model, even though the conventional wisdom in Silicon Valley is to stick to a single revenue model. We were criticized for having a "mishmash" of revenue streams, such as pro subscriptions, job listing fees, and enterprise licensing for our recruiter product. It's true that there was a cost to this strategy in terms of focus, but I believed that we didn't have enough information to pick a single revenue stream and have it be sufficient to build our intended scale of business. Multithreading to support multiple revenue lines both mitigated strategic risk and helped us get to scale.

One important technique for making this decision is to consider both the magnitude of the opportunity as well as its potential for gain. If you have a billion-dollar opportunity, it makes sense to invest more resources and eke out a 5 percent gain

($50 million) than to grow a nascent million-dollar opportunity by a factor of 1,000 percent ($10 million). This is why it's generally better to have your ten best people working on a single important project rather than splitting them to attack two different opportunities. For example, AdWords is such an enormous revenue driver for Google that even tiny percentage increases make a huge difference to the bottom line.

Conversely, when the potential for gain associated with your core opportunity declines, multithreading is often the answer to attack better growth opportunities. The company eBay can be thought of as a collection of markets. While eBay might have started with collectibles, multithreading to expand into different markets like cars and apparel was essential to reaching its current scale. More recently, Tencent's creation of WeChat is an example of aggressive multithreading.

Assuming that you make the decision to multithread your organization, the optimal management approach is to think of each thread as a different company. For each thread, you'll need to identify a leadership team ("cofounders") and create an incentive structure that allows it to operate with a great deal of independence and reap the benefits of success, without making your current managers so envious that it tears the organization apart. This is always challenging!

Further complicating matters, people with the entrepreneurial drive required to make multithreading successful usually want to start their own companies, or apply their skills to the company's main thread. One thing that can keep these employees motivated is making the various threads discrete projects—the equivalent of "apps" running on the main thread's "platform." This makes it easy to answer the question "Why shouldn't I just start my own company?" by pointing out the benefits of building on the platform. This structure also makes it easier to manage multiple threads, since the individual threads are less likely to come into conflict.

The incentives of multithreading have to reflect the success of each thread, while still keeping the leadership of each thread invested in the success of all the rest. Without this balance, the different threads might engage in internecine warfare over resources, and the individual leadership teams might prioritize the success of a secondary thread over the health of the entire company. You want to give leadership a reason to make each thread work, but not at the expense of the others; in other words, you want the "owners" of each of the threads thinking like an owner of the overall company. Poorly designed incentives can make it nearly impossible to shut down a thread, even if its performance is poor, since its leadership might fight tooth and nail to stay open.

You might be tempted to simply treat each thread like a separate company within an overall holding company. After all, doesn't that work for Warren Buffett at Berkshire Hathaway? The difference is that Berkshire Hathaway's companies are separate, noncompetitive, cash-generating businesses that have a history of independent operations and complete management teams. In contrast, when a blitzscaling company starts setting up multiple threads, they are still attached, might be competitive, are likely consuming the same pool of cash, and have no history of independent operations.

One of the people I've personally seen handle these issues with exceptional skill is Deep Nishar, LinkedIn's former head of product and now at SoftBank. Deep set up LinkedIn's different product threads and expertly managed the product leaders to create a broader sense of ownership via a web of alignment. Each product leader was the owner of a primary thread, but was also partially accountable and compensated for his or her work in supporting a fellow product leader as a secondary thread. This produced an additional layer of alignment, which reinforced the alignment of all being part of the LinkedIn "holding company."

TRANSITION #7: PIRATE TO NAVY

This key transition is the shift from playing offense to playing offense *and* defense at the same time. More poetically, it's the shift from being a pirate to being part of the navy. It requires an evolution in strategy as well as an evolution in company culture.

For decades, technology entrepreneurs have had an affinity for pirates. As with many of the classic tropes of the start-up world, the link between start-ups and pirates was codified by the late Steve Jobs. Andy Hertzfeld, a legendary serial entrepreneur who worked at Apple and helped design the original Macintosh, related the story on his website Folklore.org. When Jobs gathered together the Macintosh team for an off-site shortly after the release of the Lisa, he famously kicked off the proceedings by laying out three "Sayings from Chairman Jobs" as guiding principles for the project.

1. Real artists ship.
2. It's better to be a pirate than to join the navy.
3. Mac in a book by 1986.

Inspired by Steve's words, the Macintosh team created a homemade pirate flag, complete with the classic skull and crossbones, with a rainbow-colored Apple logo decal as an eye patch. The image of a pirate continued to be so widely associated with start-ups that when the cable network TNT released a movie in 1999 about the heated rivalry between Steve Jobs/Apple and Bill Gates/Microsoft, it was titled *Pirates of Silicon Valley*.

The reality is that many start-ups *are* like pirates: they lack formal processes and are willing to question and even break rules. This flexibility is critical in the early stages of building a great company. Pirates don't convene a committee meeting to decide what to do when an enemy ship is approaching—they act quickly and decisively, and are willing to take risks because they know that the default outcome is death.

Early-stage start-ups are also on the full offensive, waging guerrilla warfare on bigger, established competitors. They are used to striking quickly, using surprise as a weapon, and taking on risks that established companies can't or won't. During the early stages of blitzscaling—Family and Tribe—it's easier to take risks because you don't have much to lose. As Kris Kristofferson wrote and Janis Joplin (among others) sang, "Freedom's just another word for nothing left to lose."

But if you succeed as a pirate, you'll eventually win enough wealth and territory to blitzscale to the Village, City, and Nation stages. At that point, even the most inveterate pirates will have to trade in their Jolly Roger for the flag of a legitimate, disciplined navy. If they don't, their organizations will devolve into chaos.

Eventually Captain Jack Sparrow has to grow up and start acting more like the sober and responsible Captain Picard.

This transition can be challenging. Founders and early employees often resist changing their approach; after all, didn't it bring about their initial success? Plus, entrepreneurs tend to have a rebellious streak; natural-born rule followers don't always fare so well in a chaotic, "move fast and break things" start-up environment. But failing to make the transition from pirate to navy can lead to disaster.

A Note on Ethical Piracy

Before we go further, we need to spend at least a little time on dispelling some of the connotations of the word "pirate." In print and on-screen, pirates are portrayed in one of two ways: (1) lovable rogues and (2) sociopathic criminals. The key differentiating characteristic of the lovable rogue, besides appearing more prominently on the movie poster, is that while she or he may question and break the laws of polite society, a lovable rogue adheres to a personal code of ethics and tries not to harm others. The lovable rogue is willing to break the rules but remains moral. He or she is an ethical or a "good" pirate. In contrast, the sociopathic criminal, as the name suggests, behaves in a purely selfish manner, breaking rules and thoughtlessly harming others in order to bring material benefits.

While start-ups and their founders may benefit from behaving like ethical pirates, they should never behave like sociopathic criminals. Besides the fact that such an approach is morally wrong, as a practical matter, you simply can't build a world-changing company as an outlaw, and it is difficult to make the shift from deviant to mainstream society. And this is particularly true in a world where social media is quick to shine a spotlight on unethical practices that can tarnish a company's reputation forever. Go afoul of the law, and your customers will neither forgive nor forget.

One of the key ways to assess whether you're being an ethical pirate or a sociopath is to ask, "Am I trying to change the rules for everyone, or just trying to get away with a personal exemption?" At PayPal, we broke the rules, but we did so because we were working toward a better set of rules for everyone. We felt that our actions were ethical because while we could technically have been in violation of the letter of certain banking regulations (we consistently argued that we weren't a bank, but not everyone agreed!), we believed that in the long run we would be in compliance once we convinced the world to change the rules, and that the world would be better off as a result. History demonstrates that we were right. The various parties that were upset by our so-called pirate mentality—eBay, banks, regulators—all see the value of PayPal today. By changing the rules for everyone, we helped pave the way for other payment companies like Square and Stripe, which have improved the world of mobile payment even further.

Rules are not holy scripture—they exist to make the world a better place, and thus if you can improve the rules, you should. On the other hand, rules usually exist for a reason. You need to have some humility when breaking rules and recognize that you might not understand all the consequences. It's not always cheating to break the rules, but it is always a high-beta activity, hence the need for caution and compassion.

A present-day example of a field where there are both ethical and unethical pirates is the rapid development of cryptocurrencies like Bitcoin and initial coin offerings (ICOs) as a financing tool. The start-ups that are creating currencies and holding ICOs are operating in a legal gray area and likely breaking rules. Some of these start-ups are ethical pirates who are working to change the rules for everyone. Others are sociopathic criminals who are simply trying to collect as much money as possible before the window closes and devil take the hindmost. Both types might make money in the short term if the market is hot enough, but only the ethical pirates will be able to build lasting businesses, and only the ethical pirates will have a positive impact on the world.

Joining the Navy

When your company reaches the Village stage, it's time to start thinking less like a pirate and more like a navy.

What does that mean? Well, you need to start following the rules, and you might want to consider playing defense. Until now, your sole focus has been offense. If you don't have customers, why do you need to worry about retaining them? Now you should ask, "How can we lock out the competition?" More blitzscaling is often the answer. Being the first scaler helps you acquire customers, lock in investors, and attract the best talent.

I like to generate fresh, innovative ways to play defense by asking my team, "If we were trying to compete with ourselves, what we would do? What if we were a start-up? Google? Facebook? Microsoft?" You can also seek outside perspectives, either by asking an independent board member or by leveraging network intelligence.

During the City stage, defense often becomes the primary focus. Establishing a new competitive edge tends to be very difficult. You should focus on strengthening your existing market position instead. There are several best practices for doing so.

First, try to establish a standard. One of the classic Silicon Valley plays is to move from an app to a platform so that you can attract people to build on and to your platform (thereby leveraging the network effect of compatibility). Salesforce.com's Force.com ecosystem is a great example of this. By offering the ability to build third-party applications on top of the Salesforce platform, Salesforce benefits from a "force multiplier." There are over 2,800 apps on the Salesforce AppExchange, and an International Data Corporation (IDC) study showed that the Salesforce ecosystem generates 2.8 times the revenues of Salesforce.com itself. That means that while Salesforce.com has revenues of "only" $8.4 billion, its platform gives it the economic impact of a $32 billion company.

Second, offer a more complete solution, and try to outflank the competition. I like to say, "Both players are holding glasses of water, and are trying to tip over the other person's glass." In other words, if your competitor suddenly started offering its core product for free, could you still make money on *your* core product?

Interestingly, this focus on defense at the City stage of blitz-scaling is different in China than in Silicon Valley. In China, companies will put teams on anything that has traction; in Silicon Valley, talent is so precious and there are so many other offensive plays that companies often can't afford to rely on a fast-follower strategy. This means that in a very real sense China is even more competitive than Silicon Valley, though I expect that over time China will evolve to become more like Silicon Valley in this respect.

At the Nation stage, the transformation from pirate to navy is complete. (If it's not, either you don't have a Nation or you have failed to make the shift and your Nation is in chaos—witness Uber in 2017.)

In this phase, acquisitions typically become important, if not essential, to defensive strategy. You can acquire an innovative technology and team, and then feed them with massive resources as they scale. This is how Google blitzscaled Android. Google acquired Android in 2005, when it was still just a small, twenty-two-month-old start-up that was working on a new operating system for mobile phones. Google let Android founder Andy Rubin hire additional engineers to complete the product, while using its market power and reputation to establish the Open Handset Alliance, a consortium to promote Android that included hardware makers Samsung, HTC, and Motorola, carriers Sprint and T-Mobile, and chipmakers Qualcomm and Texas

Instruments. With this backing, Android grew quickly after its launch in the fall of 2008. Android exceeded the iPhone in number of phones shipped in 2010, and at over one billion phones per year, today makes up nearly 80 percent of global smartphone unit shipments.

Acquisitions are the biggest offensive and defensive plays in your Nation playbook. Think about how certain key acquisitions won a major market for their acquirers. The YouTube, Instagram, and WhatsApp acquisitions were both defensive and offensive. Acquiring YouTube allowed Google to recover from its failed Google Video initiative, but it also kept YouTube out of the hands of competitors like Microsoft. The Instagram and WhatsApp acquisitions helped Facebook defend against mobile incursions, but they also made Facebook the leader in mobile.

Financial strategy can also become competitive strategy. For example, Apple's cash hoard allows it to move quickly and pay cash for any acquisition—two key advantages during a competitive bidding process.

Finally, you may order your naval task forces to launch diversionary attacks that yield little tactical advantage but that help the overall strategic situation. For example, Microsoft needs to field a search engine to compete with Google, even though it is unlikely to capture much market share, because Google is fielding productivity apps against Microsoft. At this phase, you should try to make your opponents defend every bit of their territories, because, if you succeed, they will be stretched too thin to ward off the attacks you actually consider important.

Just remember to save a few ships to fend off attacks from those pesky pirates!

From Captain to Admiral

At the time of the writing of this book, the ridesharing company Uber was Silicon Valley's most valuable start-up (and second globally to its frenemy, China's Didi Chuxing), despite having spent most of 2017 in the news for a number of serious problems and scandals.

Some of these issues were due to clearly unethical behavior, including internal problems, such as the sexual harassment reported by the former Uber engineer Susan Fowler, and various external attempts to subvert free competition, regulation, and the press, such as creating fake accounts to poach drivers from its rival Lyft (as reported by The Verge), developing software (Greyball) to prevent law enforcement and regulators from accessing the service, and then-COO Emil Michael suggesting that the company spend money to hire opposition researchers to intimidate journalists.

This kind of behavior is unacceptable, regardless of the size or stage of the company undertaking it, and has rightfully been widely condemned.

Yet even if Uber had never engaged in the unethical behaviors outlined above, the company would still have faced real issues because of its reluctance to abandon its pirate-like strategies (many of them benign in its earlier days) despite its much greater size and scope.

When Uber's board picked Dara Khosrowshahi as the company's new CEO in September 2017, it certainly helped that Dara had a well-deserved reputation for running a no-drama operation (a classic naval officer, in other words). But just as important was his experience in successfully growing Expedia into a profitable $20 billion twenty-thousand-employee giant that has won praise as one of the best-managed companies in its industry and a great place for work-life balance.

While Dara will be dealing with many flashy, well-publicized issues at Uber, his biggest challenge—and greatest opportunity—will be steering Uber through the difficult but critical transition from "pirate" to "navy." To create a friendlier culture and halt the mass defection of top talent, win back the loyalty of drivers and riders, and put an end to the legal battles that have plagued the company, Uber's new chief executive will need to start behaving more like an admiral and less like a pirate captain. All start-ups recognize that there is a value to being small: innovation, nimbleness, focus, outcome versus process. All successful entrepreneurs have the desire to stay small in this way. But the most successful scale-ups are those that have managed to keep the positives of staying small while reaping the benefits of being big.

Dara was trying to strike this balance when he reset Uber's cultural norms in November 2017. He announced the changes in a post on LinkedIn.

> As we move from an era of growth at all costs to one of responsible growth, our culture needs to evolve. Rather than ditching everything, I'm focused on preserving what works while quickly changing what doesn't.
>
> This is the approach we've taken with our new cultural values, which we announced to employees today. Our values define who we are and how we work, but I had heard from many employees that some of them simply didn't represent the kind of company we want to be.

A firm believer that culture must be written from the bottom up, Dara didn't come up with a new set of values alone, behind the closed door of a conference room. Instead, he asked employees to submit ideas for how to improve Uber's culture. Over 1,200 people sent in submissions that were voted on more than twenty-two times.

The new cultural norms that Dara unveiled reflect his different approach even in the simple nature of their language. Instead of highlighting "lone wolf" mottos like "Always be hustlin'," the new culture emphasizes the group by starting each norm with the word "We":

We celebrate differences.
We do the right thing.
We act like owners.
We make big bold bets.

Dara deserves credit for working hard to add "navy" values such as responsibility and doing the right thing to Uber's "ethical pirate" values of boldness and aggression.

But cultural change, while necessary, is not sufficient to turn a pirate gang into a real navy. When the CEO of a large organization like Uber makes the transition from captain of a single pirate ship to an admiral running a fleet with naval-like discipline, there are well-established techniques and approaches that can help make this transition smoother and more effective. For example, if you're building a global business, there are three key elements you need to put in place.

1. A set of managers who are responsible for, and have strong executive control over, their individual markets globally

2. An understanding of how those markets differ, which leads to a variety of plans for how to grow in each of those markets

3. A unified executive team to coordinate global operations, including the activity of the individual managers leading operations in each country

The first two elements involve a decentralized command structure that allows the individual "captains" of the ships in the fleet to operate with entrepreneurial vigor. The third involves a centralized staff that can help the "admiral" coordinate the actions of the fleet for maximum impact.

Uber actually did a good job with the first two elements. Uber's general managers are like individual ship captains, and their ability to act independently helped Uber develop innovations like surge pricing (which was an independent experiment conducted in the Boston market). Where Uber failed was its inability to commit to the third element, a unified executive team. When you have strong individual captains and an admiral who can't or won't build a staff to help him or her actually manage the fleet, you end up with a pirate mob.

The failure to build a unified executive team is sadly common. Some entrepreneurs find it difficult to accept the increased structure and decreased freedom of a formal staff; many of these people started companies precisely because they disliked the feeling of working in a large organization. In his book on Uber, *Wild Ride,* the journalist Adam Lashinsky describes how Uber's Travis Kalanick viewed his role at the helm of his giant company:

> "The way I do it, it doesn't feel big," [Kalanick] says, falling back on a favorite trope: that he approaches his day as a series of problems to be solved. . . . "I would say you constantly want to make your company feel small," he says. "You need to create mechanisms and cultural values so that you feel

as small as possible. That's how you stay innovative and fast. But how you do that at different sizes is different. Like when you're super small, you go fast by just tribal knowledge. But if you did tribal knowledge when you're super big it would be chaotic and you'd actually go really slow. So you have to constantly find that line between order and chaos."

Kalanick's words reveal a pirate's discomfort with running a large organization. "He obviously thinks of himself as troubleshooter in chief as much as a CEO," Lashinsky writes. But while acting as a troubleshooter in chief might be a good fit for his personality, at the City or Nation stage, getting too involved in the details of individual problems is probably a poor use of a CEO's time.

Kalanick, in other words, was doing what felt good to him rather than what the organization needed.

The purpose of hiring a management team is to solve the organization's problems in a more scalable way. The CEO should be the hub, and the executive team the spokes that connect the CEO to the frontline managers and employees operating where the rubber hits the road. Kalanick was trying to be the hub and the spokes rather than helping the organization build the ability to get things done without his personal oversight. Another symptom of this dysfunction was Kalanick's habit of canceling his executive staff meetings. Without spending time together, it is difficult for a management team to build a group culture or to coordinate the many initiatives of the organization. A strong executive team meets on a regular basis and focuses on the most important initiatives and issues, including active planning for the future. According to a 2018 *Forbes* article, "Inside Uber's Effort to Fix Its Culture Through a Harvard-Inspired 'University'," Uber's SVP of Leadership and Strategy, Frances Frei, described the management team's lack of cohesion as one of the largest problems facing the company. The article reports that "Uber's senior executives weren't working as a team and only had one-on-one relationships with Kalanick who oversaw them all."

Kalanick is absolutely correct when he argues that staying small helps organizations stay innovative and fast, but staying small isn't always a possibility. It is better to build an organizational structure that you can iterate multiple times rather than to avoid scaling the organization as long as possible and make the shift in a single giant leap "someday."

In other words, you have to build management strategies that scale. Even someone as smart as Larry Page learned this during the early days of Google; he tried to run Google's engineering department without management by having all four hundred employees report directly to then-VP of engineering Wayne Rosing. The failure of this experiment convinced him to allow then-CEO Eric Schmidt to build a real organizational structure at Google.

Any given management structure is likely to be temporary. You can't run a Village the same way you run a Tribe, and you can't run a City the same way you run a Village. But without structure, you won't make it to the next stage of growth.

It appears that Kalanick's discomfort with Uber feeling "big" led to a dysfunctional organizational structure in which he clung to his previous ways. In the absence of a cohesive management team, Uber seemed to operate on a model that Susan Fowler described in her personal blog as "a game-of-thrones political war" with managers fighting for advancement:

> The ramifications of these political games were signifi-
> cant: projects were abandoned left and right, OKRs were
> changed multiple times each quarter, nobody knew what
> our organizational priorities would be one day to the next,

and very little ever got done. We all lived under fear that our teams would be dissolved, there would be another re-org, and we'd have to start on yet another new project with an impossible deadline. It was an organization in complete, unrelenting chaos.

When Uber tried to scale its management by hiring experienced executives like Jeff Jones from Target, they ended up resigning rather than changing the organization. During the first half of 2017 alone, Uber lost eight VPs or department heads.

In contrast, companies like Facebook and Amazon, and leaders like Mark Zuckerberg and Jeff Bezos, found ways to successfully recruit leadership from the outside, blending them with existing team members to change and strengthen the organization. Facebook promoted insiders like Chief Product Officer Chris Cox (who joined Facebook as a software engineer in 2005 after dropping out of Stanford), but also brought in compatible outsiders like Sheryl Sandberg and Mike Schroepfer. Jeff Bezos's top lieutenants like Jeff Blackburn and Andy Jassy are Amazon lifers, but he also brought in key outsiders like Jeff Wilke from AlliedSignal and former Chief Information Officer Rick Dalzell from Walmart. These outside hires can help even at massive scale; one of the benefits to Microsoft of buying LinkedIn has been adding Jeff Weiner and CTO Kevin Scott to Microsoft's executive team.

As your fleet of pirate ships and followers grows, you need to intentionally shape them into a disciplined navy. A fleet of ships requires strong captains *and* a strong centralized staff that can coordinate and harness their entrepreneurial vigor.

Every successful founder and every successful organization must go through these changes. But as Uber has discovered, blitzscaling makes these changes simultaneously harder (because of the speed at which they must happen) and more important (because of the risk inherent in investing in speed over efficiency).

TRANSITION #8: SCALING YOURSELF: FOUNDER TO LEADER

All founders need some universal skills to succeed. They need the ability to take bold risks in pursuit of a vision that isn't self-evident to others. They need the ability to learn (since they're trying to do something brand-new). And to play a long-term role at their start-up turned scale-up, they need the ability to live with and resolve the inevitable paradoxes of being a founder. When I asked Dropbox founder Drew Houston to look back on his experience, he told me, "I think a lot of entrepreneurs start with a lot of insecurity about what they don't know. What you want is not to be paralyzed by it, but to harness it—to use that nervous energy to learn and make yourself better. You've got to keep your personal learning curve ahead of the company's growth curve."

Maintaining a certain humility and a sense of perspective can help you navigate the changes in your role as you blitzscale your company. If you truly want to blitzscale, then speed has to take priority over everything—including your own ego.

There are only three ways to scale *yourself*: delegation, amplification, and just plain making yourself better.

Delegation

Can you find, hire, and manage good people, then transfer work over to them so you can tackle the challenges you're uniquely suited to tackle? Many founders are so talented that they have a hard time letting go of tasks once they start performing them. They often think things like "Will someone else be able to do this as well as I can?" The answer is almost certainly "No, especially not at first, but they'll probably figure it out over time, just like you did."

Start-ups get off the ground thanks to the individual talent and hard work of founders like Mark Zuckerberg and Brian Chesky, but they blitzscale into giant companies like Facebook and Airbnb because these founders learn how to delegate.

One of the most important aspects of delegation, and often the most challenging for a founder, is to hire an executive and hand off functional leadership. For example, a lot of great founders are product people. Initial product/market fit and success are achieved because of their product instincts. But as the company grows, these founders will almost always need to hire an executive to take over leadership of the product organization—it's too important to be a founder's part-time job.

A key technique I use to overcome this challenge is to picture the hire as a specific living, breathing person rather than as a role written down on a piece of paper. When you try to picture an abstract "head of product," for example, you might have a hard time visualizing this faceless entity doing a better job than you are. But when you picture a particular individual (say, Joe Zadeh of Airbnb), all of a sudden your mind shifts to thinking, "Wow, just imagine how awesome it would be to have someone like this running our product team." It might be difficult to hire this paragon—executives who are that good are hard to pry loose from their current companies—but it doesn't hurt to try, and at the least, you'll have a great reference to which you can compare the people you actually consider hiring.

Amplification

Rather than delegate work you're doing to others, can you hire people who *amplify* the work you do? The goal here isn't to free you up from your work so that you can do other things; it's to make the things you do much more impactful. This is actually one of the areas I've tried to develop and refine in my own life.

Like many founders and executives, I have an amazing executive assistant, Saida Sapieva, to help me with scheduling and logistics. But I've discovered that you can take the concept of amplification much further. For example, I was one of the first start-up leaders in Silicon Valley to borrow the "chief of staff" concept from the realm of politics and established corporations. Unlike a traditional assistant or even a technical assistant, your chief of staff should amplify your business impact: he or she should be a businessperson who can not only make certain decisions for you but also triage the important decisions that you have to make yourself. A chief of staff can also make sure that all the people who want to meet or interact with you are "briefed" in advance so that your time together can be as efficient and effective as possible. My first chief of staff, Ben Casnocha, was a successful author and entrepreneur before we began working together; my second, David Sanford, had worked with me at LinkedIn and had also been an entrepreneur (and a restaurateur!). It turned out that Ben and David were better at organizing my own life than I was; I've become significantly more productive since they started amplifying my efforts. To learn more about the role and value of a chief of staff, I recommend that you read Ben's essay on the topic, "10,000 Hours with Reid Hoffman," which you can find on his personal website, Casnocha.com.

Once you begin to appreciate the power of amplification, you can find many ways to scale yourself. For example, one of the things you need to do is to process information about your company, your industry, and the world as a whole. I have a freelance researcher on my team, Brett Bolkowy, who helps me learn new things and answer key questions by finding the best information on any particular topic. Another key team member, Ian Alas, helps me with creative projects like the visual summaries I prepare for my books. The slide shows he created for my book *The Start-up of You* have been viewed nearly fifteen million times. Now that's amplification!

Nor am I unique in this. For example, Mark Zuckerberg has a substantial team to help him manage his social media communications so that when he travels and meets people, he can maximize the impact of his interactions.

Trusted employees, freelancers, or even a team of outside consultants can be your amplifiers. The official nature of the relationship is less important than having assistance that you can trust.

Making Yourself Better

Because your company grows and changes so quickly as you blitzscale, it's crucial for you to figure out how to make yourself better just as quickly so that you don't become the bottleneck that holds your company back. As our friend Jerry Chen likes to say, "There are no job descriptions for founders. If the role doesn't change, there's something wrong."

Since you're going to face new challenges during every stage of blitzscaling, you have to **make yourself into a learning machine**. My friend Elon Musk is a great example. He dropped out of Stanford's PhD program in applied physics because he thought he could learn more on his own! He started SpaceX and Tesla by learning literal rocket science and carmaking. So how do you accelerate your learning curve so that you can learn more faster? The key is to stand, as Isaac Newton wrote, "on the shoulders of giants."

This means talking with other smart people, often, so that

you can learn from their successes and failures. It's usually easier and less painful to learn from another's mistakes than from your own. When I need to learn about a new subject, I'll definitely devour some books on the topic, but I almost always supplement this reading by seeking out dialogue with leading experts in the field. Brian Chesky at Airbnb, another amazing learning machine, does something similar, seeking advice from mentors like Sheryl Sandberg and Warren Buffett. Brian told our class at Stanford, "If you find the right source, you don't have to read everything. I've had to learn to seek out the experts. I wanted to learn about safety, so I went to George Tenet, the ex-head of the CIA. Even if you can't meet the best, you can read about the best." Brian lives this advice; he got many of his ideas by assiduously poring over biographies of great entrepreneurs like Walt Disney.

Another helpful approach to seeking mentorship is to get help from experts who might be less famous than the Sheryl Sandbergs of the world, but who have faced (and solved) similar issues in the recent past. In an interview for Reid's *Masters of Scale* podcast, Dropbox's Drew Houston described how he tries to learn from fellow entrepreneurs who are on the same journey:

> Talk with other entrepreneurs. Not just famous entrepreneurs, but people who are one year ahead, two years ahead, five years ahead. You learn very different and important things from those kinds of people. It really helps to have a sense of the longer-term arc, because the game changes quietly from phase to phase.

In addition to seeking help on an ad hoc basis, I believe it's a good idea to be systematic about learning from others. I advise entrepreneurs to have a personal board of advisers or "board of directors" who can proffer advice and help you fill the gaps in your knowledge. For example, I have a set of informal advisers who help me learn about the areas that matter to me, including very specific topics like virality or people management. If you're serious about someday blitzscaling a company, you should think of your mentors as a board of directors. Regularly report to them on your progress, and ask them how you can do better. Everyone needs feedback. Brian Chesky, for example, likes to say, "I'm shameless about getting feedback." He and I have a scheduled dinner every month where (among other things) we share what we've learned and provide feedback. Leveraging a board like this can help you manage risks and increase the potential upside of your actions.

This may sound like a lot of work, but it's important to leave yourself time and space for reflection and feedback. It's easy to get caught up in an endless to-do list and to lose sight of what is important. That's one of the things I learned from Mark Zuckerberg and Sheryl Sandberg. Mark and Sheryl meet first thing every Monday and at the end of every Friday—no matter how busy they are or what else has come up. The Friday meeting is especially important because it gives them time to look back over the week and reflect on what they've learned.

You might feel like you can't afford to take time out from your busy schedule to make yourself better. After all, you might think, everyone is counting on me. This feeling, while natural, is counterproductive. Netflix CEO Reed Hastings warned our Stanford class, "[When I was running Pure Software,] I felt like investing in me was selfish. I thought, 'I should be working.' I was invited to join YPO [Young President's Organization], but I thought, 'I can't take a day off.' I was too busy chopping wood to sharpen the axe. I should have spent more time with other entrepreneurs. I should have done yoga or meditation. I didn't understand that by making myself better, I was helping the company, even if I was away from work." Plus, when you model the behavior of taking the time to improve yourself, you help encourage the rest of the company to develop a culture of learning.

NINE COUNTERINTUITIVE RULES OF BLITZSCALING

Blitzscaling a company isn't easy; if it were, everyone would do it. Like most things of value in this world, blitzscaling is contrarian. To succeed, you'll have to violate many of the management "rules" that are designed for efficiency and risk minimization. In fact, to achieve your aggressive growth goals in the face of uncertainty and change, you need to follow a new set of rules that fly in the face of what is taught in business schools and are completely counterintuitive to accepted "best practices" of either early-stage start-ups or classic corporate management.

RULE #1: EMBRACE CHAOS

Annual plans. Revenue guidance. Traditional business strives for order and regularity in management, operations, and financial results. This desire for order and regularity makes sense, because it allows companies to fine-tune their approach to be as efficient as possible, and gives shareholders a pleasing sense of stability. But when you're blitzscaling, you're explicitly choosing to sacrifice efficiency for speed, which means that the traditional focus on order and regularity needs to be replaced with a unique willingness to embrace a level of chaos that would horrify most Harvard MBAs and their professors.

When you start a company, almost everything is an unknown, from the product/market fit, to the competitive landscape, to the composition of your future team. There is no way to eliminate all of these uncertainties with careful planning; most can only be resolved by doing. As a result, you have to take action even if you know you still have issues to resolve (and sometimes even if you don't yet know exactly what those issues are). For example, many entrepreneurs start building product before they have a go-to-market strategy.

Yet simply throwing up your hands is unlikely to bring success; passively succumbing to chaos is not a winning strategy. *Embracing* chaos, on the other hand, means accepting that uncertainty exists and therefore taking steps to manage it. If you know that you'll make mistakes, the answer isn't to sit back and wait for answers to find you, nor is it to charge ahead without preparation or forethought. You can still make smart decisions based on your estimate of the probabilities, even without certainty. And, perhaps most important, you can make sure that you have the ability to correct your mistakes.

My earlier book, *The Start-up of You,* introduces the useful concept of "ABZ planning." Entrepreneurs should always have a Plan A, a Plan B, and a Plan Z. Plan A is your best current plan; Plan B is an alternate plan, based on the "adjacent possible" to which you can pivot if Plan A isn't working or you learn of an even better opportunity; Plan Z is your fallback plan for surviving a worst-case scenario. ABZ planning gives you multiple opportunities to recover from mistakes or setbacks.

At my first start-up, SocialNet, we were delighted when we managed to hire a brilliant server engineer (Plan A). That delight turned to horror when he asked to defer his start date for a year! Needless to say, a start-up can't simply put itself on hold for a year—even if you had the money to wait out the delay, the loss of momentum would probably convince most of the team to quit. We kept looking for other brilliant server engineers (Plan B), but when we couldn't find them, we kept building the service anyway by asking other members of the team to do their best, knowing that we'd have to rebuild the service later (Plan Z).

Even if you do manage to hire the people you want, you'll often have to scramble their roles and job titles as the organization changes in response to market feedback. At PayPal, we thought we were a mobile encryption product, and we hired accordingly. Then we shifted rapidly in turn to cash on mobile phones, then cash on PalmPilots, then payments between PalmPilots, and finally payments via e-mail. We couldn't have done so if our people were tied to neat and tidy jobs like "mobile encryption engineer."

Take Jamie Templeton, one of our key early employees at PayPal. We hired Jamie to work on the product, but over the course of just three years, he shifted from product to engineering to systems to policy, depending on what the company needed. Jamie is exactly the kind of employee you need in the early days—someone who is willing to embrace the chaos of a start-up—which is why I made sure he joined me in the early days of LinkedIn as well.

RULE #2: HIRE MS. RIGHT NOW, NOT MS. RIGHT

For most of Silicon Valley's history, the conventional wisdom on hiring executives into a start-up was to quickly bring in an executive who could scale. This meant hiring someone who had experience with much bigger organizations, the idea being that their experience would come in handy at a later stage.

In today's start-up world, this rule no longer applies. The Darwinian competition is so fierce that your organization needs to be "all in" on the current stage of scaling. You need managers and executives who are "just right" for the current phase of growth; after all, you won't have to worry about that next phase if your team can't actually get you there. Hiring someone who has been managing a thousand people to run a ten-person company is actually counterproductive, because the skills needed to succeed during those two phases are very different.

The ideal, of course, is to hire executives who can not only excel at your current phase but stretch to cover the next phase as well. But that "scalability" should be a secondary concern. The primary concern is current value. You can worry about whether to scale or replace an individual executive when the company approaches its next phase.

For example, entrepreneurs are sometimes advised to avoid hiring salespeople until they are able to secure a VP of sales who has shown that he or she can scale the company to $100 million in sales. This is hogwash. The salespeople you need to ignite hypergrowth are totally different from the salespeople you'll need at scale. When you're trying to sell your product for the first time, you need aggressive, adaptable salespeople who aren't big on following rules. By the time you've achieved scale, you'll need thorough, process-oriented salespeople who can keep a machine running smoothly. You're not going to find one person who is great at both.

One thing to look for when evaluating a potential hire is whether the person seems self-aware of which stages of the process he or she excels at and prefers. For example, some people will tend to gravitate toward early-stage companies where they will have more opportunities to take on a broad portfolio of responsibilities. Others might prefer early stages because they enjoy the direct and tangible impact of being a key individual contributor or an important team leader over tackling the very different and more abstract work of being a full-time manager or executive. I've known a number of talented people who prefer joining early-stage companies because while they don't want to take on the challenge of being founders, they do want to be, in the words of Aaron Burr in *Hamilton,* "in the room where it happens."

Very few people excel at being an individual contributor, a manager, *and* an executive, and even those rare employees are likely to have a preferred role. Seasoned Silicon Valley professionals tend to be aware of their preferred stage and role because the disproportionate prevalence of blitzscaling companies gives people a chance to experience more of the different stages. These repeated experiences with different stages let employees zero in on the best fit for their skills and desires.

Part of hiring Ms. Right Now also means knowing when to let someone go when the moment passes. For example, a great designer might excel running a one-woman show at a Family or a Tribe, but be less effective working as part of a larger design team.

At LinkedIn, one of the key employees who fit the description of Ms. Right Now was Minna King. Minna is an incredibly accomplished professional who has carved out a valuable niche at a very specific stage in the life of a start-up. You see, Minna specializes in taking a successful software product and helping it go global. She has a very particular set of skills that she has acquired over a long career dating back to the dot-com era. She knows exactly what a software development and product team needs to do in order to make Internet software work in different languages and markets, in areas ranging from database schemas to user interface. She then works with a cross-functional team to implement these changes in advance of a global rollout. It's not easy to find people who fit your needs so perfectly; you can't just go on LinkedIn and filter by "preferred stage of blitzscaling." (Though come to think of it, that might not be a bad idea . . .) You'll probably have to rely on your network for recommendations, which is where your investors and board of directors can help. But when you find Ms. Right Now, she can add huge value to the organization.

This is precisely what Minna did for me at LinkedIn, just as she did for Overture and eBay before joining LinkedIn, which is exactly the same thing she did for two other highly successful software companies, SurveyMonkey and Nextdoor, after she left LinkedIn. In each case, she came to the company at the early Village stage because in order for her work to add the most value, the company needed to be big and successful enough to need to globalize, but small enough to not have the internal skills to do so.

RULE 3: TOLERATE "BAD" MANAGEMENT

When blitzscaling, speed is more important than having a "well-run" organization. Under normal circumstances, you should strive for organizational coherence and stability. Chaotic, unstable organizations make employees nervous and hurt morale. But when you're scaling up at lightning speed, you may need to reorganize the company three times in a single year, or repeatedly churn through members of your management team. When your organization is growing 300 percent per year, you might have to promote people before they're ready and then swap them out if they sink rather than swim. You don't have time to be patient and wait for things to "work out"; you have to act quickly and decisively. There's always a lot of change, and much of it isn't voluntary. You're building teams and the company simultaneously. In the interests of speed, you might even surprise or blindside your people to cut down the time required to make and implement important decisions.

Problems relating to job titles are one common symptom of

this messiness. In the Family and Tribe stages, you don't have time for a careful promotion process, and you don't have time to sit around debating whether someone's business card should read "head of engineering" or "senior VP of product" (nor, for that matter, do you have time to design and order business cards). You might just keep employees' titles the same even as they fail to reflect organizational progress and level of responsibility, or you might do things that no rational company would do, such as deliberately inflating job titles to keep people happy and counting on the ability to correct the situation "later." Either way, you're taking on organizational risk in exchange for being able to focus efforts wholly on growth.

Consider the example of PayPal. While PayPal was a great success, the company was badly managed—and I write that statement as one of its senior managers. We did a few good things, such as making sure that every employee had a clear primary job and staying focused when working on certain important projects, but for the most part PayPal's management was a lack of management. There were no one-on-one career development conversations with employees. There was no work done to form teams beyond simply picking who was going to belong to them. The few rules we had were more about individual incentives rather than team management. For example, when people were late to a meeting, the last person to arrive was fined $100 to enforce discipline. Yet while we knew meetings were important, we didn't designate a note taker to capture key points and action items, a common and basic practice in Silicon Valley.

But PayPal's "bad" management provided a number of counterintuitive strengths while we were blitzscaling. During the critical times when PayPal was developing its business model innovations and scaling up, we found ourselves needing to navigate a series of make-or-break challenges, or, as I like to call them, "Oh shit!" moments.

Oh shit, we have a fraud problem and we're losing millions of dollars we don't have. Oh shit, Visa says we have to change the product or they'll shut us down. Oh shit, eBay, our most important business partner, just started its own venture to directly compete with us.

Because of our "bad" management, we didn't have any preconceived notions of "this is what the company must look like in three years." The chaotic nature of our management actually kept us nimble in the face of these serious, unexpected land mines. When everyone in the organization has roles that are undefined and in flux, it's easier to say, "I know this is what you've been working on for the past four days, but now we're doing something different." The internal chaos had the effect of normalizing radical change for our people, which meant they were better able to adjust to the radical changes the outside world was throwing at us. We knew that we were slaloming through a minefield while other people shot at us. To paraphrase Bruce Banner/the Incredible Hulk from the movie *The Avengers,* the secret behind our superpower was that we were always changing.

We were also fortunate in our timing. One thing that holds teams together in the absence of management is an opportunity to win. After the dot-com bust began, a lot of tech companies were failing, but PayPal still had a chance to succeed. All you had to do was to look at the chart showing the continuing rise in daily transaction volume! So our people put up with more than they would normally put up with because they wanted to win and liked being part of a team of high-powered, high-IQ players.

Classic "good" management and planning presume a certain amount of stability that isn't always available when you're blitzscaling. One of the misconceptions of entrepreneurship is that you work out a plan and then execute it. Think of the embedded metaphor in "building" a business—the very language suggests that you're following an architectural plan. But when you're creating and scaling an innovative business model, you often don't have any detailed blueprints. Instead, it's more like "I think a building over there would be a good idea. Let's start digging!" Then once the cement is poured and the walls go up you realize, "It should be a hotel, and therefore we need to do this kind of a floor plan."

Is that "bad" management? Maybe. But if bad management saves you from building a warehouse in the wrong part of town and lets you quickly turn that structure into a successful hotel (or saves you from losing money on mobile cash and lets you quickly capture the market for global payments), then it might be the best approach you can take.

RULE 4: LAUNCH A PRODUCT THAT EMBARRASSES YOU

It's not that you should strive to produce a bad product. Rather, if you need to choose between getting to market quickly with an imperfect product or getting to market slowly with a "perfect" product, choose the imperfect product nearly every time. Getting to market fast allows you to start getting the feedback you need to improve it. Any product that you've carefully refined based on your instincts rather than real user reactions and data is likely to miss the mark and will require significant iteration anyway. The ideal is a tight OODA loop—observe, orient, decide, act—over and over again. Speed really matters, and launching early lets you climb the learning curve to a great product faster.

Mark Zuckerberg credits speed for the success of Facebook. In an interview for Reid's *Masters of Scale* podcast, Mark told us, "Learn and go as quickly as you can. Even if not every single release is perfect, I think you're going to end up doing better over a year or two than you would be if you just waited a year to get feedback on all of your ideas. That focus on learning quickly is the focus of the company."

I learned this lesson the hard way when I was running my first start-up, SocialNet. I didn't want to be embarrassed by our first release, so the approach we took was to complete the entire product before we pulled back the curtain and let people sign up. This approach delayed SocialNet's launch by a year, and when we finally did launch, we quickly realized that half of the features we'd painstakingly implemented weren't important, and half of the important things that our service would be useless without were missing because we hadn't thought of them. While there were other reasons why SocialNet failed, not launching early and iterating based on market feedback was probably the main cause of death.

After my experiences at PayPal, and the success we found through rapid launches and product iteration, I was determined to launch LinkedIn as soon as possible. Our team defined a list of features that we thought were the minimum required to enter the market. Years later, Steve Blank and Eric Ries would dub this a "minimum viable product" (MVP). For LinkedIn, the MVP included a user's professional profile, the ability to connect to other users, a search function to find other users, and a mechanism for sending messages to friends.

Shortly before launch, we started worrying about whether LinkedIn would be useful without a critical mass of profiles. If a user logged in to LinkedIn, how could we make it useful even if none of that user's friends had signed up yet? We decided that what was missing was a Contact Finder, a version of search that would let a LinkedIn user find potential vendors. For example, if you needed a consultant to help you figure out how to globalize your service, you could use Contact Finder to find Minna King. Our engineering team estimated that it would take us a month to build this feature. We were presented with a difficult choice—delay the launch by a month, or launch without a feature that we thought might be essential to our success. Operating on the embarrassment principle, we launched without Contact Finder. And quickly we discovered a far bigger problem: Unlike users of personal social networks like Friendster, which were growing explosively as new users invited their friends to join, LinkedIn users weren't sending any invites. Our user growth was stalled. Our baseline product was embarrassing because no one was using it! If we had delayed the launch a month to build Contact Finder, there still wouldn't have been enough people hanging around to use it, meaning that we would have lost a month building a feature that didn't address the core problem. We estimated that we would need at least one million users before search (and Contact Finder) would be useful, and solving that problem was the top priority.

Based on the launch data, we focused on trying to increase virality, which is how we became the first social network to allow you to upload your address book. This feature helped LinkedIn get to a critical mass of over one million user profiles, and the rest is history.

Keep in mind that you should be *embarrassed* by your initial release—not ashamed or indicted! The desire for speed is not an excuse to cut dangerous corners. If you trigger lawsuits or burn through your money without learning, it means you *did* launch too soon. The point of launching your product early is to learn as quickly as possible. But your learning is useless if you don't have the ability to iterate. If your product bursts into flames and kills someone, you probably won't get another chance. The first launch of LinkedIn fell well short of our expectations, but we didn't do any harm. Before you release your product, make sure you know what you're trying to learn, and how much risk you can take without endangering your customers or your reputation. Entrepreneurs have to walk a fine line between fixable and fatal flaws!

The line between fixable and fatal often depends on the nature of your product. If we consider just two dimensions of product—free (or freemium) versus paid and consumer versus enterprise—each combination can be placed along a continuum:

- A free consumer product can get away with the most flaws, because consumers tend to be very tolerant when it comes to something that doesn't cost them anything.

- A free enterprise product needs to be more refined; even if it is free, the stakes are higher in a professional setting.

- A paid enterprise product needs to be even more refined, but it can still have significant flaws, because these types of products are intended for expert users who may have no choice but to use the product.

- A paid consumer product has the least room for error. While consumers are very tolerant of flaws in free products, they expect products they pay for to be nearly perfect and will grouse loudly about any significant flaws they find: "What am I paying for here?"

Sometimes you can reduce the risks and uncertainties by obtaining user feedback without actually launching. Design thinking often calls for rapid prototyping and user testing through paper prototypes or visualization tools like InVision and testing tools like UserTesting.com. Yet even these techniques adhere to the rule—the goal is to test as early as possible rather than try to get things right before unveiling them to users.

Once you've launched your product, you have to make sure you learn the right lessons from market feedback. As the example of LinkedIn's initial launch shows, the key lessons might not be found in what your customers say but in what they do. The first users of LinkedIn were largely our friends and family, and they didn't tell us, "This crap is useless without more users!" Instead, they told us things like "It seems like it will be pretty useful"—yet even they weren't sending out a ton of invites. Yes, you need to listen carefully to what your users have to say, but you also need to know when to selectively ignore them. When anecdotal user feedback and data contradict each other, listen to the data. People are often quite bad at predicting how they'll react to changes. The scientific term is the inconsistency between predicted and observed behavior. For example, when Facebook was considering adding a feature that would use facial recognition to automatically tag members' faces in photographs, the focus group participants were very negative toward the concept, calling it "creepy" and an invasion of privacy. Yet when Facebook tested the feature, auto-tagging boosted engagement and users loved it!

When I offer this advice, I sometimes hear the objection "That's not the way Steve Jobs did it." Well, hold on a minute. First of all, contrary to the popular narrative, not all of Steve's products were perfect from the start. The original Mac didn't come with a hard drive. The original iPhone didn't come with an App Store. It is true that we can point to a number of entrepreneurs who did launch a great product at the very beginning. For example, when Elon Musk launched the Tesla Model S, it immediately became the highest-rated car on the road, being named *Motor Trend* Car of the Year in its debut year, and achieving a higher *Consumer Reports* rating than any other car that organization had ever tested. But to do this, you have to believe that you can nail the product/market fit of a new market before you launch, and invest substantial amounts of capital based solely on that confidence. Elon bet his own fortune, and hundreds of millions of dollars of investor and government money, that Tesla could build a better car than any of his century-old competitors. The number of entrepreneurs who are able and willing to bet so aggressively is low. The number who can do so successfully is even lower, and the number who can do it successfully more than once is lower still.

So, yes, if you are a rare genius and can accurately and consistently predict what the market wants, trusting your instincts will be faster than using trial and error to iterate your way to a better product. Good luck with that approach! As a mere mortal, I prefer market feedback.

RULE 5: LET FIRES BURN

I often tell entrepreneurs that starting a company is like jumping off a cliff and assembling an airplane on the way down. The default outcome for any start-up is death, which means that you have to move quickly and decisively to avoid that default outcome at all costs. That doesn't leave a lot of time for dotting each *i* or crossing each *t*.

At every stage of blitzscaling, there are always far more problems and issues clamoring for your attention than you have the resources to address. You might feel like a firefighter, except instead of trying to extinguish a blaze in one contained spot, you can see separate fires all around you—and you don't have time to put out all of them. One of the ways that blitzscaling entrepreneurs can stay alive is by deciding to let certain fires burn so that they can focus on the fires that if allowed to rage unchecked really will destroy the company. My Greylock colleague Joseph Ansanelli says, "What you say 'no' to is more important than what you say 'yes' to."

You can't ignore those fires forever—they are actually dangerous and will eventually require attention, but they aren't relevant at most points during blitzscaling because extinguishing them doesn't move the needle on the expected outcome. Picture an emergency room surgeon trying to save the life of a trauma patient; as she's conducting emergency surgery, she might notice a suspicious-looking mass, but she's going to focus on patching the patient's arteries first—there will be time for biopsies and tests later. After all, if the patient dies on the operating table, even a potential tumor will be irrelevant.

The art, of course, is knowing which fires to let burn. Prioritizing your fires tends to be a function of a combination of different factors. The first is *urgency*: Which fire is going to damage or kill your business the soonest? This doesn't have to be limited to fires that endanger the existence of the business; for a start-up, a fire that kills your ability to grow is nearly as deadly in the long run as one that threatens to put you out of business tomorrow. Usually, your first step is to decide whether you can simply punt on the problem and tackle it later. When Selina Tobaccowala joined SurveyMonkey, one of the first fires she considered fighting was the design of the product. It was ugly, outdated, and frankly somewhat embarrassing. But it was also extremely effective and successful—user engagement was good, and customers were happy. Selina decided to defer redesigning the product in favor of more urgent fires. This decision made it harder for her to recruit aesthetically sensitive engineers, but it didn't kill the company.

In some cases, if the fires at your start-up are burning money but not touching the customer, and if you're able to afford the waste, you might be able to literally buy time and ignore them. Frequently, raising more capital is an easy (though often expensive) way to keep less urgent fires contained.

The second factor you want to look at is *efficacy*: Which fires do you have the ability to extinguish right now, and which will be easier to extinguish later (and vice versa)? If a fire is urgent, but you can't effectively fight it right now, you might have to ignore it and hope that external circumstances put it out. Likewise, if it isn't necessarily urgent right now, but will wreak a lot more havoc if allowed to spread, you might consider saving yourself the ordeal later by nipping it in the bud.

The final factor to consider is *dependency*: Will extinguishing Fire A make it easier to extinguish Fires B and C? These knock-on effects can be very important, because there are always more fires burning than you have time to fight at any given time.

I believe that there is a Maslovian hierarchy of fires that applies to most rapidly growing start-ups, where the top of the list is the most important fire to fight first:

Distribution
Product
Revenue model
Operations
Competition
What's next?

What this means is that for most consumer Internet start-ups, the most important fire is distribution; if your distribution goes up in flames, your company is doomed. If you are able to contain that fire, however, it will make fighting the other fires a whole lot easier. Acquiring users gives you feedback on how to improve your product. Acquiring millions of users or thousands of customers makes it a lot easier to generate revenue. Generating revenue makes it easier to pay for the infrastructure and personnel to scale up your operations, either out of cash flow or by raising investment. And if you have a successful and growing business, then it makes sense to worry about the competition.

In the case of LinkedIn, after we had fixed our distribution problem by building in virality and generating a significant user base, we had people harping on the revenue model fire. If I received a nickel for every time someone asked me, "How is LinkedIn going to make money?" during those days I probably wouldn't have needed another revenue model! But I knew that we should ignore that fire, because (1) the lack of revenue wasn't going to be the proximate cause of death unless it prevented us from raising money and (2) the product fire was far more urgent and required our focused attention. If we couldn't find the distribution to acquire a critical mass of at least a million users, and build a product they found compelling enough to become regular users of the service (or at least respond to LinkedIn requests), the revenue model would be irrelevant.

At the time, potential Series A investors wanted to see a business model that showed how LinkedIn would get to profitability. I told potential investors that we weren't going to generate revenue until after the next round of funding, and that therefore it shouldn't matter to them. They insisted anyway, so the team and I generated a financial model that included revenue sources. I don't even remember what we put in it! Rather than waste weeks on it, we simply set aside a single evening, drank a couple of glasses of wine, and put together the model (I might have been a little miffed at having to spend even a single evening, but it was pretty good wine, so it wasn't a total waste).

This story also highlights why you need people on your team who have a tolerance for chaos, risk, and uncertainty. Most of us are willing to fight fires; it's a smaller subset of people who are capable of noting the presence of a roaring blaze that might soon cut off all escape routes without allowing it to distract them from their laser-focused effort to fight an even more urgent fire. The members of the LinkedIn team were comfortable with that uncertainty, and could still work at full effectiveness even though we didn't have a defined revenue model. Plus, if your people can't let fires burn, they'll spend all of their time fighting them, which won't leave any time for coming up with breakthrough opportunities to advance the business.

RULE #6: DO THINGS THAT DON'T SCALE (THROWAWAY WORK)

Paul Graham, the cofounder of Y Combinator, wrote a famous essay in which he advised entrepreneurs to do things that don't scale. This advice is spot-on for young start-ups, but it's even more important for blitzscaling start-ups.

Engineers hate doing throwaway work. Not only is it wasteful, it offends their sense of efficiency. They are firm believers in the conventional wisdom that says it's better to build your product right the first time, so you only have to build it once. But when you're blitzscaling, inefficiency is the rule, not the exception. To prioritize speed, you might invest less in security, write code that isn't scalable, and wait for things to start breaking before you build QA tools and processes. It's true that all of these decisions will lead to problems later on, but you might not have a later on if you take too long to build the product. A hack that takes a tenth of the time may be more useful than an elegantly engineered solution, even if it has to be thrown away later.

Much the same logic applies to nearly every aspect of your business. You'll often have to do things that don't scale when it comes to sales (e.g., founder Marc Benioff brought in Salesforce .com's first customer, Blue Martini Software, by calling in a favor from its CEO Monte Zweben), operations (e.g., Paul English listed his personal cell phone number as the original customer service line for Kayak), and so on.

Nor is the world neatly divided into "things that don't scale" and "things that scale," with the former smoothly—and permanently—giving way to the latter. The code or process that scales during one stage of blitzscaling may break down at the very next stage, and whatever you replace it with might not scale at first either. Consider how the founders of Airbnb solved the problem of hosts posting poor-quality photos of their rental properties on Airbnb.com: they became the photographers. As Brian Chesky told me, "We would borrow cameras from our RISD [Rhode Island School of Design] friends in Brooklyn, then literally knock on the doors of all our hosts."

Together, Brian and cofounder Joe Gebbia could photograph about ten homes per day (cofounder Nathan Blecharczyk had to stay at the apartment that doubled as their office, making sure the site didn't crash). Talk about doing things that don't scale! Once, a host asked Brian when he'd get paid, and Brian pulled the company checkbook out of his backpack and wrote him a check. "I guess you're not a very big company," the host said as he pocketed the check.

As Airbnb took off, the photography function had to scale up considerably. So the founders hired photographers from Craigs- list, hit up their RISD friends, and even recruited Airbnb hosts who listed photography as a hobby. By tapping these sources, the company was able to build a stable of five to ten photographers who were paid $50 per home, and whom they tracked using the sophisticated management tool of a spreadsheet with photographers and their assignments.

Pretty soon, this system too was overwhelmed. So they hired Ellie Thiele as a summer intern from Syracuse University, and made managing photographers her full-time job. By focusing solely on managing the photography, Ellie was able to increase the number of active photographers to about fifty. It was only at this point that Airbnb went to a truly scalable solution: software. Nathan wrote some code, adding two buttons to the site; one for hosts to request a photographer and the other for Ellie to trigger a payment when a photographer finished an assignment. Eventually the founders hired Joe Zadeh as an entry-level engineer and asked him to work with Ellie to fully automate the photography process.

Airbnb worked its way through three different ways of handling photography before building any code, and has rewritten the photography system multiple times since then. It wouldn't have made sense for Airbnb to start by building a scalable automated photography system; at the point when the company began this journey, the site was receiving a mere ten visitors per day, and the only engineering resource was Nathan Blecharczyk. Any work he did on this problem would have delayed all the other engineering work Airbnb needed to get done to grow its business. By doing things that didn't scale, the company was able to grow despite the resource constraints and the "wasted" work of building spreadsheets that would have to be thrown away later.

RULE #7: IGNORE YOUR CUSTOMERS

The fundamental rule of customer service has long been "The customer is always right." But for many blitzscaling companies, the key rule is "Provide whatever customer service you can as long as it doesn't slow you down . . . and that may mean no service!" Many blitzscaling start-ups will offer e-mail support only, or no support at all, relying on users to find and help one another on discussion forums.

On an absolute scale, ignoring your customers is rarely going to be a positive. Customers like to feel heard, and ignoring them will eventually deplete your company's supply of goodwill. But for blitzscaling companies, letting customers feel ignored is often one of the fires that's easier for you to let burn until you have finished fighting the bigger, more deadly fires.

Our experiences at PayPal offer a telling example of how hypergrowth requires rapid changes in your approach to customer service. In February 2000, transaction volume was increasing 3 to 5 percent per day, on a compounding basis. Each day we were falling behind to the tune of thousands of unanswered e-mails, which compounded the problem because the users who didn't get a response to their initial e-mail would simply write in again.

Conventional wisdom would have called for us to devote as many people as possible to customer support. But that's the opposite of what we did. Out of a forty-person team, we had two support people (and our office manager was spending half of his time to help out). We had much more urgent fires to fight. For example, during that same time period, we were (1) raising our first major round of venture capital, (2) starting to compete with Billpoint, our biggest partner eBay's attempt to clone our business, and (3) negotiating a merger with Elon Musk's X.com. Suffice it to say that things were busy, and we didn't have the bandwidth to solve the customer service problem. So we ignored our customers! After all, none of their complaints stopped transaction volume from growing exponentially.

Of course, ignoring our customers had its own cost. Even

though PayPal was only listed in the local Palo Alto phone directory, enough people looked up the number and dialed random extensions that at any time of day, every phone would be ringing with an angry customer on the other end. We stopped picking up the phones.

Ignoring customers is a *temporary* solution. Eventually, after we raised a significant round of venture capital and had announced the X.com merger, we had the time and resources to deal with the problem. We forged an alliance with the governor of Nebraska and announced that we were hiring for customer support positions in Omaha. Why Omaha? X.com already had a small customer service team located there. Why had X.com picked Omaha? One of its early employees had a sister living there who offered to help the fledgling start-up take customer service calls.

We ended up flying out most of the company to hold group interviews so we could hire and train one hundred new support employees within thirty days. The PayPal employee we hired to lead the charge, Sarah Imbach, ended up moving to Omaha for eighteen months. Fortunately, there was a happy ending to the story for everyone involved: Our product was useful enough that our customers stuck with us until we were able to start serving them. We beat Billpoint, went public, and ended up selling the company to eBay for $1.5 billion. As for Sarah, her eighteen months in Omaha were productive on several levels; in addition to building a service and operations organization that still employs over a thousand people in Omaha, she also met her husband there.

RULE 8: RAISE TOO MUCH MONEY

Entrepreneurs generally try to avoid raising more capital than they need. Raising excessive amounts of capital dilutes their stake in the company and introduces a preference overhang (all that money has to be paid back to investors before the founders and employees get to participate in the upside). Yet when blitzscaling, you should always raise more—preferably much more—than you need.

"Excess" cash allows you to better account for the unforeseeable—and the only thing that's foreseeable about blitzscaling is that you will at some point encounter the unforeseeable. That includes anything from a stock market crash or outlandish expenses to an opportunity you couldn't predict in a market that didn't exist when you started out.

The fact is, most entrepreneurs are far more likely to raise too little rather than too much money. Nobel Prize–winning economist Daniel Kahneman and his longtime collaborator, the late Amos Tversky, described this general phenomenon when they wrote about the "planning fallacy" in their 1979 paper "Intuitive Prediction: Biases and Corrective Procedures."

> The planning fallacy is that you make a plan, which is usually a best-case scenario. Then you assume that the outcome will follow your plan, even when you should know better.

Almost every entrepreneur I've ever worked with falls prey to the planning fallacy, especially first-time entrepreneurs!

Having "extra" capital gives you a cushion for when outcomes do not in fact follow your plan. Moreover, it increases your optionality—if you need to invest in growth, you can do much more without having to go through the time-consuming process of raising another round. As Mariam Naficy, CEO of Minted, told me, "Act like you've got half the amount you have in the bank because you've got to factor in all the failures and all the optimizations that kill great entrepreneurs and businesses all the time. Both of us know so many people who had good ideas and were on the right track, but just ran out of money."

At both PayPal and LinkedIn, we raised large financing rounds right before a market meltdown (2000, 2008), and we sure were glad we did. In the case of PayPal, that money allowed us to keep growing during the dot-com bust; without it, we wouldn't have made it to our IPO. In the case of LinkedIn, the situation wasn't as dire, but I realized that the value of the optionality from additional funding far outweighed the potential negatives of equity dilution.

Even if the money doesn't prove to be necessary, a major financing round can also have positive signaling effects—it helps convince the rest of the world that your company is likely to emerge as the market leader, and can discourage investors from backing additional competitors.

Most blitzscaling start-ups have a high burn rate. This is because the drivers of growth, such as sales and marketing, often require significant investments that exceed the cash coming from product sales. It usually takes a lot of money to make a killer company, which is why we have venture capitalists!

But while it may make sense to burn cash in order to grow (and finance the difference with capital you raise from investors), you should make this investment with long-term profitability in mind. If the unit economics are positive in the long run, and capital is available at low cost, then it makes sense to take in investment capital to fuel rapid growth. The company won't be profitable in the short term, but it is building a customer base that will drive long-term value in the form of greater revenues and profits in the far-off future.

For technology start-ups, the amount of money you need to raise will tend to be a function of two primary factors: people costs and the cost of outbound customer acquisition. The good news is that these costs are largely predictable, which gives you a chance to act thoughtfully rather than just react. The classic rule of thumb in Silicon Valley is to raise enough cash for eighteen to twenty-four months of operations. This is because it usually takes about six months to raise your next round of venture capital, which means unless you have at least eighteen months of "runway," you'll have less than a year to make enough progress to convince venture capitalists that you've justified another round of investment.

This is important because all financing events are better played as a long game than a short game. We're not the first to observe that investors always prefer to give their money to someone who doesn't need it. Few things trigger a more positive Pavlovian response from a venture capitalist than the words "We don't need to raise any money." Unfortunately, this is easier said than done.

When you are blitzscaling your start-up, growth is so rapid and your organization is pushing its limits in so many ways that multiple things are always breaking. It's tempting to fix these things with money, but you have to resist that temptation. Only spend money to fix things that are on the critical path to reach the next phase of scale; everything else can wait. As I described earlier, at PayPal we deliberately avoided spending money on customer service because we knew it wasn't a critical path. The more you can keep juggling and defer spending, the more likely you'll be able to raise money without the pressure of a short runway.

Remember, starting a company is like jumping off a cliff and assembling an airplane on the way down. If you run out of money for the fuel and parts you need to get airborne, no one will ever get to find out how efficiently you spent it along the way!

RULE #9: EVOLVE YOUR CULTURE

Nearly all founders, business gurus, and academics agree that organizational culture is important. While there are a lot of inefficiencies you can tolerate and fires you can let burn during your blitzscaling journey, ignoring your culture is not an option. Brian Chesky of Airbnb defines culture in a simple and concise way: "a shared way of doing things." Clearly defining the way an organization does things matters, because blitzscaling requires aggressive, focused action, and unclear, hazy cultures get in the way of actually implementing strategy. Netflix cofounder and CEO Reed Hastings told me, "Weak cultures are diffuse; people act differently, and don't understand each other, and it becomes political."

Mark Zuckerberg and Sheryl Sandberg have done many wonderful things at Facebook, and one of them is building a unified culture that is devoted to aggressive experimentation and data-driven decision making, as summarized by Mark's original motto "Move fast and break things." Facebook's culture helps employees understand that they shouldn't be afraid to try things that might fail. This allows Facebook to move faster, and to move on from failed experiments quickly.

Imagine if someone asked a random employee from your start-up the following questions:

What is your organization trying to do?

How are you trying to achieve those goals?

What acceptable risks are you incurring to achieve those goals more quickly?

When you have to trade off certain values, which ones take priority?

What kind of behavior do you hire, promote, or fire for?

Would she be able to answer those questions? If you asked another employee, would he give the same answers? When organizations have strong cultures, their employees give consistent answers and act accordingly.

A strong commitment to a culture will sometimes mean passing on hiring "A players" who don't fit that culture. At PayPal, for example, Max Levchin instituted a problem-solving test as part of the hiring process for joining our engineering group. He wanted a culture that was focused on solving big-picture problems, not simply writing good code. If a person was a great programmer but didn't have a problem-solving orientation, we didn't hire him or her. At LinkedIn, we tried to recruit people who were hard-working but also family-oriented. Our founding team members had families, and we wanted to establish the norm that employees could go home to have dinner with their families (and then work remotely later in the evening). Candidates who believed that a start-up needed everyone at the office until ten o'clock every night would inevitably frustrate colleagues and themselves, so they were screened out. Conversely, candidates who wanted to work a nine-to-five job would also be screened out, no matter how talented.

Culture is critical because it influences how people act in the absence of specific directives and rules, or when those rules reach their breaking point. In a notorious example from 2017, acting at the request of United Airlines, Chicago Department of Aviation employees forcibly dragged passenger David Dao off an over-booked flight, breaking his nose, knocking out two of his teeth, and giving him a significant concussion in the process. The next morning, United CEO Oscar Munoz sent a rather perplexing e-mail to United Airlines employees.

> Our employees followed established procedures for dealing with situations like this. While I deeply regret this situation arose, I also emphatically stand behind all of you, and I want to commend you for continuing to go above and beyond to ensure we fly right.
>
> I do, however, believe there are lessons we can learn from this experience, and we are taking a close look at the circumstances surrounding this incident. Treating our customers and each other with respect and dignity is at the core of who we are, and we must always remember this no matter how challenging the situation.

The David Dao incident is a classic example of how a poor articulation of company values can weaken the culture. The employees on the ground believed they needed to bump passengers from the flight so that United could get another flight crew to their plane (i.e., "flying right") and that meeting metrics such as on-time departures and flight cancellations was more important than treating customers with "respect and dignity" (which most of us would agree does not include breaking their noses and knocking out their teeth).

In contrast, Southwest Airlines is not only clear about its company values but makes them the emphasis of hiring and management. The mentality isn't: "We'll know it when we see it." Instead, it is: "Does this person already live the way we do?"

The company uses behavioral interview questions to determine whether candidates are a cultural fit. For example, to determine someone's ability to be a selfless team player, they might ask her to describe a time when she went above and beyond to help a coworker succeed.

The airline acknowledges that certain positions call for specific skill sets. As Southwest puts it, "We're not going to hire a pilot who has a great attitude but can't fly a plane!" But, when it comes down to two equally qualified candidates, the one who lives Southwest's values receives the offer. And, even when Southwest finds a qualified candidate who doesn't have the right values, it will keep looking until it finds someone who does—no matter how long the job has gone unfilled.

Southwest's development and promotion practices are also explicitly tied to company values. In performance reviews, employees are assessed not just on results but also on how they got those results; in fact, people are actually rated on things like their "warrior spirit," "servant's heart," and "fun-LUVing attitude."

In other words, culture isn't just manifested as a mission statement on Southwest's website; it's woven into the airline's processes and practices.

In both cases, culture has real business implications. In the case of United Airlines, a culture without strong values led to a disastrous public relations fiasco. For Southwest Airlines, the value of employees' "servant's heart" and "fun-LUVing attitude" shows up in the concrete metrics of customer satisfaction. Even though Southwest's performance on metrics such as on-time arrival is decent to above average, the airline consistently has the fewest customer complaints per passenger carried.

Organizational culture has played a key role in the rise of Silicon Valley. Most of the iconic companies that have shaped and defined the technology industry—Hewlett-Packard, Intel, Apple, Google, Facebook—are known for their distinctive cultures, regardless of their era. The same can be said for more recent start-up market leaders like Airbnb and Salesforce.com.

Typically, the credit for these cultures goes to the founders. Bill Hewlett and David Packard are synonymous with the HP Way. Bob Noyce, Gordon Moore, and Andy Grove are referred to as the Intel Trinity. Steve Jobs, Larry Page and Sergey Brin, and Mark Zuckerberg are seen as the sources of Apple's, Google's, and Facebook's cultures. Yet while the personalities of the founding team play a critical role in defining an organization's culture, it is more accurate to say that an organization's culture emerges over time based on the actions of many people, not just the founders.

The primary culture of an organization typically originates in the functional area that is most critical to the success of the company. Early on, engineering predominated, and engineering culture formed the basis of things like the HP Way. As the technology industry matured, sales assumed a greater importance, and sales-oriented cultures arose at companies like Oracle and Cisco. Companies today might also have a product culture, design culture, marketing culture, finance culture, or even an operations culture. Any and all of these cultures can be successful, but you should focus on whichever function is key for your organization to succeed. In addition to the role this choice plays in the company's values, the executive in charge of the functional area that drives the culture also tends to be the most likely successor to the CEO.

The development of organizational culture is intimately intertwined with branding. Culture is central to the story that we tell ourselves and others about who we are and our place in the world, as well as the stories others tell about us! You can list all the values you want on your website, but the only way that they become an integral part of your culture is if you make them a part of your strategy, and make sure that you and others can tell stories (backed with hard evidence and concrete details) about living up to them.

So how do you develop a strong culture at your organization? I believe that the best approach represents a middle ground between hoping that the culture evolves organically through benign neglect and trying to define a comprehensive culture up front. The former approach risks developing a weak culture or one that doesn't fit the company's needs; the latter may be too rigid and inflexible.

Most cultures begin to form organically. As we've discussed previously, the founders of the organization have a major influence on the culture, simply because of who they are. If a founder believes that certain beliefs and practices are fundamental keys to winning, those beliefs and practices tend to be transmitted to the people who work closely with him or her. This might occur via filtering during the hiring process, as a result of working closely together, or both. For example, Larry Page of Google is a technologist with a strong academic background. As a result, Google developed a technology-oriented, academic culture that strongly resembled Stanford's graduate Computer Science Department. For example, Google engineers sat in four-person offices because that is how Stanford organized graduate students' offices. Google hired Eric Schmidt to bring in stronger business experience, knowing that Eric's own academic background (he earned a PhD in Electrical Engineering and Computer Science [EECS] at UC Berkeley) would allow him to effectively synchronize culturally with Larry and cofounder Sergey Brin.

In blitzscaling companies, culture becomes increasingly important—and increasingly difficult to maintain—as the organization grows. In the beginning, the bond that employees form in the early days of the company can be a powerful force in shaping the culture, but this gets more challenging as more people come on board and spontaneous interactions give way to more formalized structures.

Transmitting culture organically requires both personal interaction and time. This osmosis works during the Family and even Tribe stages of blitzscaling, but breaks down at later stages. If the founders don't have personal interactions with all employees, or if those interactions are brief and sporadic, osmosis doesn't work. And when a company is doubling or tripling in size every year, even brief and sporadic personal interactions with the founders are a best-case scenario!

By the time an organization reaches the Village stage of blitzscaling (at least one hundred employees), the mesh of person-to-person interaction is insufficient, especially when culture needs to be synchronized across multiple offices.

Drew Houston makes sure that all Dropbox employees are aware that they need to help re-create the culture. "We tell people, 'You might have just joined last week, but sooner or later, you'll be an old-school Dropboxer too. So remember the things you like about this place now, because it'll be your responsibility to make sure those things stick around.'"

It's not always easy to move from organic to deliberate cultural transmission. Reed Hastings's experience is typical. "When we [Netflix] went public, we had 150 people," Reed told me. "People were worried that now that we were public, everything would go to shit—we'd put in a lot of process, and stop taking risks. What we've done is to promote employee freedom. If you want to operate with very few rules, you need to set context." Yet while early employees often fear that deliberate cultural development will bring bureaucracy, as Reed argues, culture is actually a substitute for bureaucracy and rules. The stronger you make your culture, the less you'll have to bind people's behavior with rigid directives.

The two key levers of deliberate cultural transmission are communications and people management. Communications are important because they provide founders with a direct channel to all employees. This can take many forms, ranging from formal in-person meetings to electronic communications to things as seemingly neutral as office layout and design.

Airbnb, for example, employs a wide range of channels to maximize cultural transmission. The weekly e-mail cofounder Brian Chesky sends to all Airbnb employees is a powerful one. "You have to continue to repeat things" Brian told our class at Stanford. "Culture is about repeating, over and over again, the things that really matter for your company." Airbnb reinforces these verbal messages with visual impact as well. Brian hired an artist from Pixar to create a storyboard of the entire experience of an Airbnb guest, from start to finish, emphasizing the customer-centered design thinking that is a hallmark of its culture. Even Airbnb conference rooms tell a story; each one is a replica of a room that's available for rent on the service. Every time Airbnb team members hold a meeting in one of those rooms, they are reminded of how guests feel when they stay there.

At Amazon, Jeff Bezos famously bans PowerPoint decks and insists on written memos, which are read in silence at the beginning of each meeting. This memo policy is one of the ways that Amazon encourages a culture of truth telling. Memos have to be specific and comprehensive, and those who read the memos have to respond in kind rather than simply sit through some broad bullet points on a PowerPoint deck and nod vague agreement. Bezos believes that memos encourage smarter questions and deeper thinking. Plus, because they're self-contained (rather than requiring a person to present a deck), they are more easily distributed and consumed by a wider population within Amazon.

The late Steve Jobs used architecture as a core part of his deliberate communications strategy at Pixar. He designed Pixar headquarters so that the front doors, main stairs, main theater, and screening rooms all led to the atrium, which contained the café and mailboxes, ensuring that employees from all departments and specialties would see people from other groups on a regular basis, thus reinforcing Pixar's collaborative, inclusive culture. In Walter Isaacson's biography of Steve Jobs, John Lasseter, Pixar's chief creative officer says, "Steve's theory worked from day one. I kept running into people I hadn't seen for months. I've never seen a building that promoted collaboration and creativity as well as this one."

Build a "Ship of Theseus"

The other main lever for cultural development is the organization's people management practices. After all, the strongest influences on organizational culture are often who you hire, promote, and fire.

When he visited our Blitzscaling class at Stanford, Eric Schmidt shared how Google's hiring strategy shaped its culture. "The people that you hire make your culture," Eric said. "We'd hire people who were special in some way. You don't hire generic people—you hire people who have had stress and achievement." Culture is a key part of the hiring process at Airbnb too. Each candidate also goes through a values interview, conducted by an Airbnb employee who isn't that candidate's hiring manager. This ensures that values are considered independently of how much the organization needs that candidate's particular job skills.

When the business is growing that quickly, it's usually desperate for bodies, and it can be tempting to simply pay whatever is necessary to get employees through the door. The problem is that you end up hiring mercenaries rather than missionaries. And if you're tripling the company's size each year, you can shift your company from a majority-missionary culture to a majority-mercenary culture in a single year.

Another side effect of rapid growth is that many, if not a majority of, employees will be reporting to inexperienced managers. A systematic approach like that laid out in *The Alliance* can help those managers better align the personal values and missions of employees with the company culture.

It can be tough to prioritize culture when other fires are burning. During the Family and even Tribe stages of blitzscaling, HR often doesn't exist as a separate department and might be outsourced to a professional employer organization like TriNet, or left as a part-time job that an office manager or administrative assistant handles as a secondary priority. As a result, the unconscious habits and patterns of early employees often form and crystallize into an organizational culture without any experienced oversight. And even after the company adds an HR function, its first priority is usually to hire more employees as quickly as possible rather than focus on culture and values. If an organization wants to make culture an HR priority, the founders and leadership need to make sure that the HR team is given the time and resources to do so, and that new hires are managed, evaluated, and rewarded accordingly.

These mechanisms need to continue to evolve as the company grows and its needs evolve. Reed Hastings and Netflix are well-known for the Netflix Culture Deck, a one-hundred-plus slide presentation that explains Netflix's high-performance culture. Reed and Patty McCord created the Netflix Culture Deck to help filter out job candidates who wouldn't want to participate in the Netflix culture. But the deck isn't carved in stone; Netflix continues to revise it on a regular basis.

One of the reasons for evolving your culture is the "Ship of Theseus" paradox. The ancient historian Plutarch coined the term in reference to the ship on which the mythical hero Theseus returned to Athens after slaying the Minotaur. As the legend goes, the Athenians had preserved the famous vessel by replacing broken parts with new wood, until at last none of the original wood remained. Plutarch reported that philosophers argued strenuously, and without resolution, over whether the ship of replacement parts was still the Ship of Theseus. (Amusingly, the philosopher Thomas Hobbes complicated matters by asking what would happen if the original wood parts were preserved after being replaced, and were then used to build a second ship!)

All companies are like the Ship of Theseus. Employees join, stay for one or more tours of duty, and leave, only to be replaced by new employees. A stable, low-growth company might persist for decades or longer, slowly replacing employees but remaining the same size and retaining a strong sense of continuity. In other words, the "planks" of the ship remain essentially unchanged from decade to decade. In contrast, a blitzscaling company like Facebook might grow from the Family to Nation stage in a single decade, doubling or tripling in size each year, so that the employees who made up the entire ship on New Year's Day end up as a small minority by the following New Year's Eve. At the same time, as we discussed in "Hire Ms. Right Now, Not Ms. Right," many early employees are likely to leave at some point along the journey, which means even fewer of the original "planks" are still part of the ship. Yet these changes are a necessary part of blitzscaling: you need new people with new skills as you grow.

The people, the product, and the offices of a company can, will, and must change as it blitzscales. Culture is one of the few mechanisms that allow the ship to retain its essential identity. Culture is what helps Apple retain its "Apple-ness" with Steve Jobs gone, and Intuit retain its, well, "Intuit(ive)-ness" even as it shifted from selling packaged personal finance software to providing a cloud accounting suite. Organizational culture has become such a hot topic in this age of blitzscaling because culture is more important when there is rapid growth and change, rather than stability and stasis.

You have to walk a fine line as you evolve your culture—evolve it too slowly, and it will hold you back from adapting to new businesses and the changing world around you. Evolve it too quickly, and the Ship of Theseus illusion breaks down, and people no longer feel like they belong.

In the words of the Dutch historian Johan Huizinga, "If we are to preserve culture, we must continue to create it."

A Lack of Diversity and Other Cultural Pitfalls

Given the popular emphasis on company culture, it's also important to offer some thoughts on the potential pitfalls that can come with trying to build a strong culture.

First, there can be a fine line between a strong culture and a cult. By definition, culture is narrowing to some degree. Building culture into your hiring processes means that you're excluding people by design, and you have to be careful not to restrict your hiring to the point of total homogeneity. Successful organizations need a combination of conformity and diversity. The right kind of sameness (e.g., smart, driven, intelligent, hardworking, mission-driven) can give a company an edge, as was certainly the case at PayPal. But too much sameness can result in groupthink, bias, and stagnation.

Far too many companies misinterpret what it means to hire for "cultural fit." In many cases, this leads to teams that are heavy on young, Caucasian men who went to a short list of elite colleges, which hinders the organization's ability to innovate or serve a broader market. But even without such problematic practices, hiring for "fit" should not mean asking, "Do you fit into this box?"

For example, many start-ups have a work culture where employees come to the office after 10 a.m., work late, and spend evenings socializing together at bars. In other words, an extended version of college! If your start-up has such a culture, you might avoid hiring employees who want to come in early and leave before 6 p.m., or who rarely socialize or go out at night. That might be good for "cultural fit," but it also means that you won't hire people who don't drink alcohol for religious or other reasons, you won't hire employees who are parents, and you probably won't even hire employees who are married (or at least those who wish to remain married). Rather than hire people who "fit" your culture in superficial ways—whether based on gender or race or alma mater—hire people who are additive to your culture. When Belinda Johnson joined Airbnb in 2011, she brought a very different background and experience to the young company. The founders were in their twenties; Belinda had been a lawyer when they were still in diapers, and had spent a dozen years as an executive at Yahoo! It was precisely these differences that helped both Belinda and Airbnb succeed as a team. Brian Chesky calls her Airbnb's "Secretary of State," and her diplomacy and knowledge helped the firm develop productive relationships with regulators and municipalities. New hires are an opportunity to refine your culture and add to its capabilities. They should be compatible with your current culture but also bring elements that help change it for the better. The art is in finding transplants that the organization's existing "immune system" doesn't reject.

Blitzscaling companies are particularly susceptible to building a culture that lacks diversity because of their relentless emphasis on speed. The fastest and easiest way to hire is usually to ask employees to refer their friends. But hiring based on homophily ("birds of a feather flock together") almost inevitably leads to homogeneity. Just as start-ups incur "technical debt" by taking shortcuts with their code, they can incur "diversity debt" by taking shortcuts with their hiring practices.

This diversity debt is a serious problem for individual companies, and for society as a whole. Homogeneity harms companies because groupthink reduces the resilience and adaptability of the companies, and it harms society if those many opportunities blitzscaling provides aren't fully open to all qualified people, whatever their gender, sexuality, religion, or ancestry.

One of the ugliest manifestations of these problems is the culture of sexism and sexual harassment that has been uncovered at various companies. In almost every case, these problems arose because one or more employees who belonged to a demographic group that represented the overwhelming majority held power over employees who were in the minority. Many times, executives abused their power, setting a disgraceful example for other employees. This is absolutely unacceptable, and begs for action. In 2017, for example, I called for the Decency Pledge to try to address the serious problems in the venture capital industry around men abusing their power and position to harm women (and some men).

Hopefully, most blitzscaling companies will never reach the

point where their cultures tolerate such bad behavior, but the best way to ensure this is to build inclusive cultures from the very beginning. This is one area in which it's insufficient to allow cultures to evolve organically. Even at the Family stage, a company should be explicit about diversity, and state in writing that it strives to be inclusive in terms of gender, sexuality, religion, ancestry, and age. And, it should make diversity a priority in hiring starting with its first ten employees, and especially in core functions like product, engineering, and marketing.

In the Tribe and Village stages, the rate at which you are adding employees will require a more systematic approach to diversity. We recommend implementing at least three key policies: First, measure your demographics and make that information transparent and available, both internally and externally. As with any metric, you can't manage what you don't measure. Second, institute the equivalent of the National Football League's Rooney Rule, which requires NFL teams to interview (but not necessarily hire) at least one minority candidate for any senior football operations position. And third, tie at least part of executive compensation to the company's progress toward its diversity goals.

In an ideal universe, all companies would build diverse workforces from the start. But the more people a company employs, the more important diversity becomes. Don't wait to make diversity goals a priority. It's much harder to shift from a "brogrammer" haven to a truly inclusive culture when you're a 10,000-person company.

Another pitfall is cultural hypocrisy. If you preach the gospel of your strong culture, you have to live up to it, or you'll be doing more harm than good. When you talk the talk but don't walk the walk, employees will recognize the hypocrisy. Credibility has to be earned, not simply asserted. This is particularly true of founders, who typically have the moral authority within a start-up, and of nonfounder CEOs, whose position magnifies the impact of their words and actions. Founders and CEOs are cultural role models; if they don't exemplify the culture, it will inevitably weaken.

THE NEVER-ENDING NEED FOR CHANGE

What do the eight key transitions and nine counterintuitive rules have in common? They reflect the fact that when you're blitz-scaling, the need for change never stops. Just when you've managed a key transition or successfully applied a counterintuitive rule, the game board changes, and you have to do it all again.

No market remains valuable forever, which means that even companies that successfully reach the Nation stage by dominating an important market have to keep searching for the next market in which to blitzscale. Every exciting new technology or market that once supported massive wealth creation eventually becomes a stable, boring industry. At various points in history, the cargo ship, railroad, and automobile industries spawned companies and innovations that changed the world and made generational fortunes. Today, they're largely sleepy backwaters (though occasionally companies like Tesla manage to revitalize them), a fate that is still better than irrelevance but unlikely to hold many exciting opportunities for large-scale growth.

The same pattern has played out on a smaller scale in Silicon Valley, where markets for Dynamic Random-Access Memory (DRAM), hard drives, and personal computers allowed companies like Intel, Seagate, and Compaq to grow to massive value before becoming low-margin commodities. (Intel continued to grow, thanks to its shift to high-margin CPUs, while Seagate and Compaq languished, and in the case of Compaq, ended up being acquired and vanishing.)

The best entrepreneurs and companies use successful blitz-scaling in one market to jump into another. Intel jumped from DRAMs to microprocessors, and rode a second wave to even greater heights. Microsoft used its dominance in operating systems to develop the even more dominant Microsoft Office platform. Amazon's e-tail blitzscaling allowed it to become the leader in cloud computing with Amazon Web Services. Perhaps Facebook will do something similar with VR.

The never-ending need for change should fill you with both fear and hope. Fear, because you can never rest or stand still. Hope, because new markets are always emerging, giving everyone, from Silicon Valley to Shanghai (and everywhere in between), the opportunity to build nothing short of a new rocket ship.

In Lewis Carroll's classic book *Through the Looking-Glass,* the Red Queen tells Alice, "Now, here, you see, it takes all the running you can do, to keep in the same place. If you want to get somewhere else, you must run at least twice as fast as that!" Sometimes blitzscaling a company might feel a bit like running as hard as you can simply to end up in the same place. But the difference between our world and the Red Queen's is that blitzscaling is a race to build things that make the world a better place. Whether your new market will be machine learning, or a new kind of wireless computing, or something that hasn't been invented yet, there's a word for the by-product of blitzscaling: "progress."

PART V

The Broader Landscape of Blitzscaling

While many of the examples you've encountered throughout this book have been Silicon Valley technology companies, the principles of blitzscaling apply far beyond this specific domain. In this section, we'll focus on the broader landscape of blitzscaling, including how it works in other geographies and industries, and what it means for the future of our global economy. Because it is such an important topic, we'll devote an entire section of this chapter solely to examining blitzscaling in China.

BLITZSCALING BEYOND HIGH TECH

While blitzscaling is probably most applicable to high tech, its techniques can benefit any industry in which opportunities can demonstrate strong growth factors (market size, distribution, gross margins, and network effects) and overcome the growth limiters (lack of product/market fit and operational scalability).

For example, consider the Spanish clothing retailer Zara. Few industries could seem farther away from the world of Internet companies like Google and Facebook. Yet while Zara's expansion took longer to get there (the company was founded in 1975, which, coincidentally, is the same year that Microsoft was founded), its scale and dominance in its industry rival those of its high-tech equivalents, and have made its founder, Amancio Ortega, the world's third-richest man (behind Jeff Bezos and Bill Gates, but ahead of Warren Buffett).

Zara plays in an enormous market; global apparel sales in 2016 were over $1.4 trillion, and even though Zara's gross margin reached a ten-year low in 2017, it still stood at a robust 57 percent (versus 61 percent for Google, and 35 percent for Amazon). Its global network of stores gives it broad distribution, and while apparel doesn't offer any strong network effects, clothing does command a fair amount of consumer loyalty, enabling Zara to lock in a degree of long-term advantage.

What's even more important, however, is that Zara actually uses the techniques of blitzscaling to run its business. Speed is the foundation of Zara's "fast fashion" business strategy, which, for decades, can be summarized in a single sentence: "Give customers what they want and get it to them faster than anyone else."

Every aspect of Zara's business is organized around achieving that speed. The results are impressive: Zara takes only two weeks to develop a new product and get it into stores—the industry average is six months—and launches over ten thousand new designs per year, a rate several times that of competitors like H&M and Gap. Zara holds just six days of inventory, while rival H&M holds nearly ten times as much. In the 1970s, Ortega established a rule that Zara had to fulfill apparel orders from its stores in less than forty-eight hours. Today, Zara still follows that rule, even though it has expanded from a local Spanish retailer into a global empire with stores in Africa and Asia.

To achieve these results, Zara has found a way to balance addressing the growth limiter of operational scalability while following the counterintuitive rules to embrace chaos and do things that don't scale. Given its massive scale, you would expect Zara to turn to China for help with improving its margins, in the way that Apple did with the iPhone. But unlike its competitors, Zara still manufactures most of its clothing in Spain. Thanks to its financial might, Zara was able to build fourteen highly automated factories in Spain, where robots create "greige goods"—newly manufactured clothes that haven't been whitened and dyed. Zara then uses a partner network of more than three hundred small shops in Spain and Portugal to process those greige goods into finished apparel. While the labor costs might be higher than in China, and thus less "efficient," the payoff is incredible responsiveness and speed.

Responsive manufacturing is critical to Zara's business model. Apparel is designed by small teams in Zara's design center, where designers work with pattern makers and commercial sales specialists. Feedback comes in daily from Zara's store managers. That feedback is analyzed by the sales specialists and then presented to the designers and pattern makers, who start sketching designs on the spot and create, on average, an astonishing three new items per day. The designs are then dispatched to those factories for manufacturing and on to partner shops for finishing.

Zara's logistics model continues this preference for responsiveness over efficiency. Zara products are distributed in small batches, which require more frequent shipments. The logistics costs are higher, but this allows Zara to get clothes to its stores in less than twenty-four hours for Europe, the Middle East, and America, and in less than forty-eight hours for Asia and Latin America.

This focus on speed comes directly from the founder and animates the entire organization. In a 2013 profile, *Fortune* told the story of how, stopped at a traffic light, Ortega spotted a young motorcyclist wearing a jean jacket covered in 1970s-style patches. Ortega grabbed his cell phone, called an aide, described the jacket over the phone, and ordered the aide to get the design into production. Loreto García, the head of Zara's woman's trends department, explained the need to be lightning fast in responding to trends when she told *Fortune,* "What seems great today, in two weeks is the worst idea ever."

Despite all the chaos, and the inefficiency of manufacturing and shipping in small batches, Zara's gross margins continue to exceed those of its competitors H&M (55 percent) and Gap (29 percent). That's because all that inefficiency incurred in the pursuit of speed allows Zara to avoid one of the biggest drags on gross margin for almost any apparel company—overstock of designs that failed to sell. Ortega devised this model when he was sixteen years old—don't order inventory and hope it sells; instead, figure out what people want, and then make it.

Another example of how blitzscaling applies to a completely different type of business is the rapid rise of the shale oil and natural gas industry in the United States during the 2000s. The energy sector scores well on the growth factors we've defined. Oil and gas is an enormous, high-margin industry, with a very efficient distribution system. And while the shale industry doesn't feature many network effects, it has its own source of powerful long-term competitive advantage. In the energy industry, rather than buy land outright, the usual practice is to lease the drilling rights for ninety-nine years for a combination of guaranteed lease payments and royalties. This means that leasing the right land is tantamount to holding an unbreakable monopoly on the oil and gas underneath that land, at least for the term of the lease.

Blitzscaling allowed shale companies to grow at an amazing rate. In 2002, leading shale player Chesapeake Energy reported revenues of $738 million. Just four years later, Chesapeake reported revenues of $7.3 billion and was added to the S&P 500. That's an order of magnitude of growth in the time it takes to go through high school.

Chesapeake's cofounders, the late Aubrey McClendon and his partner Tom Ward, didn't have the usual industry background in exploration or refining. Instead of working drilling rigs or operating refineries, McClendon and Ward were "land men," specialists who went out into the field to negotiate mineral rights leases with landowners. This expertise would be key to their blitzscaling effort.

In the late 1990s, the combination of horizontal drilling and improved hydraulic fracturing techniques (fracking) made extracting hydrocarbons from shale rock formations economically feasible for the first time. Essentially, energy companies could drill horizontal shafts into rock formations and then pump high-pressure liquids into the wells to fracture the rock and release more oil and gas. Because traditional drilling techniques didn't work on shale rock formations, the land above those formations had never been leased, which meant that when fracking made those hydrocarbons accessible for the first time, the market to acquire those mineral rights was completely wide open.

While Chesapeake wasn't the first company to employ fracking—it was in fact Mitchell Energy, which brought fracking to the Barnett Shale formation in Texas in 1997—it combined this technology innovation with McClendon's business innovation to become the fastest-growing energy company in history.

Chesapeake moved faster than any other company in its industry, deploying an army of land men to aggressively lease as much land as possible, with instructions to pay whatever was necessary, without knowing whether the gas deposits would justify the price. Hiring an army of land men and paying top dollar for leases sight unseen seemed inefficient . . . until the wells started producing. Chesapeake's willingness to blitzscale paid off as improvements in fracking technology made its wells insanely profitable—at first.

The case of McClendon and Chesapeake also illustrates the inherent risks of sacrificing efficiency in the name of hypergrowth. Blitzscaling can lead to big wins *and* big losses, sometimes at the same company. Chesapeake continued to borrow money to lease more land at ever higher prices. McClendon acted as though his blitzscaling strategy was guaranteed to succeed, and Chesapeake was hit hard by the global recession of 2008. After peaking at $62.40 in June 2008, its stock price has declined sharply, falling as low as $2.61 in early 2016 (in 2017, it traded between $4 and $8 per share). McClendon had taken on a lot of risk in his personal finances as well, borrowing money to buy Chesapeake stock. A margin call in 2008 forced him to sell 94 percent of his Chesapeake stock at a massive loss.

McClendon was eventually forced to step down from his position as CEO of Chesapeake in 2013, but remained a resolute blitzscaler. At the time of his death in 2016, McClendon was running American Energy Partners, a company he founded after his departure from Chesapeake, and for which he had raised $15 billion from investors.

Even if you are not able to fully apply the business model patterns of software-driven high tech to your industry, a careful analysis of growth factors and growth limiters might just show you where to find an opportunity to blitzscale and reap the associated rewards. After all, if you can blitzscale T-shirts and oil wells, you might very well be able to blitzscale any business.

BLITZSCALING WITHIN A LARGER ORGANIZATION

While the hypergrowth of blitzscaling is often synonymous with scrappy start-ups, blitzscaling can take place within larger, established organizations as well. None of the growth factors or limiters, and none of the proven patterns or business models, require a business to be an independently owned, privately held, venture-backed corporation. Even if your organization can't offer stock options that will make your employees rich if your blitzscaling is successful, you can and should adopt and adapt the lessons of blitzscaling to help you achieve rapid growth and first-scaler advantage.

Trying to blitzscale within a larger organization has both advantages and disadvantages over doing so within a start-up. It's critical to be realistic—start-ups have some inherent advantages when it comes to blitzscaling. Blitzscaling is all about speed and risk taking, and with far less to lose, start-ups are much more nimble. Established companies that want to blitzscale need to find major advantages to overcome their inherent disadvantages in speed and risk taking.

ADVANTAGE #1: SCALE

This might sound obvious, but there are some opportunities that you can only tackle if you already have the scale that comes with being a large, established player. For example, Amazon couldn't have launched Amazon Web Services (AWS) without achieving massive scale in its data centers, and becoming the world leader in managing those data centers. Trying to build that product from scratch, without being able to leverage Amazon's economies of scale and reputation for operational excellence, would have been nearly impossible. Even today, AWS's main competitors come from other scale companies like Microsoft, Google, and IBM.

Outside of tech, scale can be an even bigger advantage. When Quicken Loans launched Rocket Mortgage, which provides mortgages online with a decision in less than ten minutes, Rocket Mortgage was able to tap into Quicken Loans' consumer marketing expertise—including a Super Bowl ad—to acquire customers, and the company's existing financial relationships to fund those mortgages. As a result, in its first full year of operation (2016), Rocket Mortgage originated $7 billion in loans, which would rank it in the top thirty of all mortgage lenders in the country if it was an independent company, and which helped push Quicken Loans' overall closed loan volume to $96 billion, up sharply from $79 billion in 2015.

On the other hand, if a start-up can play the same game, scale may not provide a significant advantage unless there is a massive difference in scale. For example, when Airbnb was blitzscaling, it was competing with HomeAway, an established player that had much greater scale. However, HomeAway had achieved its scale via a string of twenty-one acquisitions, which meant that all of its acquisitions were running on different technology platforms and serving different clienteles. Indeed, HomeAway's scale was actually a disadvantage! HomeAway itself was later acquired by Expedia, as part of that company's response to the competitive threat of Airbnb.

ADVANTAGE #2: ITERATION

Another advantage that established companies have is the ability to make multiple, iterative blitzscaling attempts. Blitzscaling is a risky strategy, and you might not achieve success on the first try. You need to have enough capital to stay in the game. Microsoft was famed for its ability to iterate its way from knockoff products to market dominance. The first and second versions of Microsoft Windows were unsuccessful attempts to copy Apple's Macintosh operating system; the third version, while still inferior to its inspiration, was good enough, and Microsoft unleashed a marketing blitz for follow-up versions such as Windows 95 and Windows NT that carried them to dominance. Microsoft later repeated this strategy with its Xbox business, which evolved from the Xbox, to the Xbox 360, to today's Xbox One.

To borrow an analogy from sports, you may need to take repeated shots on goal before scoring. Established players have a much easier time financing multiple shots on goal.

Nor is this advantage limited to technology. In the shale oil industry, financial wherewithal played a major role in the success of pioneers like Chesapeake Energy. The late Aubrey McClendon told *Rolling Stone* in 2012, "To be able to borrow money for ten years and ride out boom-and-bust cycles was almost as important an insight as horizontal drilling. . . . If something didn't work for a little bit of time, we could regroup and find something that did work."

ADVANTAGE #3: LONGEVITY

While the ability to undertake multiple attempts at blitzscaling is an advantage, so is the ability to be patient with a single attempt. Large companies can (if they have patient shareholders) have longer time horizons than start-ups, which need to show immediate results to continue raising money. Google often plays this long game with technologies ranging from self-driving cars to a cure for aging. Facebook is also playing the long game with Oculus Rift and VR. The key is knowing when to scale up. Microsoft tried to scale smartphones too early with Windows CE; as it turns out, the modern smartphone only became practical once Moore's Law made mobile CPUs powerful enough, and Apple combined software with capacitive touch screens, Corning's damage-resistant Gorilla Glass, and high-volume Chinese manufacturing.

ADVANTAGE #4: MERGERS & ACQUISITIONS (M&A)

One final advantage that established players have is the ability to use acquisitions to drive blitzscaling. Acquiring a business that is already blitzscaling or has the potential to blitzscale can transform an existing company. Priceline, for example, best known for "name your price" airfares, executed this strategy to perfection when it acquired Booking.com, allowing it to achieve a lasting advantage in the hotel booking market. Many American consumers who are only familiar with Priceline because of its catchy "Priceline Negotiator" commercials starring the actor William Shatner probably have no idea that nearly two-thirds of Priceline's revenues come from hotel bookings outside the United States. In 2015, Priceline actually had the highest ten-year return of any stock in the Fortune 500.

As with direct blitzscaling, succeeding with an M&A strategy requires having a rare or unique insight into the market; had all the players in the travel space known the value of online hotel booking, Priceline wouldn't have been able to afford the Booking .com acquisition. Established players can also use a string of acquisitions to blitzscale, provided they do a better job of integration than HomeAway did. For example, Facebook's acquisitions of Instagram and WhatsApp helped it fend off a dangerous competitor in Snap to achieve a dominant position in social networking for a younger generation.

But established companies also have a number of disadvantages—beyond simply being less quick and nimble—to take into account when implementing a blitzscaling strategy.

DISADVANTAGE #1: INCENTIVES

A major issue faced by established players is that the incentives tend to favor cautious expansion rather than aggressive blitzscaling. Successful companies generally assume that they already have something valuable, which means risk taking tends to be penalized. If you make the play and fail, you've destroyed a valuable thing. That's not something a start-up faces—a start-up is dead by default, so there is nothing to lose. Companies also face pressures from shareholders, analysts, and the press. The thing is, big company leaders are not wrong to be cautious! A large and public failure can tank an established player's stock price—and its reputation. Moreover, the potential rewards have to be huge to matter. A $10 million opportunity that a start-up might see as a life-changing bet is pocket change to a big company.

The incentives that drive individual employees can also have a negative impact on blitzscaling attempts inside an established company. The employee or executive who proposes a risky blitzscaling initiative is the one who stands to gain the most (promotions, bonuses, clout, etc.) from its success. In contrast, other employees gain little from that success, and might even end up losing if that success allows its champion to jump over them for promotions or bonuses. And if the initiative is unsuccessful and costs the company a large sum of money, its employees all bear the cost of failure as well. Is it any wonder that so many bold initiatives are killed in committee?

DISADVANTAGE #2: UNSTAGED COMMITMENT

Another (largely self-inflicted) disadvantage for large companies is the inability or unwillingness to stage their investments. This results from internal incentives, which tend to reward managers based on the revenues that they oversee, while penalizing failure and undervaluing growth opportunities. Staged investments let managers minimize their companies' downsides when performing experiments. But since most such experiments fail, big company managers try to reduce the risk of failure by committing more resources. Unfortunately, most blitzscaling opportunities are so risky and uncertain, and require so much capital to succeed, that making an unstaged commitment effectively bets the company. That may not be a big deal to a start-up, which must succeed or die, but it is a very big deal for a going concern whose business might otherwise chug along profitably for years or even decades!

Senior managers may also, for ego reasons, prefer splashy announcements and major commitments to small experiments that can be blitzscaled if successful. Larger companies also impose a great deal more managerial overhead; by the time you get approval on a proposal, competitors might have already locked up the market.

It should come as no surprise that one big company that continues to value and encourage staged commitments and experiments is Amazon. Jeff Bezos talked about this in one of his famed shareholder letters. Bezos wants to make sure that Amazon continues to have the start-up mindset, which he calls

"Day 1." Bezos writes, "Staying in Day 1 requires you to experiment patiently, accept failures, plant seeds, protect saplings, and double down when you see customer delight."

DISADVANTAGE #3: PUBLIC MARKET PRESSURE

Finally, established companies that are publicly traded face an additional set of pressures to deliver short-term (i.e., quarterly) financial results. Blitzscaling generally requires sacrificing short-term efficiency (and thus financial results) to achieve long-term value creation. Privately held companies are usually closely held; this can make it easier to get the major shareholders to agree on a risky, long-term investment—if you have shareholders who are willing to incur risk for a chance at a much greater reward. But a widely held public company may face activist investors and other such shareholder rebellions if it attempts to carry out a blitzscaling strategy. This could even lead to the worst of possibilities—incurring the initial expense of blitzscaling without the necessary commitment and follow-through to reap the long-term rewards. Many publicly traded blitzscalers like Google and Facebook have tried to avoid public market pressure by issuing two classes of stock so that decision-making authority is vested in a small number of people (i.e., Larry, Sergey, and Mark).

With these advantages and disadvantages in mind, here are a few specific management techniques or "hacks" that large companies can use when they set out to blitzscale.

BLITZSCALING HACKS

One productive hack to help your existing company blitzscale is to **find ways to leverage people and businesses with prior blitzscaling experience**. One obvious play is to partner with a blitzscaling start-up. For example, GM responded to the rise of Uber and the corresponding threat it represents to the market for cars for human drivers by investing $500 million in Lyft, Uber's blitz-scaling rival. GM also hedged its bets by acquiring Cruise for its self-driving car technology.

A less obvious technique is to **leverage the knowledge of venture capitalists.** Venture capitalists are keen fans of blitzscaling and the returns it brings, even if they didn't know the specific term before the book came out. If you ask them to become minority investors in your project, they will provide a realistic assessment of your situation. For example, many large companies misprice their own assets or overvalue their own advantages, and attempt to blitzscale even if an objective observer would consider the attempt ill-advised. Approaching venture capitalists is a quick way to get a sense of how knowledgeable professionals assess the value of your assets.

One final way to mitigate the inherent pitfalls of blitzscaling within a larger organization is to **treat the new initiative as a company within a company.** Once your blitzscaling project is under way, you will need to manage it differently than your regular projects. Blitzscaling's increased pace and decreased efficiency can seem reckless and wasteful when evaluated against conventional initiatives that are designed to provide steady growth. As a result, a blitzscaling project needs to be insulated from the rest of the company so that the executive in charge can run it effectively. The classic example is Steve Jobs's approach to managing the original Macintosh team, which had separate offices that were off-limits to regular Apple employees. More recently, Larry Page applied this same technique to Android by allowing Andy Rubin's team to work in separate offices—Google employee badges didn't grant access to Android offices—and adopt different hiring practices from those of the parent company. Much the same was true for the PlayStation project at Sony, the Kindle project at Amazon, and the Watson team at IBM.

BLITZSCALING BEYOND BUSINESS

While we've focused on the application of blitzscaling in the world of business, the basic principle of sacrificing efficiency for speed in the face of uncertainty can be applied in just about any context.

Let's consider how the growth factors and growth limiters of blitzscaling translate to nonbusiness settings.

MARKET SIZE

In the nonprofit world, we need to find new measures of market size, since we can't rely on financial metrics like revenue. Often, the best measure might simply be the number of people whose lives are improved, but other measures such as "years of healthy life" or "metric tons of carbon sequestered" could also serve this role. While the metrics might change, the principle of market size still applies—without a large market, it makes little sense to blitzscale. One of the main reasons that the Bill & Melinda Gates Foundation decided to tackle malaria prevention and treatment is the enormous size of the malaria "market." In 2012, 207 million people suffered from the disease and 627,000 died from it, with 77 percent of those deaths affecting children under the age of five. Those figures include a 42 percent reduction in annual deaths from 2000 to 2012, thanks in part to the efforts of the Gates Foundation. That is a large market where the ability to blitzscale makes a huge impact.

DISTRIBUTION

Distribution is just as critical outside of the business context as it is for profit-seeking companies. No matter how potentially effective your "product"—whether that product is a social service, a political candidate, or anything else—is at improving the lives of those who adopt it, its impact is directly proportional to your ability to execute an effective distribution strategy. The Mozilla Foundation wasn't the only open-source organization to create a Web browser (Firefox), but it was the only nonprofit organization that was able to leverage distribution to achieve a leading market share. In 2008, Barack Obama won the presidency in part because his campaign was the first to leverage the distribution possibilities of the Internet, including leveraging existing grassroots networks and achieving virality via social media.

GROSS MARGIN

Since many nonprofits don't charge the people they serve, gross margin doesn't apply. However, we can use metrics that align with the spirit of gross margin, such as economic impact. At a high level, gross margin is a measure of impact per dollar, and the greater the impact per dollar, the more amenable a not-for-profit business should be to blitzscaling. For example, the International Civil Society Support estimates that each $1 spent on malaria prevention and treatment generates $20 of economic benefit, with insecticide-impregnated mosquito bed nets representing the single most cost-effective intervention. That's the kind of impact that compares favorably even to software gross margins.

NETWORK EFFECTS

Network effects are relatively rare in the nonprofit world. While there are mega-NGOs such as the Red Cross and the United Way, their market position is largely due to economies of scale rather than true network effects. But it is still worth considering whether or not it is possible to tap into network effects, since doing so can have such a major impact.

For example, Sal Khan's Khan Academy began when Sal started tutoring one of his young cousins over the Internet. When other cousins started signing up, he decided to post his lectures on YouTube so that anyone in the world could use them. The critical decision to leverage the YouTube platform meant that Khan Academy had both an enormous market (anyone who could access YouTube, which is to say, most of humanity) and a powerful distribution platform (anyone searching for educational content on YouTube was likely to run across Khan Academy). As the Khan Academy gained a massive user base, it began to benefit from both indirect and standard-based network effects. Educators began incorporating Khan Academy videos into their official curriculum, and creating lesson plans that they shared with other educators. Today, the Khan Academy is used by 40 million students and 2 million educators every month (the entire United States has only 50.7 million K–12 students), and volunteers have translated its videos into thirty-six languages.

LACK OF PRODUCT/MARKET FIT

In the case of for-profit businesses, the remorseless logic of the market economy quickly eliminates companies that fail to achieve product/market fit. Without the ability to achieve traction, businesses lack the revenue to survive and have little ability to raise additional funding from investors. In contrast, nonprofits often receive grants and donations for noneconomic reasons, and the flow of funds isn't always correlated with the effectiveness of the organization being funded. The "clients" are the people it serves, but the "customers" are the funders. Yet product/market fit is still important for those organizations if they want to blitzscale. In general, the more effectively a nonprofit organization serves its "clients," the better it is able to raise more money from "customers." Charity: Water is a nonprofit that provides clean, safe drinking water to people in developing nations. It is also a model of product/market fit for its users, who have benefited from the more than twenty-three thousand water projects it has funded, and for its funders, who can see photos of the wells it builds and know that 100 percent of their donations will go to fund those projects (the organization's operating costs are covered by foundations and sponsors). As a result, in the decade since its founding in 2006, Charity: Water has raised over $252 million from more than three hundred thousand individual donors.

OPERATIONAL SCALABILITY

If anything, operational scalability is a bigger challenge outside the business world. As a business scales, it usually has the revenues or VC dollars to invest heavily in a scalable infrastructure or to hire additional employees. The business world is also full of companies that have successfully scaled, which means that it is easier to bring in employees who can help you manage rapid growth. In contrast, nonprofits usually don't have the same financial capital, and certainly don't have access to the same kind of experienced human capital. This places a greater premium on designing a business model that does not require as many resources to scale, as in the case of an open-source organization like the Mozilla Foundation.

Aside from the growth factors and growth limiters, one other major potential difference is how nonprofits and impact organizations look at competition. In the business world (and certain nonbusiness organizations like political campaigns), competition—specifically, beating that competition—is one of the most important motivations for blitzscaling. In contrast, the Gates Foundation would welcome another major player that spent billions of dollars to try to "beat" the Gates Foundation to achieving the goal of malaria eradication. This may help explain why blitzscaling has been relatively less common in the world beyond business. However, given the scale of the challenges before us today, from climate change to poverty to an education system in need of reform, we believe that the time is ripe to consider how to apply scalable technology solutions to traditionally unscalable issues.

Let's examine two very specific but very different examples to see some of the ways in which you can apply the principles of blitzscaling beyond business.

Example #1: Dress for Success

Dress for Success (DFS) helps low-income women get jobs by providing them with donated professional attire and coaching them through the interview process. Ninety-nine percent of its operating funds come from grants, government funding, and donations.

Without investor dollars or revenues to fund expansion, DFS founder Nancy Lublin had to find clever ways to circumvent the challenges of operational scalability without consuming cash.

One particularly clever strategy was to leverage its infrastructure limitations to get around the limitations in manpower. To achieve scale, DFS needed to find a way to screen potential clients (to ensure the organization was serving those who most needed it) and staff its clothing "shop," both of which would normally require either paid employees or extensive recruiting of volunteers. Instead, Lublin partnered with organizations like domestic violence shelters that were serving the same clients, and accomplished both at zero cost. DFS only accepted clients who were referred by partners; in exchange, those partners were required to provide volunteers to help staff the shops. This allowed DFS to scale the number of people it served along with the workforce needed to provide that service, all without costing it a dime!

Lublin also leveraged the power of an innovative distribution model by "franchising" DFS. Anyone who wanted to start a DFS shop was invited to fly to New York and stay on a futon in her apartment. She then trained those entrepreneurs and sent them back to their hometowns to start up new DFS shops. When Lublin left DFS in 2002, she had expanded the organization to seventy-six shops. Today, DFS has expanded into twenty-one different countries and helped nearly one million women.

Example #2: Barack Obama for President

In 2008, the presidential campaign of Barack Obama used the power of blitzscaling—especially business model innovation—and the tools of Silicon Valley to catapult a little-known first-term senator from Illinois to the White House, despite running against a series of prominent national politicians, including former First Lady and fellow senator Hillary Clinton.

The key business model innovation behind Barack Obama's long-shot campaign for the presidency was an unprecedented use of connectivity to enable and coordinate a decentralized movement. Obama announced his candidacy on February 10, 2007. According to campaign adviser Steve Spinner, the campaign grew from zero to seven hundred employees (and orders of magnitude more volunteers) in a single year. The key to this rapid growth was the use of technology to leverage large existing networks and achieve powerful distribution.

First, Obama focused on raising small donations from individuals via the Internet rather than raising large donations from well-heeled, traditional Democratic Party donors. This was partially out of necessity, since he was running for the Democratic nomination against Hillary Clinton, who was both viewed as a presumptive favorite and had deep relationships with big donors from her years in the White House and the Senate. But as it turned out, this new business model allowed Obama to raise more money than any previous candidate: more than $650 million in campaign contributions, nearly $300 million more than the previous record, which had been set by President George W. Bush during his 2004 reelection campaign. Over half that amount came from donations of less than $200; in contrast, only 27 percent of the money raised during the 2004 election cycle came from small donors.

Second, the Obama campaign also utilized technology to build and manage an army of volunteers to get out the vote. Here, the Obama campaign benefited from a remarkable piece of luck; shortly before announcing his candidacy, the campaign reached out to the young social network Facebook to set up an official page. The person they reached, Facebook cofounder Chris Hughes, became convinced that Barack Obama could win the presidency and change the world, and Hughes left Facebook to join the campaign. Hughes brought with him his personal experiences working at one of the world's great blitzscaling companies, and moved quickly to apply the tools of Silicon Valley to the Obama campaign.

Hughes and his team ended up creating three key tools that leveraged growth factors to help Obama win the election. The first was my.barackobama.com, or MyBO for short. MyBO was a social network that leveraged existing networks of Obama supporters, allowing them to connect with one another, as well as create groups, plan events, and raise funds. Over the course of the campaign, volunteers used MyBO to create two million profiles, host two hundred thousand off-line events, and raise $30 million.

The second tool was the Neighbor-to-Neighbor canvassing tool. When MyBO users logged in, Neighbor-to-Neighbor provided a list of undecided voters they could call or visit. Neighbor-to-Neighbor tapped into online databases to match volunteers with people they would likely connect with, taking into account factors like age, profession, languages spoken, and military service. Neighbor-to-Neighbor generated some eight million calls— and tremendous word of mouth.

The final tool was the Vote for Change voter registration site, which automatically sorted out the fiendishly complicated nest of local voter registration rules to help potential Obama voters register correctly. For example, college students would log in and be asked for the location of both their college and childhood home; Vote for Change would then help them register in the state where a student's vote was more badly needed. During the campaign, Vote for Change helped one million people register to vote—roughly the same number that two thousand paid staff could handle using the old-fashioned door-to-door method.

On Tuesday, November 4, 2008, Barack Obama was elected the forty-fourth president of the United States of America.

Thanks in part to the blitzscaling techniques his campaign employed, he received over sixty-nine million votes, still a record for any US presidential candidate.

As these examples demonstrate, blitzscaling can be as powerful a tool for social impact and change as it can be for building a massively profitable business. It's not easy; you'll need either access to significant capital (as we saw with Barack Obama's 2008 presidential campaign), the ability to leverage the contributions of a community or another existing network (as we saw with Dress for Success), or both. But if you are able to support this kind of rapid growth, the lessons of blitzscaling can help you manage the strains of that growth and maximize the impact you have on the world.

BLITZSCALING IN GREATER SILICON VALLEY

One of the interesting developments in the business world over the past decade is how other high-tech ecosystems on the Pacific coast of the United States have become more tightly integrated with Silicon Valley. For most of the twentieth century, Seattle, Los Angeles, and Silicon Valley were very different and differentiated industry hubs. While Silicon Valley specialized in computers, Seattle and Los Angeles both had strong aerospace and defense industries, and each ecosystem also boasted its own market leadership positions in coffee (Seattle) and the entertainment industry (Los Angeles). But in the twenty-first century, Seattle and Los Angeles have also become home to high-tech ecosystems that are increasingly tied to Silicon Valley.

In a 2017 article titled "How America's Two Tech Hubs Are Converging," the *Economist* argued that Seattle and Silicon Valley were becoming increasingly intertwined, citing as evidence the fact that most of the venture capital investment in Seattle start-ups has come from Silicon Valley VC firms, and that about thirty Silicon Valley firms had opened Seattle offices to tap into that city's plentiful supply of computer scientists, while Seattle's two dominant blitzscalers, Amazon and Microsoft, have thousands of employees working in Silicon Valley. Meanwhile, Seattle's Amazon Web Services has become the cloud computing platform of choice for Silicon Valley start-ups and scale-ups.

Los Angeles has also seen impressive growth as a start-up and scale-up hub. According to the research firm CB Insights, Los Angeles–based start-ups took in $3 billion in funding in 2016, up sixfold since 2012. The LA ecosystem, including the so-called Silicon Beach area along the Pacific coastline, has produced a number of important companies, including Snap and SpaceX, each of which is worth over $10 billion, as well as other success stories like Dollar Shave Club. It is worth noting that Snap's founders met while studying at Stanford, that SpaceX was founded by former San Franciscan Elon Musk, and that the majority of their investors were Silicon Valley venture capital firms like Lightspeed, Founders Fund, and Venrock. Like Seattle, Los Angeles is an operations base for major Silicon Valley companies such as Google. These relationships aren't particularly surprising when you consider that both Seattle and Los Angeles are close enough to Silicon Valley to allow the intertwining of their networks of capital, talent, and learning: either a short flight—Seattle is two hours away, Los Angeles just an hour—or a six-hour drive from LA, with plenty of Tesla Superchargers along I-5 so that venture capitalists can make the journey! This helps to integrate the capital networks; it's easy for Silicon Valley investors to invest in Seattle- and Los Angeles–based deals because they can simply fly in and out for board meetings. This also helps integrate the talent networks, since entrepreneurs can easily travel between hubs to develop and maintain relationships and to share insights and learning face-to-face. For example, geography allows Elon Musk to run both Tesla (Silicon Valley) and SpaceX (Los Angeles). Seattle and Los Angeles also offer good quality-of-life benefits to individual professionals, since they are major cultural centers and popular tourist destinations, with less expensive housing markets than Silicon Valley (though hardly inexpensive).

These ties will likely get even closer if the cities are connected via additional transportation links like high-speed rail or Elon's proposed Hyperloop, or with the advent of self-driving cars, all of which would make travel and commuting between these cities and Silicon Valley faster and cheaper. Thus, LA and Seattle are becoming increasingly fertile grounds for entrepreneurship, and good places to set up a company that you are planning on blitzscaling. It will be interesting to see if Amazon's HQ2 project to set up a second headquarters (Amazon intends to spend $5 billion to construct a new corporate campus that will accommodate fifty thousand employees) ends up expanding "Greater Silicon Valley" even further (and farther). Moody's picked Austin as the most likely city to be chosen, while the *New York Times* believed Denver to have a good chance. Either would be a logical expansion point, given the long-standing pattern of migration from Silicon Valley to Colorado, and the "nerd bird" flights that Southwest operates between San Jose and Austin.

OTHER BLITZSCALING REGIONS TO WATCH

Within the United States, cities like Boston and Austin have emerged as powerful tech hubs, followed more recently by Boulder, Colorado, and even New York City. Over in Europe, cities like London, Stockholm, and Berlin (where the Samwer brothers' Rocket Internet is attempting to industrialize blitzscaling as a business model, with notable successes and failures) have begun producing interesting companies as well. According to research at Wharton, Stockholm actually produces the second highest number of billion-dollar "unicorn" start-ups after Silicon Valley itself. Around 65 percent of working-age (eighteen to sixty-four years old) Swedish adults think there are good opportunities to start a company in Sweden, compared with 47 percent of working-age Americans.

For example, Stockholm's streaming music giant, Spotify, has a record of blitzscaling that most Silicon Valley unicorns would envy. Spotify's cofounders, Daniel Ek and Martin Lorentzon, are both serial entrepreneurs with prior blitzscaling experience—Ek was the CTO of Stardoll, while Lorentzon cofounded Tradedoubler. Spotify uses the proven freemium business model, offering a basic free service and encouraging users to subscribe for higher-quality audio and zero ads. Since its launch in 2008, Spotify has pursued a course of extremely aggressive investment, raising over $2.5 billion in funding from Silicon Valley VCs, such as Founders Fund, Accel, and Kleiner Perkins Caufield & Byers, as well as global investors with scale experience, such as Li Ka-shing's Horizons and Yuri Milner's Digital Sky Technologies (DST), while growing from one million paying subscribers in 2011 to sixty million paying subscribers in 2017.

It's worth noting that despite their success in Stockholm, in 2016 Ek and Lorentzon began to fear that policies like restrictive and expensive housing regulations for immigrants and heavy taxation of stock options could make it difficult for Spotify to remain there. Sure enough, in February 2017, Spotify announced that it would add 1,000 new jobs in its New York office, making the United States the home to the majority of Spotify's workforce.

Outside the Western world, the prospects might be even brighter. We know about China, of course, but India is also projected to overtake the US economy this century. Indian e-commerce giant Flipkart has raised nearly $7.3 billion from investors around the world, including Accel (Silicon Valley), Tiger Global (New York), Naspers (South Africa), GIC (Singapore), and SoftBank (Japan). Its founders, Sachin Bansal and Binny Bansal—the two are not related—both worked for Amazon. Africa is pioneering mobile services like the M-Pesa mobile payment system, which was developed in the UK, managed by IBM in America, and whose technology is now managed by Huawei in China. M-Pesa accounted for $28 billion in transactions in Kenya in 2015; for comparison, Kenya's GDP that year was $63 billion. Latin America represents a fast-growing, largely Spanish-language market. Israel, which boasts more start-ups per capita than any other nation, is a leading center for cybersecurity companies and is also home to a thriving venture capital community. Even Australia has produced successful technology companies like Atlassian.

Blitzscaling in emerging ecosystems poses both different challenges and different opportunities. Emerging ecosystems lack many of the platforms that established ecosystems like Silicon Valley or, more broadly, the US market provide—for example, payment systems and shipping vendors, let alone professional service providers (lawyers, accountants, etc.), experienced executives, and aggressive venture capitalists. This makes blitzscaling more difficult and leads to slower rates of growth. It's far easier to leverage existing platforms than to build your own.

On the other hand, once you are successful, having built your own platforms represents a major competitive advantage, which often compounds over time, resulting in faster long-term growth. MercadoLibre grew much more slowly than Amazon during its early years. In Latin America, fewer than half of consumers even have a bank account. The company couldn't simply tap into ubiquitous credit card networks and established shipping vendors the way Amazon did; instead, it had to build its own payment and logistics systems.

Today, however, owning platforms like Mercado Pago, the leading e-commerce payment system in Latin America, allows MercadoLibre to sustain a higher growth rate while creating barriers to potential competition. Whereas rivals who want to compete with Amazon in the US market can start and grow quickly thanks to Visa and UPS, a rival to MercadoLibre would have to use MercadoLibre's payment and logistics platforms, making it much more difficult to gain significant traction.

MercadoLibre was also able to take advantage of lessons learned by previous blitzscalers like eBay. In 2001, eBay acquired a French company called iBazar, which had a Brazilian subsidiary. Because eBay wanted to focus on Europe, it made MercadoLibre an offer: take over the Brazilian operation in exchange for 19.9 percent of MercadoLibre. The deal included both a five-year noncompete agreement (which meant that MercadoLibre didn't have to worry about eBay expanding into the Latin American market for at least that time period) and a best practices sharing agreement. While CEO Marcos Galperin did the deal for the noncompete agreement, during an interview for Reid's *Masters of Scale* podcast, he said that the most important element of the deal for MercadoLibre ended up being the best practices sharing agreement:

> What ended up being incredibly valuable for us was that really, really intense best practices sharing process. We were basically like an eBay subsidiary for five years! We would go up there [to eBay HQ in Silicon Valley] every quarter, and every different sector of our company would exchange best practices with different sectors of eBay. It helped us scale

and see all the different problems eBay was having in different parts of the world and with different competitors. We were able to pick and choose; there were things eBay was doing that we really liked, and things eBay was doing that we didn't think applied to Latin America, which we would do differently.

Marcos and his team didn't just imitate eBay. They learned from eBay's best practices, and adapted them to the specific characteristics of their own market.

All these new ecosystems around the globe represent interesting and potentially differentiated opportunities, much like China fifteen years ago or Silicon Valley twenty-five years ago. Boston has won a leadership position in health, for example, because of its world-class hospitals and universities, while New York is the leader in fashion-related businesses like Rent the Runway and Birchbox. Countries like Estonia have made their dependence on international markets a strength; Skype (founded by Estonian programmers Priit Kasesalu and Jaan Tallinn) wasn't likely to have started in the United States because international phone calls simply weren't as important to the US consumer.

CHINA: THE LAND OF BLITZSCALING

Remember Pony Ma's decision to launch and then blitzscale WeChat in 2010? He did this despite the massive risks that WeChat would pose to his mature QQ desktop product, and thus to Tencent's overall bottom line. By taking these risks and launching WeChat, Ma was able to rejuvenate his company and push it to even greater heights.

The story of WeChat exemplifies why, if anything, China may very well end up being an even better ecosystem for blitzscaling than Silicon Valley. Like Silicon Valley, China has an entrepreneurial culture that encourages risk taking, a highly developed financial sector that is willing to fund aggressive growth, and a plentiful supply of high-value technology talent. But thanks to its incredible recent growth, China's market is both massive and open to disruption.

China has been one of the world's fastest-growing economies for decades, and PricewaterhouseCoopers projects that China's economy will overtake that of the United States in size by 2030. In many areas, it already has. In 2016, the volume of mobile payments in China was $8.6 *trillion*. In comparison, the same figure for the United States was $112 billion. In other words, China's mobile payments market was nearly seventy-seven times that of the United States. Didi Chuxing provides *twenty million* rides per day in China, over triple the volume of Uber worldwide. These factors give China a major advantage over almost every other ecosystem when it comes to the growth factor of market size.

China also has major advantages when it comes to overcoming the growth limitations of operational scalability, thanks to its flexible labor market, which was explored in a 2012 *New York Times* article about Apple's manufacturing operations in China: "Apple's executives had estimated that about 8,700 industrial engineers were needed to oversee and guide the 200,000 assembly-line workers eventually involved in manufacturing iPhones. The company's analysts had forecast it would take as long as nine months to find that many qualified engineers in the United States. In China, it took 15 days."

The result is an ecosystem in which companies grow, break apart, and recombine with incredible speed. "Innovation moves faster here," said Kai-Fu Lee, who runs Sinovation Ventures, and used to be the head of Google's China operations. The Chinese market views growth as the first, last, and best solution to almost any issue. Perhaps this is why Chinese start-ups tend to scale up at an even faster tempo than Silicon Valley firms.

For example, it took less than five years for Chinese smartphone maker Xiaomi to go from founding to the world's most valuable start-up in 2014—it has since been surpassed by Uber and Didi Chuxing, no blitzscaling slouches themselves. Lei Jun founded Xiaomi in 2010; by 2015, it was the third-largest smartphone manufacturer in the world after Samsung and Apple.

But just as companies can rise faster in China, companies can also fall faster in China. In 2016, IDC reported that Xiaomi's sales dropped 40 percent year over year, as its online-only sales strategy began to falter and competitors like OPPO and Vivo gained market share by selling through brick-and-mortar distributors. At least one analyst predicted that Xiaomi's value would drop over 90 percent.

Xiaomi's response to this crisis demonstrates both the fierce competitiveness of Lei Jun and the amazing tempo possible in China. The company attacked its distribution problems with a rapid, massive effort to build up its off-line sales channel, opening one hundred Mi Home retail stores in a single year, with a target of opening two thousand stores by 2019. In the first quarter of 2017, an astounding 34 percent of Xiaomi's smartphone sales in China came from its one hundred retail stores, which the company claims generate sales per square foot second only to Apple's famed Apple Stores. In 2017, IDC reported that Xiaomi's sales had rebounded 59 percent from the previous year, placing it back among the world's top five smartphone makers. That's a rags to riches to rags to riches story, all compressed into less than a decade.

As founders, investors, and authors, we have a personal, in-depth familiarity with the Silicon Valley way; in contrast, our knowledge of China is necessarily that of outsiders. Yet we can't help but be struck by how many valuable lessons these two eco-systems can learn from each other.

For example, China's speed demonstrates the value of intense competition as a motivator. On one occasion, Xiaomi's Lei Jun told me, "You American entrepreneurs are lazy. The vast major-ity of my company is still working at nine o'clock on a Saturday night." In some ways, he's right. Chinese blitzscalers work with an intensity that few in Silicon Valley can match. Rather than staying open during the standard American business hours of 9 a.m. to 5 p.m., Xiaomi operates on a "996" model—get in at 9 a.m., leave the office at 9 p.m., and work six days a week. I saw the same thing at LinkedIn China. To make a tight deadline for our "Red Horse" project, our China team leader Derek Shen simply moved the entire development team to a hotel for two weeks so that its members could work around the clock without any of the distractions of normal life.

A by-product of this intense work ethic is that it allows for much faster decision making, a key advantage in blitzscaling. When I interviewed him for my *Masters of Scale* podcast, An-drew Ng, a professor at Stanford who cofounded Coursera and led major machine learning efforts at Google and Baidu (China's leading search engine), told me that when he was at Baidu, he once had an HR question come up while he was at dinner. He texted his HR lead at 7 p.m.; she texted her team for input, and by 7:30, Andrew had his answer. "If she had taken longer than an hour to respond," Andrew said, "I would have gotten wor-ried." That kind of rapid decision making might make many feel uncomfortable, but by consistently making quick decisions, Chinese entrepreneurs become comfortable with the discomfort and uncertainty, allowing them to move even faster.

Another advantage comes from China's massive talent pool. The sheer abundance of human capital allows companies in

China to scale their organizations more quickly, including opening multiple offices in multiple cities. China also has a thing or two to teach Silicon Valley about tapping the entire talent pool. For example, China has proven an amazing environment for women entrepreneurs. Of the seventy-three women in the world who are self-made billionaires, forty-nine (over two-thirds!) live in China. Eight of the ten wealthiest self-made women in the world are Chinese.

Finally, China's relatively recent rise into its status as an industrial power means that more of its industries are still nascent and thus up for grabs. Where Silicon Valley might have cornered the market on software and the Internet, with a sideline in hardware, China has fast-growing companies in every industry from farming to chemicals.

Yet despite these impressive strengths, China can also learn from Silicon Valley. For one thing, Silicon Valley's comparatively less frenetic pace means that it can pursue deeper tech and longer time horizons like Elon Musk's commitment to interplanetary travel and Google's famous $750 million investment in Calico, a project to "cure death." Silicon Valley still has a lead in most deep technology innovations such as artificial intelligence (AI), virtual reality (VR), space flight, and nuclear power.

While Silicon Valley is certainly home to plenty of ruthless competition, the culture also encourages more collaboration between companies. This collaboration leverages network connections across companies to drive greater innovation and productivity for the entire region. When Google open-sourced the TensorFlow software library in 2015, it allowed Google to leverage external brainpower to improve its machine learning projects, but it also allowed companies throughout Silicon Valley (and the rest of the world) to accelerate their own machine learning projects as well.

Moreover, Silicon Valley's history of blitzscaling put it several decades ahead of China in terms of concentrated experience and institutional knowledge. Remember, half of the world's most valuable technology companies are clustered in this small region with a population of less than four million. That's about 10 times smaller than the metropolitan area of Guangzhou, and 350 times smaller than the population of China. Meanwhile, China's two companies worth more than $100 billion, Alibaba and Tencent, are both less than twenty years old. Together, these facts mean that despite China's massive labor pool and incredible supply of technical talent, it lacks the density of Silicon Valley, and is still limited in terms of the bench strength of scale executives available to help manage blitzscaling companies.

Finally, China's more insular management and hiring practices can present obstacles to blitzscaling. My friend Jerry Yang, who cofounded Yahoo! and led that company's prescient investment in Alibaba—when Jerry made his first trip to China in 1997, the guide the Chinese government provided him was an English teacher named Jack Ma—has observed that Chinese companies try to breed their leaders from within the organization. Unlike in Silicon Valley, in China senior managers are rarely brought in from external companies, and the few that have been hired typically haven't worked out well. For example, Hugo Barra was a well-regarded executive at Google who joined Xiaomi as its vice president of international, but left the company after a little over two years to lead Facebook's VR efforts.

This internal approach has major implications for blitzscaling; you have to start thinking about how to fill leadership positions years in advance and start grooming people for them right away. This also means that there is far less mobility between firms, and, as a consequence, less intermixing of ideas and innovation. This may be changing; Jerry pointed out that the first generation of Chinese start-up giants is already beginning to provide the seeds of the next. For example, Cheng Wei, the founder of ride-hailing giant Didi Chuxing, learned how to scale at Alibaba, where he worked for eight years before starting his own firm. That experience probably helped Cheng scale Didi at a pace that makes Uber envious. Despite being founded three years later than Uber, Didi completed more rides in 2015 than Uber had during its entire existence to that point. Meanwhile, the fact that first-generation companies like Alibaba, Tencent, and Baidu are all Didi investors affords Didi's management access to knowledge networks helpful for blitzscaling.

Overall, we think China's technology industry leaders are doing a good job of learning from Silicon Valley. When I travel and speak in China, I find that my audiences are familiar with what is happening in Silicon Valley. Most Chinese executives speak and read English, and are reading the latest English-language news on a daily basis. How many American or European executives read Chinese and are staying abreast of developments in China? If you wait for an innovation to make its way into the English-language press, perhaps because a Silicon Valley company is now doing it, you might be giving China's blitzscalers a one-year head start on the global market.

The biggest opportunity is for Silicon Valley and China to work together and combine their respective strengths. According to Andrew Ng, it took a combination of ideas from both sides of the Pacific to drive breakthrough progress in speech recognition. Silicon Valley companies like Nvidia provided the graphical processor units (GPUs) to power machine learning networks, while progress came from combining Silicon Valley's expertise in GPU programming with China's expertise in supercomputing. As of November 2016, the world's most powerful supercomputer was the Sunway TaihuLight at the National Supercomputing Center in Wuxi, China, while number two was the Tianhe-2. America's most powerful supercomputer, the Titan at Oak Ridge National Laboratory in Tennessee, was less than one-fifth as powerful as the Sunway TaihuLight.

There is no telling what kind of wealth and progress might emerge out of future collaboration between the leading innovators in these two ecosystems.

DEFENDING AGAINST BLITZSCALING

Thus far, we've focused on helping you understand how you can use blitzscaling to build a start-up into a scale-up, or to rapidly scale a new product or business unit. In other words, you've learned how to use blitzscaling to play offense.

But what if you're the incumbent? What if, instead of having nothing to lose, and everything to gain, the opposite is true?

If you find yourself in a position where competitors are trying to blitzscale your existing business out of existence, you have three basic options to defend yourself: beat them, join them, or avoid them.

OPTION #1: BEAT THEM

The first option to defend against blitzscaling is to beat them by continuing to play your traditional game. As we've discussed, many attempts to blitzscale are doomed to failure. You should assess the growth factors and growth limiters of the business model, and if they seem ill-suited to blitzscaling, not overreacting is probably your best strategy.

Fans of the late Muhammad Ali may recall his "rope-a-dope"

strategy from his "Rumble in the Jungle" boxing match against George Foreman. The rope-a-dope calls for allowing an opponent to punch himself out; when that opponent is exhausted, you can beat him with a counterattack.

In the case of Webvan during the dot-com boom, the many problems with its business model (low margins, massive operational scalability issues) meant that its attempt to blitzscale was probably doomed from the start. Established grocers essentially rope-a-doped: they set up their own online grocery initiatives, but these were incremental, low-investment efforts. Safeway even exploited Webvan's failure by allowing Webvan to convince early adopters to order groceries online and then setting up its own grocery delivery service to serve those stranded customers.

Of course, those same grocers now face a much different competitor in the form of Amazon and its acquisition of Whole Foods. These circumstances seem to call for a very different response. Amazon is unlikely to punch itself out!

OPTION #2: JOIN THEM

If your market does seem ripe for blitzscaling, one obvious response is to launch your own blitzscaling effort. The problem with doing so, especially if you're an established company, is that you might not have the technology or expertise to win a head-to-head competition. You might be able to buy the technology or expertise, but this brings its own set of risks.

First, if blitzscaling is occurring, that almost certainly means that investors (public or private) are enthused enough about the market to provide cheap capital. That means that any acquisitions are likely to be very expensive.

Second, as I warned Brian Chesky about buying Wimdu, any merger or acquisition brings with it the possibility of a culture clash. The cultures of an established, stable company and a risk-taking blitzscaler are about as different as can be.

In its battle against Amazon, Walmart spent $3.3 billion to acquire Jet.com, a high price for a thirteen-month-old start-up (the price represented a revenue multiple double that of Amazon's already-rich valuation). The two companies have already experienced some culture clash moments, such as when Walmart asked Jet to stop holding its regular office happy hours, stocking bottles of liquor in the office kitchen, and allowing employees to drink at their desks. According to a 2017 *Wall Street Journal* article, Jet executives complained, and Walmart allowed Jet to revive its office happy hours.

On the other hand, Walmart's e-commerce sales got a big boost from the acquisition, and Jet has allowed Walmart to appeal to urban millennials—a key demographic that has typically shunned Walmart's traditional stores. Blitzscaling is risky, but so is doing nothing if a competitor seems likely to succeed in scaling up.

OPTION #3: AVOID THEM

The final and perhaps most often "successful" option is to cede the current market to blitzscalers and use your current assets to migrate to a new, less vulnerable market. Recall our list of $100 billion technology companies from the introduction; the oldest member of that list successfully pursued this exact strategy.

IBM was one of the original computer blitzscalers. IBM's willingness to invest in the growth of breakthrough products like the System/360 mainframe allowed it to dominate computing for decades. Under the leadership of Thomas Watson Jr., IBM invested $5 billion to develop and launch System/360 ($30 billion in today's dollars). But by April 1993, when Lou Gerstner took over as CEO, IBM posted an $8 billion loss—the largest in the history of American business to that point—and seemed in danger of being surpassed by younger blitzscalers like Dell.

Rather than ignore the problem or try to compete directly in the PC market that it had created in 1981, Gerstner successfully repositioned IBM as a trusted system integrator and technology consultant for corporate America. The scope of IBM's migration can be seen in two transactions: in 2002, Gerstner's last year as CEO, IBM acquired the consulting business of Pricewater-houseCoopers, and in 2005, it sold its personal computer business (including its iconic ThinkPad brand) to a new blitzscaler from China named Lenovo (which also acquired IBM's server business in 2014).

Another powerful example can be found in how independent bookstores were able to weather the onslaught from Amazon and actually mount a comeback. No independent bookstore can possibly compete with Amazon on available selection or price. But the number of independent bookstores has increased for each of the last seven years, even as Amazon has continued to scale, because they've migrated out of the bookselling business and into the literary community business, becoming destinations for cultural events like author signings, book club meetings, spoken word performances, and more. Independent bookstores offer something that Amazon cannot (at least until VR becomes more advanced): the experience of being in a bookstore, complete with the smell of books, friendly staff, and the presence of fellow bibliophiles.

Finding yourself in the crosshairs of a blitzscaling competitor can and should be frightening, but it is not a death sentence if you choose the right response. But decide quickly; the speed of blitzscaling means that taking your time is the same as doing nothing.

PART VI

Responsible Blitzscaling

In an ideal world, blitzscaling organizations would embody all the virtues that society might desire from its businesses— a diverse and inclusive workforce, a strong sense of responsibility to shareholders and stakeholders, an ample supply of well-paying jobs, and executives who serve as moral role models and leaders of society. The unfortunate truth is that for all the good that blitzscaling produces, blitzscaling organizations can be guilty of the same sins committed by other types of companies, and face some inherent challenges even when trying to behave responsibly.

Blitzscaling companies almost always operate in fiercely competitive markets where, in order to survive and thrive, they need to outgrow their rivals. In the best case, they do this by focusing relentlessly on building the business while also trying to achieve broader social goals. In the worst case, they try to get big fast by any means necessary.

These pressures are compounded by the fact that blitzscaling companies grow so quickly that they often become key players in society before they've had time to fully mature. This can result in problematic corporate cultures, adversarial relationships with regulators, and questionable decision making.

These challenges are real but shouldn't discourage us from

blitzscaling. The art lies in marrying responsibility and velocity so that we are able to successfully capture the first-scaler advantage while still developing and adhering to a strong moral compass.

Skeptics might argue that the kind of scale that blitzscaling produces is inherently bad, and that society should simply prevent companies from growing too big. Testifying before Congress in 1911, future Supreme Court justice Louis Brandeis argued, "I think we are in a position, after the experience of the last twenty years, to state two things: In the first place, that a corporation may well be too large to be the most efficient instrument of production and of distribution, and, in the second place, whether it has exceeded the point of greatest economic efficiency or not, it may be too large to be tolerated among the people who desire to be free."

We disagree with this position on the harmfulness of scale in today's world. First, Brandeis was speaking during the era of "trusts," when figures like J. P. Morgan consolidated American industry into powerful, giant companies like U.S. Steel. But we believe that today's blitzscalers are qualitatively different than Gilded Age trusts. Those trusts held virtual monopolies over the supply of key physical resources like steel and oil. Consumers had no alternatives and were forced to do business with them. In contrast, companies like Apple and Amazon have to win their customers every day, and if they fail to do so, those consumers can simply buy Dell laptops and order books from Barnes & Noble.

Second, we believe that while big can sometimes be bad, big can also be great. Scale creates dominant companies, but scale also creates enormous value. The smartphones we love, for example, are mass-market consumer electronics that depend on economies of scale. While Brandeis is right that society needs to prevent monopolies that block technology or business innovation in the way that the old AT&T monopoly suppressed the progress of telecommunications, today's largest companies have actually enabled innovation and the creation of even more value by providing a platform for everything from business productivity software (Slack) to entertainment (Netflix). Even the concentration of capital that scale has produced isn't all bad; it has allowed blitzscalers to tackle "moonshots" like space travel (SpaceX) and autonomous vehicles (Google's Waymo) that may dramatically improve our lives.

As opposed to reflexively calling for the breakup of big companies, the better approach to tempering the potential abuses of scale is to leverage the principles for a healthy republic that James Madison laid out in "Federalist No. 10." Madison was addressing the dangers of "factions;" that is, specific groups that act against the interests of the entire community. Madison argued that factions were a natural consequence of liberty and, to safeguard against them, the best strategy was to create a diverse society in which no particular faction would be able to dominate. Madison wrote, "Extend the sphere, and you take in a greater variety of parties and interests; you make it less probable that a majority of the whole will have a common motive to invade the rights of other citizens; or if such a common motive exists, it will be more difficult for all who feel it to discover their own strength, and to act in unison with each other." We believe the same approach applies to economics as well as politics; in other words, that a greater variety of powerful companies—if they are prevented from colluding—can counterbalance the malevolent or selfish goals of any one particular entity.

It's true that, as with anything in life, blitzscaling produces winners and losers. Start-ups can and will fail, and all entrepreneurial enterprises create risk for founders, employees, and investors. At the same time, they also create the possibility for new businesses, new innovations, and new jobs. But the most successful modern societies err on the side of freedom rather than trying to outlaw all risks, and on the whole we are all better off because we allow entrepreneurs to take those risks.

It also tempting to believe that the easiest way to ensure responsible behavior is to legislate it. The problem is, we live in a globally competitive marketplace. A government that slows the growth of companies within its borders by weighing them down with inflexible legislation is just making it easier for irresponsible blitzscalers from outside those borders to dominate emerging industries.

Take the uproar that ensued when it was revealed that Facebook and Twitter were exploited by parties—both foreign and domestic—to hack the American election process. That's clearly bad, and measures should be taken to understand and address the vulnerabilities that left user data exposed. But imagine if all those users had instead adopted a social media platform under the jurisdiction of some other government? Most likely the American public wouldn't have known about the issue, let alone have the ability to remedy it.

The fact that Facebook is a global network makes it far easier for users to connect with people from around the world. There is, for example, no "Facebook of the UK." But Facebook is under the jurisdiction of the United States, not the UK, which means that when British users' data was compromised and a Member of Parliament sent a letter to Mark Zuckerberg requesting that he appear before a Parliamentary committee, Zuckerberg had no obligation to do so. Such are the limitations of regulating businesses in a globalized world.

BLITZSCALING IN SOCIETY

Responsible blitzscaling matters because successful blitzscalers often reach a point where they are more than just a business; they actually affect the fabric of the society in which they operate. Social media like Facebook and Twitter have changed how we consume information and how we communicate. Marketplaces like Alibaba and eBay provide economic opportunity—some dedicated sellers even rely on them for their livelihoods. Sharing economy services like Airbnb can bring more tourism and diversity into the cities in which they operate. And Amazon is changing the entire retail industry, which affects everyone. As Spider-Man teaches us, with great power comes great responsibility.

We believe that the responsibilities of a blitzscaler go beyond simply maximizing shareholder value while obeying the law; you are also responsible for how the actions of your business impact the larger society. But even beyond the moral imperatives, responsible blitzscaling is good business strategy. Society provides the ecosystem in which you live, and in which your business operates, which means that it can rightly claim some responsibility for your success. In other words, your success is contingent upon society functioning properly. Here in Silicon Valley, some might fantasize about floating cities in international waters, but the fact is that blitzscaling businesses rely on the rule of law, robust financial markets, and an education system that produces talented employees and a healthy market of consumers. To paraphrase Warren Buffett, we win the "ovarian lottery" when we're born into blitzscaling ecosystems.

Moreover, responsible blitzscaling can actually protect against legislation that threatens to slow growth trajectories. Regulation typically arises when government believes that an industry isn't behaving responsibly. For example, America (along with many other nations) has environmental regulations because companies were once polluting with abandon and causing harm to citizens and nature. Smart blitzscalers realize that self-regulating can actually delay or preempt government regulation. Entrepreneurs often complain that regulators write bad policy because they don't understand the intricacies of business; self-regulation lets businesses apply their expertise to finding the most cost-effective ways to achieve social goals.

FRAMEWORK FOR RESPONSIBLE BLITZSCALING

The key to blitzscaling responsibly without sacrificing pace of growth is developing the ability to distinguish between various forms of risk. Our suggested framework for risk evaluation is to consider two separate axes: Known versus Unknown and Systemic versus Nonsystemic.

	Known	Unknown
Systemic	Known/Systemic	Unknown/Systemic
Nonsystemic	Known/Nonsystemic	Unknown/Nonsystemic

Uncertainty by itself isn't risk; it simply produces unknowns, and unknowns aren't inherently negative. As anyone who has ever read a mystery novel or traveled to a new city or learned a new language can attest, one of the great joys of life is the journey of discovery, of turning the unknown into the known.

However, when you combine uncertainty with the possibility of a negative outcome, you produce risk. The magnitude of the risk is a function of the probability, and severity, of that potential negative outcome. Blitzscaling always involves risks, but all risks aren't equal. This is why you need to distinguish between systemic and nonsystemic risk.

Nonsystemic risk is localized and, at most, affects a part of the system. Systemic risk can impact or even destroy the entire system, either directly or as the result of cascading problems. For example, the possibility of nuclear war is a clear example of systemic—even extinction-level—risk. Even if we don't believe that we can eliminate this risk entirely, the magnitude of the risk makes it worth expending a great deal of effort to reduce the probability that it occurs.

Applying this analysis shows that a number of common fears about blitzscaling are actually nonsystemic risks. For example, one common fear is that blitzscaling will produce an oligarchy of powerful technology executives with too much power over our government and our society. But even today, with technology firms dominating the ranks of the world's most valuable companies, traditional business moguls such as Rupert Murdoch and the Koch brothers have had a far greater influence over public policy than tech leaders such as Jeff Bezos, Larry Page, or Mark Zuckerberg.

An additional fear that is starting to be broadly voiced is that social media (largely a product of blitzscaling companies) is a uniquely dangerous technology that is harming consumers—especially the young—by addicting them and consuming all their attention. It is certainly true that some people are spending more time producing and consuming social media than is optimal for their health and productivity. But is this really a systemic risk? In 2010, an article in *Slate* entitled "Don't Touch That Dial!" enumerated the many times in history that critics have argued that new mediums for consuming information would ruin society. Socrates warned against the pernicious effects of the written word, which he believed would harm memory. In the sixteenth century, Conrad Gessner tried to compile a list of every book, an effort that led him to conclude that the newfangled printing press had resulted in an overabundance of data that was "confusing and harmful" to the mind. The French statesman Guillaume-Chrétien de Lamoignon de Malesherbes wrote that newspapers socially isolated their readers, who would otherwise get their news from their church pulpits. Despite these warnings, the written word, the printing press, and newspapers have brought tremendous benefits to humanity. It's possible but unlikely that social media will have a qualitatively different impact than any previous form of media, but we generally find that when people start saying, "This time it's different," it usually isn't.

New technologies have always had the potential to lead to new problems. Newspapers led to demagogic "yellow journalism." Advertising led to snake oil salesmen. The answer wasn't to ban newspapers or advertising, but to build policies and institutions to mitigate the risks involved. That's why we have libel laws and regulators like the FCC. And with time, audiences themselves become more sophisticated and develop their own "immune responses."

Critics of social media are correct when they point out the corrosive effect social media have had on both the civility of political discourse and the ideal of objective, evidence-based truth. These are real problems, and that means we should try to fix them. Social media should be more transparent about who is paying for advertisements, and should require the same standards for truth in advertising as any other medium.

On the other hand, there are technologies emerging from blitzscaling companies that could pose real, systemic problems (yet get far less media attention). Synthetic biology, driven by CRISPR-Cas9 targeted genome editing, has the potential to produce huge benefits in medicine and agribusiness, but brings with it the systemic risk of bad actors engineering a deadly global pandemic. Changes and developments in this field have occurred so quickly that it is difficult for governments to create intelligent regulatory regimes to manage these risks. Responsible blitzscalers should give serious considerations to systemic risks and seek structural dialogue that involves a broad set of stakeholders rather than defying or stonewalling regulators. Conversely, regulators shouldn't assume that they know better than industry and make unilateral decisions. Broad collaboration with transparency and open communications is the best way to both identify the systemic risks and figure out the least costly interventions to reduce them while still encouraging rapid innovation.

The systemic/nonsystemic distinction is dynamic, not static, and blitzscalers should be prepared to change their approach accordingly. For example, Facebook has been extensively criticized for its role in the 2016 US presidential election, both for distributing deceptive content (aka "fake news") and for not doing enough to protect its users' personal data from being exploited by political consulting firms like Cambridge Analytica. Both of these issues are legitimate concerns, since they both erode the trust that Facebook users have in the content they find on Facebook and in Facebook itself.

Facebook's scale has made it the keeper of vast troves of data on more than 200 million Americans, as well as the primary way in which most Americans get their news and share it with their friends. This means that the issues of data privacy and deceptive content not only affect Facebook and its users, but the fabric of society itself. If Facebook were still a niche social network for students at Ivy League colleges, the impact would largely be localized, but if these issues did in fact sway the outcome of the 2016 presidential election, then that would undoubtedly represent a systemic jolt.

In instances like these, a company may have to work together with the government in order to address a serious issue. In cases of such magnitude, the default impulse is often to call for the creation of a new regulatory agency, but government regulation alone has proven too slow to keep up with the rapid changes of blitzscaling. At the same time, pure self-regulation hasn't proven sufficient. What's needed is a dynamic public/private partnership where government input meshes with private implementation.

Similarly, in the wake of all the revelations that misinformation spread via social networks may have compromised the outcome of the election, the response of traditional media outlets like the *New York Times* and the *Washington Post* was to call for Facebook to hire human editors to police "fake news." This seems like a classic example of "When you have a hammer, everything looks like a nail." You can't simply apply the traditional editorial processes designed for a fifty-person newsroom to a platform with a billion potential "reporters" writing billions of "articles" per day. Instead of trying to copy and paste a solution, Facebook should come up with its own ideas for how to address the problem and then find scalable ways to implement them. These solutions don't need to be perfect; they just need to be better than what came before, and importantly, continue to improve over time. It will be a challenge, but we wouldn't be surprised if the solutions ultimately produce a final product that is even better than that of the old system, incorporating more voices, transparent fact-checking, and social proof.

THE RESPONSE SPECTRUM

Once you have categorized a risk as known versus unknown or systemic versus nonsystemic, you need to decide how you will respond. We believe that potential responses fall into four broad categories.

#1: TAKE DECISIVE ACTION NOW.

Systemic risks may require an immediate, "stop the presses" response. In 2011, for example, an Airbnb host in San Francisco came home and discovered that an Airbnb guest had trashed her house and stolen her possessions, including her grandmother's jewelry. Airbnb's initial response, which was to coordinate with the police department and compensate the host financially but to emphasize that such incidents would be dealt with on a case-by-case basis, may have been legally sound, but didn't address the systemic issue—hosts losing trust in Airbnb.

After he recognized the magnitude of the problem, Brian Chesky took decisive action. First, he accepted full responsibility, in writing, on the official Airbnb blog, "With regards to EJ, we let her down, and for that we are very sorry. We should have responded faster, communicated more sensitively, and taken more decisive action to make sure she felt safe and secure. But we weren't prepared for the crisis and we dropped the ball." Second, he announced the Airbnb Guarantee, whereby the company would protect hosts against up to $50,000 in property damage. These actions were absolutely necessary given the scope and potential impact of the crisis, not just for Airbnb but for the whole industry. (You can read Brian's full response, "Our Commitment to Trust and Safety," on the official Airbnb blog.)

#2: TAKE SHORT-TERM ACTION NOW, BUT DEFER PERMANENT ACTION UNTIL LATER.

Even if a risk is systemic, it may be possible to employ a short-term patch that can later be replaced by a permanent fix. At Pay-Pal, credit card fraud was definitely a systemic and existential issue. After all, a payments system that users don't trust is worthless. But we didn't have an immediate solution for preventing such fraud. So our response was to eat the costs ourselves so that our users weren't affected. We knew this was a temporary solution, but it bought us the time we needed to build stronger fraud detection into the product.

#3: NOTE THE PROBLEM NOW, AND COMMIT TO TAKING ACTION LATER.

If the risk is manageable now but will become systemic in the future, you can't simply ignore the problem. Even if you don't take any immediate action, you should commit to action later so that when the risk does become systemic, you aren't caught off guard.

In the early days of PayPal, in addition to the problem of credit card fraud, we also faced the issue of illegal transactions. We obviously didn't want people using PayPal for buying and selling drugs or funding criminals and terrorists, which would represent a systemic risk. On the other hand, we didn't have in-house expertise in forensic accounting or police work. Because our transaction volume was still low, and because we judged the probability of illegal transactions occurring to be very low, we deferred working on the problem, but we also committed to building the necessary expertise and infrastructure to better manage the issue later on.

#4: LET IT BURN.

When you are facing an unknown/nonsystemic risk, it may not even be worth expending the effort to analyze it—it's probably a small fire that you should let burn.

BALANCING RESPONSIBILITY AND VELOCITY AS THE ORGANIZATION GROWS

Balancing the dual priorities of responsibility and velocity is a tricky dance that may look very different at each stage of growth. We've observed some broad patterns that seem to apply to most companies.

Early on, during the Family and Tribe stages, responsible blitzscaling means clearly defining the company's mission and laying the foundation for a culture that values being a responsible part of a larger society. To do so, you should imagine a future in which the company has succeeded in becoming a global giant, and then evaluate the likely impact of that success on your key stakeholders and on society as a whole.

For example, does your company produce negative externalities in which transactions between you and your customers impose costs on external parties? John D. Rockefeller might not have realized the impact that blitzscaling Standard Oil would ultimately have on the global climate, but his descendants seem to have done so, given that in 2016 the Rockefeller Family Fund announced that it would immediately divest its holdings in Exxon-Mobil ... the largest corporate descendant of Standard Oil. Ideally, you want to predict these externalities while you still have time to either radically reshape the business model or simply get into another business, since it's easier to institute radical change or abandon the project altogether when you're still very small.

At this stage you should also take actions that anticipate the internal effects of growth. For example, blitzscaling companies need to hire so quickly that they often rely on personal networks to source job candidates. Applied carelessly, this technique can result in a homogenous and noninclusive culture. But if you build a diverse and inclusive network before you scale, hiring within the network doesn't pose as many diversity challenges later on.

As the company achieves success and grows into the Village stage, it's time to ask yourself, "What things, if I don't fix them now, will be functionally impossible to fix at scale?" It's especially difficult to find the balance between morality and velocity during this stage, because the company is probably firing on all cylinders and pursuing all-out lightning-fast growth, and if you pause or slow down to fix things, a competitor might grab the first-scaler advantage from right under your nose. That's why the question asks what is "impossible," not just what is "difficult."

You should also continue to give serious thought to the potential negative impact of your success. In earlier stages, you were simply speculating about the future; by the Village stage, you have enough data to extrapolate into the future with reasonable accuracy. You might still be wrong, but if you don't perform this exercise you'll be culpably negligent when it comes to your moral obligations if the worst happens.

Once your company reaches the City or Nation stage, it now needs to take on the responsibilities of an incumbent, which are very different from the responsibilities of a challenger. Remember when you asked yourself which problems you could fix later? Well, later just arrived. If you previously ignored issues such as diversity, legal compliance, or social justice, you need to understand that all eyes are now on you, and you'll be expected to behave as a responsible citizen and role model. Plus, if you don't tackle these responsibilities proactively, you'll have to tackle them reactively—which will almost certainly be more costly and more painful. Like it or not, when your company is a City or a Nation, you need to start thinking like a mayor or a president and set rules for the good of humanity as a whole rather than just for the good of your profits.

Over the past few decades, blitzscaling has redefined countless industries and helped shape nearly every part of our lives. Each waking hour, you probably use multiple products from companies that blitzscaled in the past or are in the process of blitzscaling today.

But what if the Blitzscaling Era is just getting started? So far, blitzscaling has been concentrated in software and the Internet, but it's likely to reshape our physical infrastructure or even our bodies in the future. Artificial intelligence will soon be ubiquitous, thanks to self-driving vehicles and better machine learning. Technology innovations in the life sciences, such as CRISPR gene editing, may change the fabric of life itself. Cryptocurrencies and blockchain technology may change the role of governments and corporations in global finance and commerce.

New technologies are emerging rapidly and promise to change everything—again. These new technologies will enable new business models, which in turn will create new industries. In the history of high tech, platform shifts, such as the move from mainframes to client-server or the move from the Web to mobile, have represented huge opportunities. Today, multiple platforms are emerging or shifting simultaneously, bringing greater complexity—and even greater rewards for speed.

Meanwhile, markets and investors are increasingly willing to fund aggressive bets on blitzscaling. Because private investors are willing to fund growth, companies are staying private longer so that they can keep making investments in blitzscaling that the public markets might frown upon. Companies like Airbnb and Xiaomi have valuations in the tens of *billions,* making them more valuable (on paper) than the vast majority of publicly traded companies. Because investors in the public markets aren't able to profit as much from post-IPO blitzscaling, those investors are looking to invest in privately held companies, which makes even more money available to fund blitzscaling!

In this book, we've tried to help the various stakeholders in society better understand the phenomenon of blitzscaling, how it's changing the world, and how to respond to it.

Entrepreneurs should be aware that blitzscaling is the main pattern by which major new technologies, business ecosystems, and companies establish themselves and replace their predecessors. With the knowledge they gain from this book, entrepreneurs can better apply its methods to their own businesses, be more aware of how their competitors might employ the same techniques to change the playing field, and be better prepared to respond to those competitive threats. They will also better understand how to blitzscale responsibly, and build companies that improve society and of which they can be proud.

Corporate executives and organizational leaders need to recognize that blitzscaling is likely to impact their industries and businesses sooner rather than later. Because technology is becoming so integral to every business—remember, all companies are becoming tech companies—the speed of technological change is increasing the speed of change for every business.

Understanding blitzscaling allows established businesses to better anticipate and adapt to changes in the market landscape. Some changes might blow over. But others will change everything, and require everyone, including market leaders, to change accordingly. Adapting is seldom easy for big companies; everything from capital structure to organizational incentives make it difficult for them to take big risks. But the market leaders who use the lessons of this book to defend themselves against blitzscaling competitors while investing in blitzscaling their own new businesses will be the ones who remain market leaders in the future.

Governments, politicians, and regulators should try to understand how blitzscaling can *help* rather than harm society. The rapid change that blitzscaling brings can be disruptive and thus frightening. The natural impulse is to try to slow down blitzscaling, whether through taxes or regulations. The problem with giving in to this understandable instinct is that change is going to happen whether it originates in your backyard or not. Slowing things down might make you feel more comfortable, but it comes at the cost of allowing competitors from other areas to gain lasting dominance of the global market. Blitzscaling attracts investment capital and creates major new industries; as a community or a nation, you want more blitzscaling companies, not fewer.

A better understanding of the positives and negatives of blitzscaling will help governments not only to make the appropriate adjustments to encourage it, but also to improve the chances of arriving at the right social outcomes.

The economic reform and growth of China over the past thirty years has lifted eight hundred million people out of poverty—more than any other policy or program during that time. Despite the very real social and environmental price of that growth, the world is much better off for it. Blitzscaling also improves social mobility. Compared with a child born to parents in Detroit's poorest 20 percent, a child born to parents in San Francisco's poorest 20 percent has double the chance of ending up in the richest 20 percent as an adult. We believe that blitz-scaling can bring that kind of economic miracle to other areas of the world, and that educated blitzscalers will be more likely to fulfill their ethical obligations to strive for positive societal impact.

Consider, for example, the positive impact that the mobile banking service M-Pesa has had in Africa since its introduction in 2007. It has raised incomes, boosted economic growth, and financially empowered women. When Alexander Hamilton proposed a nationwide banking system for the United States in the 1790s, it took nearly a century for his vision to be realized. Thanks to blitzscaling, M-Pesa did this for multiple countries in just ten years.

Progress occurs when new ideas emerge and spread. Sometimes these ideas take the form of technologies like the printing press or the smartphone, and other times they remain abstract, like democracy or capitalism. Blitzscaling may be an abstract meme, but it has had a very concrete impact on the world. The meme of blitzscaling got its start in Silicon Valley, took root in China, and is spreading quickly—the only way that blitzscaling knows how. As it spreads, it also acts as a catalyst, helping to accelerate the impact of other ideas. We would love to see this book help to transform every region—Africa, the Middle East, Europe, Latin America, as well as North America and Asia (where the United States and China have led the way).

Here's what all of us need to realize about the Blitzscaling Era:

Speed and uncertainty are the new stability.

The only way to thrive in this fast-changing world is to accept the inevitability of change. Use it to your advantage, whether you're focused on your individual life or the fate of a nation.

This book is actually the third in a series that covers adapting to the Networked Age. *The Start-up of You* focuses on how individuals can adapt their careers to a rapidly changing world by remaining in a state of "Permanent Beta." (Visit thestartup ofyou.com for more resources and inspiration.) *The Alliance* analyzes how companies and managers should adapt their talent-management strategies to build stronger relationships with employees despite an uncertain future. (Visit alliedtalent.com to get help introducing these frameworks into your organization.) This volume is both a prequel and a sequel; it explains how blitzscaling helped create the Networked Age, and how entrepreneurs, leaders, companies, and governments can shape the coming change.

First, be an infinite learner. The best and worst thing about the rapid pace of change today is that there are no experts with ten-plus years of experience in *any* emerging phenomenon. If you're able to climb the learning curve faster than others, you have the opportunity to create massive value from it. While we wish we could write a simple, comprehensive list of rules that would guarantee your success, it's unclear how anyone could describe a strategy that would apply to all the potential changes that will occur in the next few years, let alone decades. The landscape is always changing, and learning is how you adapt.

Second, be a first responder. As new technologies and trends emerge, the uncertainty of where they are headed will paralyze many people and keep them from acting. Those who are willing to act—and act quickly—despite the uncertainty will have a disproportionate advantage. Seek out blitzscaling companies and markets; that's where you'll find the greatest growth and opportunity.

Finally, and somewhat paradoxically, be a source of stability. In a world of constant change and uncertainty, people will need reassurance and support. Offering stability and calm in the middle of the storm while others are caught in the tumult will make you a natural leader.

This prescription may seem scary, but we believe that this era of intense competition can be a good thing. Competition may be challenging for the individual person or company, but it is good for the collective whole. As more regions and ecosystems promote blitzscaling, more net value will be created. Like biodiversity, this "blitz-diversity" supports different types of growth and will allow blitzscaling to be applied to a broader array of important problems. Blitzscaling also helps guard against stasis and complacency, because it allows new domains to emerge and grow quickly, forcing incumbents to adapt.

If you believe the future will be better than the past, blitzscaling is heartening, because we'll get there faster. If you believe that the future will be worse than the past, blitzscaling is terrifying, because it overturns the existing order faster.

Here is how we personally feel about blitzscaling:

We believe that the future can and should be better than the past, and that it's worth tolerating the discomfort we feel when blitzscaling to get to the future as quickly as we can.

We hope to see blitzscaling enable more entrepreneurs to build transformative companies and succeed at a massive scale.

We hope to see more established companies leveraging the lessons of blitzscaling to be more adaptable and better equipped to tackle the challenges of the future.

We hope to see activists and governments use the tools of blitzscaling to change the world for the better.

The companies that choose to blitzscale will soon set the pace of progress in every industry. It's up to you to lead this change— for yourself, for your company, and for society as a whole.

Race you to the future.

ACKNOWLEDGMENTS

Thanks to our families for their support and patience through this long process—Michelle, Alisha, Jason, and Marissa. Thank you to our editor, Talia Krohn, and her colleagues at Currency for giving a home to our ideas. Lisa DiMona, Megan Casey, David Sanford, Saida Sapieva, Brett Bolkowy, and Ian Alas on our team offered critical support throughout this journey.

Mehran Sahami, sponsored our CS183C class at Stanford, which we taught with our friends and fellow instructors Allen Blue and John Lilly. Thanks as well to the guests who shared their stories with the class, many of which made it into the book, including Sam Altman, Brian Chesky, Patrick Collison, Michael Deering, Diane Greene, Reed Hastings, Marissa Mayer, Shishir Mehrotra, Ann Miura-Ko, Mariam Naficy, Jennifer Pahlka, Eric Schmidt, Selina Tobaccowala, Nirav Tolia, and Jeff Weiner.

Many thanks to everyone at Greylock Partners for their support of this project, including Joseph Ansanelli, Jerry Chen, Josh Elman, Chris McCann, Stacey Ngo, Simon Rothman, and Elisa Schreiber.

We owe much to June Cohen, Deron Triff, and the rest of the WaitWhat team, who produce the *Masters of Scale* podcast. Many of the stories in the book come from the guests who appeared in

Season 1 and Season 2, including Aneel Bhusri, Sara Blakely, Stewart Butterfield, Barry Diller, John Elkann, Caterina Fake, Tim Ferriss, Payal Kadakia, Nancy Lublin, Mark Pincus, Linda Rottenberg, Sheryl Sandberg, Howard Schultz, Peter Thiel, Tristan Walker, Ev Williams, and Mark Zuckerberg.

Thanks also to those who made a cameo on those episodes, including Umber Ahmad, Dominique Ansel, Greg Baldwin, Alexa Christon, Paulette Mae Cole, Chris Costa, Lisa Curtis, Susan Danziger, Angela Duckworth, Kara Goldin, Natasha Hastings, Margaret Heffernan, Drew Houston, Joi Ito, Leila Janah, Daniel Kahneman, Cheryl Kellond, Dara Khosrowshahi, Josh Kopelman, Omid Kordestani, Michelle Lee, Tim Lefler, Kristen Marhaver, Kathryn Minshew, Andrew Ng, Aubrie Pagano, Hadi Partovi, Robert Pasin, Juliana Rotich, Andrés Ruzo, Dick Stockton, Tony Tjan, Yossi Vardi, and Darryl Woodson.

The authors of the Silicon Guild provided valuable feedback on earlier drafts, including Peter Sims, Jennifer Aaker, Nancy Duarte, Morten Hansen, Frans Johansson, Charlene Li, Tina Seelig, Chris Shipley, Anne-Marie Slaughter, and Caroline Webb.

So many others helped us along the way, including Ben Casnocha, Elad Gil, Bing Gordon, Fred Kofman, Dmitri Mehlhorn, Marten Mickos, Christopher Schroeder, Mike Volpi, and Pat Wadors.

And thank you to Bill Gates for generously taking the time to contribute the foreword to this book.

As an entrepreneur and investor, either Reid Hoffman or the venture firm Greylock Partners, where he is a general partner, have the following relationships with companies mentioned in this book:

Airbnb: Greylock portfolio company; investor and board observer
Cloudera: Greylock portfolio company
Dropbox: Greylock portfolio company
Facebook: Greylock portfolio company; personal investment
Friendster: personal investment
Gladly: Greylock portfolio company
Greylock Partners: general partner
Groupon: Greylock portfolio company
Instagram: Greylock portfolio company
LinkedIn: cofounder, Greylock portfolio company
Medium: Greylock portfolio company
Microsoft: board member
Mozilla: former board member
Nextdoor: Greylock portfolio company
Pandora: Greylock portfolio company
PayPal: founding board member and executive
Pure Storage: Greylock portfolio company
Red Hat: Greylock portfolio company
SocialNet: cofounder
Tumblr: Greylock portfolio company
Zynga: former board member; personal investment

Throughout this book, we tell the stories of various blitzscalers. This appendix includes brief profiles that provide basic context for the curious reader.

AIRBNB
Airbnb.com

Airbnb is an online marketplace and hospitality service, enabling people to lease or rent short-term lodging including vacation rentals, apartment rentals, homestays, hostel beds, or hotel rooms. Founded August 2008, San Francisco, CA

ALIBABA
Alibaba.com

The Alibaba Group is an e-commerce, retail, and technology conglomerate that provides consumer-to-consumer, business-to-consumer, and business-to-business services including electronic payments and cloud computing. Founded April 1999, Hangzhou, China

AMAZON
Amazon.com

Amazon is an e-commerce company that also produces consumer electronics like the Kindle and Echo and is the world's largest provider of cloud computing services. Founded July 1994, Seattle, WA

APPLE
Apple.com

Apple designs, develops, and sells consumer electronics, computer software, and online services, such as the iPhone, iOS operating system, and Mac personal computers. Founded April 1976, Los Altos, CA

CHARITY: WATER
Charitywater.org

Charity: Water is a not-for-profit organization that provides clean and safe drinking water to people in developing nations. Founded Summer 2006, New York, NY

CHESAPEAKE ENERGY
Chk.com

Chesapeake Energy is a petroleum and natural gas exploration and production company. Founded May 1989, Oklahoma City, OK

CLASSPASS
ClassPass.com

ClassPass offers a flat-rate monthly subscription service that allows subscribers to attend participating fitness classes around the world. Founded June 2013, New York, NY

DRESS FOR SUCCESS
Dressforsuccess.org

Dress for Success is a not-for-profit organization that provides a network of support, professional attire, and the development tools to help women thrive in work and in life. Founded 1997, New York, NY

DROPBOX
Dropbox.com

Dropbox is a file hosting service that offers cloud storage, file synchronization, personal cloud, and client software. Founded 2007, Mountain View, CA

FACEBOOK
Facebook.com

Facebook provides products such as Facebook, Instagram, and Whatsapp that enable people to connect, share, discover, and communicate with each other. Founded February 2004, Cambridge, MA

FLIPKART
Flipkart.com

Flipkart is an e-commerce company that focuses on serving the India market. Founded October 2007, Bangalore, India

GOOGLE
Google.com

Alphabet Inc. is a holding company that includes Google (the company's core internet businesses), as well as other non-internet companies such as Calico, Verily, Waymo, X, and Nest Labs. In this book, we refer to the company as Google, both because it is the name by which most people know the company, and because we focus on the company's Internet businesses. Founded September 1998, Palo Alto, CA

GROUPON
Groupon.com

Groupon is an e-commerce marketplace that connects its subscribers with offers from local merchants. Its primary focus areas are activities, travel, goods, and services. Founded January 2008, Chicago, IL

KHAN ACADEMY

Khanacademy.org

Khan Academy's mission is to provide a free, world-class education for anyone, anywhere. It does this by offering online practice exercises and instructional videos. Founded October 2006, Mountain View, CA

LINKEDIN

LinkedIn.com

LinkedIn is the world's largest professional network and seeks to connect the world's professionals to make them more productive and successful. Founded December 2002, Mountain View, CA

MERCADOLIBRE

MercadoLibre.com

MercadoLibre provides solutions to individuals and companies buying, selling, advertising, and paying for goods online. Founded May 1999, Buenos Aires, Argentina/Stanford, CA

MICROSOFT

Microsoft.com

Microsoft develops, manufactures, licenses, supports, and sells computer software, consumer electronics, personal computers, and services. Based on revenue, it is the world's largest computer software maker. Founded April 1975, Albuquerque, NM

M-PESA

vodafone.com/content/index/what/m-pesa.html

M-Pesa is a mobile phone-based money transfer, financing, and micro-financing service that launched in Kenya but serves markets around the world. Founded March 2007, Nairobi, Kenya

NETFLIX
Netflix.com

Netflix is an Internet entertainment service that offers its members TV shows and movies, including original series, documentaries, and feature films. Members can watch as much as they want, anytime, anywhere, with no commercial interruptions. Founded August 1997, Scotts Valley, CA

PAYPAL
PayPal.com

PayPal operates a worldwide online payments system that supports online money transfers and serves as an electronic alternative to traditional paper methods like checks and money orders. Founded December 1998, Palo Alto, CA

PRICELINE
Priceline.com

Priceline provides online travel and related services to consumers and local partners. Its primary brands are Booking.com, priceline.com, agoda.com, KAYAK, Rentalcars.com, and OpenTable. Founded 1997, Stamford, CT

ROCKET MORTGAGE
RocketMortgage.com

Through the Rocket Mortgage website or mobile app, users can upload financial details and get a mortgage loan decision in minutes. Quicken Loans launched Rocket Mortgage in November 2015, Detroit, MI

SALESFORCE.COM
Salesforce.com

Salesforce.com provides cloud-based applications for sales, service, and marketing, as well as enabling partners to offer and run their own solutions on the Salesforce Platform. Founded February 1999, San Francisco, CA

SLACK
Slack.com

Slack provides cloud-based collaboration tools and services that connect teams with the apps, services, and resources they need to get work done. Founded 2009, Vancouver, British Columbia, Canada

SPOTIFY
Spotify.com

Spotify is a music and podcast streaming service that allows users to create and listen to playlists as well as individual tracks. Founded April 2006, Stockholm, Sweden

STRIPE
Stripe.com

Stripe helps businesses accept payments online and in mobile apps. Founded 2010, Palo Alto, CA

TENCENT
Tencent.com

Tencent is a holding company whose subsidiaries provide various Internet-related services, products, and technology both in China and globally. Its major services include QQ and WeChat. Founded November 1998, Shenzhen, China

TESLA
Tesla.com

Tesla is an automaker, energy storage company, and solar panel manufacturer. Founded July 2003, San Carlos, CA

TWITTER
Twitter.com

Twitter is an online news and social networking service where users post and interact with messages called "tweets." Founded March 2006, San Francisco, CA

UBER
Uber.com

Uber is a transportation technology company. It develops, markets, and operates the Uber car transportation and food delivery mobile apps. Founded March 2009, San Francisco, CA

XIAOMI
Mi.com

Xiaomi is a electronics and software company that designs, develops, and sells smartphones, mobile apps, laptops, and related consumer electronics. Founded April 2010, Beijing, China

ZARA
Zara.com

Zara (and its holding company, Inditex) is the world's largest clothing and fashion retailer. Founded May 1974, Arteixo, Spain

One of the ways we developed the material in this book was by teaching a class at Stanford University in the fall of 2015. This class, CS183C: Technology-enabled Blitzscaling, helped us refine our ideas and provided some of the content in the form of quotes from the various distinguished guests who visited our class.

During the course of our class, we asked our students to write two essays and a final reflection. We've included links to the best of the essays, and a sample of the final reflections, both to reward our students for their hard work, and to give you, the reader, some additional perspectives on the topic of blitzscaling. For those of you who are reading the paper version of this book, you can find the links below on the Blitzscaling.com website.

THE BEST OF ESSAY 1
medium.com/cs183c-blitzscaling-class-collection/featured-essays-for
-assignment-1-f8b34938e5e2

Oguzhan Atay
Robert Chun
Jorge Cueto
Axel Ericsson
Jocelyn Neff

THE BEST OF ESSAY 2
medium.com/cs183c-blitzscaling-class-collection/featured-essays-for
-assignment-2-c620149f8eb5

Jorge Cueto
Skylar Dorosin

Aaron Kalb
Jocelyn Neff

A SAMPLE OF FINAL REFLECTIONS

Chaitanya Asawa: medium.com/@casawa/ride-of-your-life
-678bea009d3f

Christina Chen: medium.com/@christina.chen/teachers-open
-the-door-you-enter-by-yourself-c9135aadef92

Jorge Cueto: medium.com/@jcueto/taking-the-leap-399ec46cf3a5

Maxine Cunningham: medium.com/@mmcunnin
/blitzscaling-with-reid-hoffman-co-final-assignment
-62e921ba2bf3

Skylar Dorosin: medium.com/@sdorosin/from-household-to
-nation-final-musings-on-blitzscaling-2b8b6e27a3ce

Axel Ericsson: medium.com/@ericsson_axel/lightning-fast
-final-essay-on-blitzscaling-612d12fc2139

Andre Esteva: medium.com/@andreesteva/cs-183c-final
-essay-blitzscaling-a-foundation-for-rapid-company-growth
-e59043d63292

Vijay Goel: medium.com/@vijaygoel/blitzscaling-knowing
-when-it-s-time-to-go-all-in-55f4cad85aaa

Marcus Gomez: medium.com/@mvgomez/final-lessons
-6ac03fdb1397

Rish Gupta: medium.com/@rish_says/what-i-learnt-from-reid
-hoffman-brian-chesky-marissa-mayer-elizabeth-holmes-jeff
-weiner-on-1e66bf61a23a

Kurt Heinrich: medium.com/@kurtjheinrich/cs183c
-blitzscaling-takeaways-final-essay-10609b080562

Brandon Hill: medium.com/@brandon_hill/how-and-when
-to-blitzscale-f54c31f2a4fd

Teddy Jungreis: medium.com/@teddyjungreis/blitzscaling-for
-dummies-c3b48272acec

Aaron Kalb: medium.com/@kalb/blitzscaling-retrospective
-b8e72bf81229

Daniel Kharitonov: medium.com/@volkfox/cs183c-final-essay
-1a3242eca9f

Charles Lu: medium.com/@charleslu/like-lightning
-638c9051beb8

Ryan McKinney: medium.com/@ryanmckinney/blitzscaling
-the-future-8c9c27c1e1e7

Joann McMaster: medium.com/@joannmacmaster/99c620beaa8a

Jocelyn Neff: medium.com/cs183c-blitzscaling-student
-collection/blitzscaling-a-chemical-reaction-bf9e318fe903

Nirmit Parikh: medium.com/@Nirmit_Parikh/cs-183c
-blitzscaling-168d208532aa

Veeral Patel: medium.com/@vral/2ab47a57a162

Dayne Rathbone: medium.com/@daynerathbone/blitzscaling
-takeaways-73570800f84b

Shikhar Shrestha: medium.com/@shikharshrestha/final
-reflections-on-blitzscaling-a8eb5aacba96

Jason Weeks: medium.com/@Weeksy_J/cs183c-final
-assignment-9be1b4af8087

#1 *NEW YORK TIMES* BESTSELLER
BY AUTHORS REID HOFFMAN AND BEN CASNOCHA

LEARN THE SKILLS YOU NEED TO ACCELERATE AND MANAGE YOUR CAREER AND BECOME THE CEO OF YOUR FUTURE.

"Whatever career you're in or want to be in, *The Start-Up of You* holds lessons for success."

—Michael Bloomberg, founder of Bloomberg, L.P. and former mayor, New York City

"Everyone, women and men alike, needs to think big to succeed. This is a practical book that shows you how to take control and build a career that will enable you to have real impact."

—Sheryl Sandberg, chief operating officer, Facebook

"LinkedIn cofounder Reid Hoffman has pulled off something extraordinary in his book-writing debut. He has challenged a well-worn idea ... and replaced it with something better."

—Fortune